Reflective Practice

Dedicated to all who heal, care, and educate.

Knowledge is limited. Imagination encircles the world.

Einstein [1929] 2002

Try to love the *questions themselves* like locked rooms and like books that are written in a very foreign tongue. Do not now seek the answers, which cannot be given to you. *Live* the questions now.

Rainer Maria Rilke 1934

Contents

Foreword

by **Anne Hudson Jones**

Narrative competence – that is, the mastery of several kinds of narrative skills – has increasingly been seen as desirable for professionals, and especially for those in medicine. One way to foster such narrative skills is the practice of reflective writing that Gillie Bolton describes in her book. This process of writing depends upon the intuitive, linguistic, and imaginative capacities rather than the rational and quantitative modes of thought that dominate much of professional training and practice.

Although the process may sound simple, if practised well, such writing requires honesty and courage and can lead to unexpected insights and new ways of knowing. The results may improve practice as well as revitalise the practitioner.

As one who has had the privilege of participating in a reflective-writing workshop led by Gillie Bolton, I can affirm the validity of testimonials to its power. I can also affirm this book's opening reminder that the best way of undertaking reflective practice is to do it rather than to read about it. But for those who have not yet had that opportunity, this book offers the next best thing. Read it as a prelude to, rather than a substitute for, engaging in the reflective practice it encourages.

Anne Hudson Jones
Institute for the Medical Humanities
The University of Texas Medical Branch at Galveston

Acknowledgements

Many practitioners and colleagues have enabled *Reflective Practice*, generously giving time, enthusiasm and insight into your experience, knowledge and feelings, and – perhaps most vitally – warmth. Heartfelt thanks is all I can offer for our adventures, your sensitivity, and permission to be quoted. I thank Sheffield University Institute of General Practice Master in Medical Science and Master in Education graduates, Institute of Public Health in Ireland Leadership Programme graduates, Nottingham Community Health nurses, participants in medical, nursing, social work counselling/therapy, education, and management development programmes.

There are some without whom I could not even have laced my boots. Rosie Field dances hand in hand with me along the most rocky and precipitous paths; Kate Billingham laughingly points out contours I'd missed, and Martyn Evans lakes; Amanda Howe, Julian Pratt, Alan Bleakley, Faith McLellan, Anne Hudson Jones, Trisha Greenhalgh, Tom Heller, John Goodwin, Lindsay Buckell illuminate our track; Leslie Boydell and Angela Mohtashemi have led me off my map; Nigel Mathers, Sir Kenneth Calman, David Hannay, Steve Dearden, Pat Lane, Craig Newnes, Tony Warnes, Sonya Yates, David Greaves, Ken Martin, Andrew Eastaugh, Jeannie Wright, Paul Schatzberger, Jonathan Knight, Lucy Henshall give support, advice and insight. Marianne Lagrange is a fearsomely able editorial guide in velvet gloves, and Emma Grant-Mills great; Abigail Campbell offers flasks opportunely. I can't sufficiently value Moira Brimacombe, Jo Cannon, Helen Drucquer, David Gelipter, Charles Heatley, Martin McShane, Bob Purdy, Caroline Walton, Jane Searle, Helen Starkey, Rosie Welch, Shirley Brierley, Clare Connolly, Naomi Dixon, Maggie Eisner, Seth Jenkinson, Sheena McMain, Mark Purvis, Becky Ship, Bev Hargreaves, Di Moss, Janet Hargreaves and Gail Young. Marilyn Lidster, whom I miss, endlessly picked up bits of me from the cliff-foot. Dan Rowland says 'oh Gillie!' but helps me again to click, and discusses everything important and unimportant. Alice Rowland advises on colours and coats, and how not to slip on mud.

Stephen Rowland has travelled this and many other roads with me so closely I am no longer sure if it's his journey or mine. This edition is another milestone in our shared adventure. He not only makes sure I have warm jerseys, compass, whistle and the right map, but fills my rucksack with goodies.

Preface: Mind the gap

> In the end I found that the reflective process itself was where the bounties lay, and no amount of reading about reflecting could help me.
>
> This writing allows you to touch things you otherwise couldn't.
>
> This is an opportunity to inhabit the unknown.
>
> Reflective practitioners

If the first speaker above is right you should shut this book now. So why do I want you to read it? Reflective practice is only effectively undertaken and understood by becoming immersed in doing it rather than reading about it or following instructions. But an initial guide can save time; this one will, I hope, enable you to engage in the process as dynamically as he did.

Bank Underground Station, London, is built on a curve, leaving a potentially dangerous gap between platform and carriage to trap the unwary. The loudspeaker voice instructs passengers to '*Mind the gap*': the boundary between train and platform. *Gap* can be used as image for other boundaries in our lives, such as between professional me and parent me. We spend our lives minding gaps to protect ourselves from being hit by trains, eaten by bears (Milne 1924) or falling into uncomfortable situations where we do not know the answers. Awareness of such gaps can lead to deep, thorough self-questioning. At such moments of openness understandings can flash: 'aha' moments of 'oh, I see!', epiphanies of allowing myself to stop thinking, stop carefully being myself, and allow other possibilities to present themselves. At these times and places professionals are open to querying, or potentially querying, situations, knowledge, feelings and understandings. Such deeply reflective questions are bridges which cross moral gulfs:

> Bridges are sort of the opposite of boundaries, and boundaries are where wars start.
>
> Levi 1988, p. 104

Borders and *frontiers* are sensitive politically. We use them to tell us who we are, and the way we will relate to others (friend or family? stranger or fellow-countryperson? colleague or client?). We take on many different roles – lover, parent, chauffeur, academic, supervisor, counsellor, friend – all with uncertain boundaries between them; we strive to clarify our roles for ourselves and others. We also strive to know the answers relevant to our roles: doctors assume patients want answers; parents want to give children correct ones. Yet, saying 'I don't know', at least to oneself, can be life-changing.

In striving for certainty in an uncertain world, for clarity of boundaries in professions where ambiguities abound, we forget to ask personally and professionally developing reflective questions about gaps, and the issues found there. Philip Pullman explored strict frontiers being breached, in award-winning *His Dark Materials* (1995): enormous fatal energy forces gaps between worlds, dangerous disturbing elements cross illicit frontiers, inter-world war ensues. *Reflective practice* deals with positive dynamic exploring of boundary gaps (licit and illicit).

> How difficult it is for professionals in such anxiety-producing work to remain open and responsive (rather than reactive); routinised responses and procedures (though an essential framework for action) can also lead to a rigidity which is inimical to the uniquely personal response needed in the caring professions.
> Effective learning is therefore dependent, at least in part, on access to that world of feeling and phantasy, which allows structures of meaning to be recognised, and to be open to change, in a way which facilitates a different (and perhaps more constructive) professional response.
>
> Yelloly and Henkel 1995, p. 9

Reflective practice: aesthetic and artistic

Reflective practice can enable a mindfulness of the gap – an awareness of and willingness to tackle border issues – excitingly, if carefully. Winter et al. (1999) maintain that reflective practice is one way of redressing the 'devaluation, deskilling and alienation' now suffered by the caring and teaching professions:

> The late 1980s saw professional staff beginning to sense their autonomy being reduced, decision-making mechanized, expertise fragmented, and their 'artistry' abolished . . .
> The reflective paradigm assembles its theoretical resources in order to defend professional values, creativity, and autonomy in a context where they are generally felt to be under attack from political and economic forces which threatened to transform the professional from an artist into an operative.
>
> Winter et al. 1999, p. 193

Working reflectively with our whole selves entails harnessing our artistic talents alongside other talents. If practice itself is an art, then reflection upon it is also an artistic process (Bleakley 1999; Winter et al. 1999). Expressive and explorative writing relies on our habitual communicating medium, words, gives validity, form and coherence over time and space, and aesthetic illumination.

This book offers an introduction to effective reflective practice using writing, based on teaching and research experience with doctors, nurses, social workers, therapists, counsellors, teachers, clinical psychologists, and in business consultantancy. Practitioners write stories, poetry or drama about their work, or their research data, then submit these to discussion with a facilitated group, supervisor, mentor or peer-mentor. A short story or poem is a slice of life, metonymically revealing the whole. The processes of writing develop and clarify writers' understanding of data or experience; discussions draw out issues and locate gaps and queries, extending the learning process for writer as well as group (mentor). Writers become readers and co-critics, listeners co-authors. A closely observed event, however small, written about, reflected upon, discussed critically, and re-explored through further writings stands metonymically for the whole of that reflective writer's practice.

This critical research also encompasses the reading of a wide range of appropriate texts, thoroughly and clearly embedding the whole reflective process consciously in the practitioner's wide political, cultural and social/professional context.

About this book

I provide background information; the how, why, where, who, when, what; a discussion of theoretical pedagogical principles and underpinnings; insight into facilitation and group work; an explanation of writing methods, learning journals, and different writing genre; and an examination of queries and problems, including those relating to ethics and values. Principles and practice of reflection and reflexivity are discussed with reference to facilitated group, supervision, or peer-mentoring.

"'What is the use of a book,' thought Alice, 'without pictures or conversation?'" (Carroll [1865], 1954 p. 1). Wise Alice knew texts have to capture heart, imagination and spirit, as well as mind, to communicate. This text is fully illustrated and exemplified throughout with original writings from colleagues, students and publications. They are first-hand accounts of practice, discussions about writings, reflections upon the usefulness of the reflection and reflexivity, and a range of descriptions of methods and their effectiveness. Reflective and reflexive processes are as old as thinking people: ancient and respected texts, some invoking child-like wisdom, offer great and simple windows on understanding.

A suggested criterion for my Masters students' final assessment is *evidence of enjoyment* (as well as *evidence of substantive reading*, etc.). My involvement in marking is increased when students' enjoyment oozes off the page. We only learn effectively when doing what we want to do. Stefano's research conclusions at Neurosciences Research Institute, New York State University, include: 'pleasure is our brain's way of subconsciously and continuously ranking what is most important to us: pleasure leads to pure rationality' (2004). This book concerns effective, enjoyable reflective practice.

The aha moment

Rowing is a precise art. You must have confidence in your boat and oars, but also confidence in your ability to let go and trust your natural instincts.

I will let you into a secret. The best way of introducing this feeling is to take away for a moment the crew's vision. To get them to shut their eyes. This lifts outside interference and pushes back those constraints of *how it ought to be* to *how it is*.

Shutting your eyes and letting those natural instincts take over can be daunting but liberating.

SEE HOW IT CAN BE DONE IF YOU JUST LET GO . . .

Jo Turner

Oars are 'wings that make ships fly', according to Odysseus (Homer trans. 1996, p. 464). If we continue Jo's metaphor of rowing for reflective practice, I hope this book will enable you, reflective practitioner readers, to fly, and to find 'goodness there':

Just halfway through this journey of our life
I reawoke to find myself inside
A dark wood, way off course, the right road lost.
How difficult a task it is to tell
What this wild, harsh, forbidding wood was like
The merest thought of which brings back my fear;
For only death exceeds its bitterness.
But I found goodness there.

Dante, Inferno, trans. 1988, Canto 1, lines 1–8

1

AN INTRODUCTION TO REFLECTIVE PRACTICE

We do not 'store' experience as data, like a computer: we 'story' it.

Winter 1988, p. 235

You understand how to act from knowledge, but you have not yet seen how to act from not-knowing.

Chuang Tsu trans. 1974, p. 68

I'm no longer uncertain about being uncertain: uncertainty is now my mantra.

Reflective practice student

Reflective practice is positioned firmly as a dynamic developmental process in this interdisciplinary second edition. The term has lost some credence, becoming a catch-all name for a wide range of activities from deep life, work and organisation-changing critique to rote box-ticking practices seeking to make professionals accountable to and controllable by increasingly beaurocratic and market-led organisations. This second edition offers practical and theorised methods for understanding and grasping authority over actions, thoughts, feelings, beliefs, values and professional identity in professional, cultural and political contexts. It clearly delineates processes for critical reflection upon the forms, values and ethics of institutional organisations and structures in which professionals work. This critique can result in radical movements for change.

Most training and post-experience courses include elements of reflective practice; the danger lies in undertaking it because it is just the thing to do. Such an attitude cannot support reflection and reflexivity.

The paradox is that reflective practice is required by the masters, by the system. Yet its nature is essentially politically and socially disruptive: it lays open to question anything taken for granted. Enquiry-based education, 'education for creativity, innovativeness, adaptability, ease with difference and comfortableness with change . . . [is] education for instabililty' (Reid and O'Donohue 2004, p. 561).

Smooth running social, political and professional systems run on the well-oiled cogs of stories we construct, and connive at being constructed around us.

Welcoming of diversity can be mere window dressing. Effective reflective practice and reflexivity are transgressive of stable and controlling orders; they lead cogs to decide to change shape, change place, even reconfigure whole systems.

The structures in which our professional and personal roles, values and everyday lives are embedded are complex and volatile. Power is subtle and slippery; its location is often different from how it appears. Deep reflection and reflexivity for development involve:

- *authority* and *responsibility* for personal and professional identity, values, action, feelings;

- *contestation*;

- willingness to stay with *uncertainty*, *unpredictability*, *questioning*.

Paradoxically the route is not through angry uncomfortable confrontation: such revolution leads to destructive cycles of action and reaction. The route is through spirited enquiry leading to constructive developmental change and personal and professional integrity based on deep understandings. It is *creative, illuminative, dynamic, self-affirming*, but not a thornless rose bed. People only learn and develop when they enjoy the process, and benefit personally. Serious professionals have cavilled at such creative methods, and use of deeply accessible varied sources of wisdom.

Einstein (1929) was successful partly because he doggedly and constantly asked questions for which everyone thought they knew the answers. Childlike, he asked why?, how?, what?, rather than accepting givens or taken-for-granteds. He 'love[d] the *questions themselves* like locked rooms', and certainly '*live[ed]* the questions' (Rilke [1934] 1993, p. 35).

Stories are the mode we use to make sense of ourselves and our world. This world and our lives within it are complex and chaotic: seemingly governed by forces not only beyond our control, but beyond our understanding. We tell and retell episodes both minor and major to our colleagues, to our loved ones, to therapists and priests, to strangers on the train, to a wedding guest (Coleridge 1834). This can merely be a process of tucking ourselves securely under a quilt patchworked out of safe and self-affirming accounts: our stories can only too easily be essentially uncritical. Or, even worse, they are censoring tools: 'cover stories' (Sharkey 2004). This self-protectiveness can ensure that our stories are not exploring sensitive issues, but are expressions of what we feel comfortable with, or would like to be.

> It was still snowing as [Pooh Bear] stumped over the white forest track, and he expected to find Piglet warming his toes in front of the fire, but to his surprise he found that the door was open, and the more he looked inside the more Piglet wasn't there.
>
> Milne [1928] 1958, p. 163

Effective reflective practice can be like looking for Piglet: the more you look, the more it seems not to be there. It is only when you have the courage to stop looking and trust the reflective and reflexive processes that you will begin to perceive the areas you need to tackle. Discovering what you need to reflect upon and the route to altering things is an exhilarating journey. Afterwards the insights and inevitable changes seem obvious. Although reflective practice has become a standard in initial and continuing professional education and development, it is a state of mind, an attitude, an approach, and therefore elusive to curriculum planners. It is an educational approach which makes the difference between twenty years of experience or one year of experience twenty times.

One way forward is to focus on NON-critical incidents, or perhaps non-'critical' aspects of such events. Insight is gained by respecting the reflective and reflexive processes to light upon and enlighten that which most needs examination. These areas might not sock us in the face as 'critical'; they are probably ones which have been allowed to pass unnoticed because focusing upon them is more problematic, often for unexamined personal or professional reasons. 'Critical' incidents, such as giving the wrong vaccine because they had been stored higgledly-piggledly in the fridge, will inevitably be examined. The events we 'forget' most need reflection, and give rise to the deepest reflexivity: 'we need to attend to the untold' (Sharkey 2004). Joy-Matthews et al. (2004; see also Goldberg 1991) recommend a human resource development exercise: writing what you *do not* remember. Plato, who said 'the life without examination is no life' (Plato trans. 2000, p. 315), reckoned education is finding pathways to what we do not know we know.

Reflective practice and reflexivity are not subjects but a pedagogical approach which should 'pervade the curriculum' (Fanghanel 2004, p. 576): the pearl grit in the oyster of practice and education. To be effective they need dynamic methods. The method of travel affects what happens along the way and the destination. A medical student commented: 'we spend so much time studying medicine that we never have time to study sick people'. Reid and O'Donohue (2004) argue that enquiry-based learning should become the organising logic of entire teacher education programmes, with students learning *through* enquiry rather than being prepared *for* enquiry. Curricula need shaking up, and more enquiry-based methods introduced. *Curriculum* is Latin for race course (Rome's Piazza Navone was one): perhaps we need to lose an association with ancient Romans.

A story is an attempt to create order and security out of a chaotic world. But for our experiences to develop us – socially, psychologically, spiritually – our world must be made to appear strange. We, and our students, must be encouraged to examine our story making processes critically: to create and recreate fresh accounts of our lives from different perspectives, different points of view, and to elicit and listen to the responses of peers. Listening critically to the stories of those peers also enables learning from their experience. It is the exploration of experience, knowledge, values, identity that matters, rather than any attempt to arrive at a 'true' account (Doyle 2004).

important knowledge about reality always comes out of [writing] . . . through a . . . transformation of reality by imagination and the use of words . . . When you succeed in creating something different out of . . . experience, you also achieve the possibility of communicating something that was not evident before . . . But you cannot plan this transmission of knowledge.

Llosa 1991, p. 79

Postulating what other actors might have thought and felt, empathising with them and the situation, as well as imaginatively reconstructing the situation in fresh ways, offers understandings and insights as no other process can. For example, a practitioner can retell a story from the point of view of students or clients, reconstruct it with the genders of the actors reversed, or create a satisfactory ending in place of a horrible one.

Effective reflective practice and reflexivity meet the paradoxical need both to tell and retell our stories in order for us to feel secure enough, and yet critically examine our actions, and those of others, in order dynamically to increase our understanding of ourselves and our practice.

What do we call it?

The term *reflective practice* is not a terribly useful one. The metaphor it embodies is limited: a mirror reflection is merely the image of an object directly in front of it – faithfully reproduced back to front. What is the reflection of shit? Shit. *Reflective practice writing*, however, is a creative adventure right through the glass to the other side of the silvering. Such reflective practice can take us out of our own narrow range of experience and help us to perceive experiences from a range of viewpoints and potential scenarios. It can do this by harnessing a vital human drive – to create stories about our lives, and communicate them.

Perhaps this approach should be called *flexive*. Flexion means 'alteration, change, modification', and 'a bend, curve, and a joint', whereas reflection means 'the action of turning [back] or fixing the thoughts on some subject' (*Shorter Oxford English Dictionary*), with the associated definition of the reversed reproduction of an image. This makes *reflection* sound as dynamic as *rumination*: a sheep chewing smelly cud. I have a cartoon of a sheep nose to nose with the reflection of herself and the surrounding meadow. She's saying: 'I'm sure the grass is greener in the mirror, but whenever I try to reach it, this ugly ewe bars the way and butts me on the nose.'

The mirror image model of reflection suggests there is a me *out there* practising in the big world, and a reflected me *in here* in my head thinking about it. If I think about it constructively enough I will be able to alter my practice and my relation to you out there. This model is located in modernist duality: *this* in dialogue with *that*, *in* and *out*, or *here* and *there*. Here is an ancient Zen text:

You must first forsake the dualities of: self and others, interior and exterior, small and large, good and bad, delusion and enlightenment, life and death, being and nothingness.

Tsai Chi Chung trans. 1994, p. 95

The through-the-looking-glass model involves far wider potential interactions, opens up more developmental reflexive and reflective space than is possible with a Cartesian-based one. 'Reflection is the central dynamic in intentional learning, problem-solving and validity testing through rational discourse' (Mezirow 1981, p. 4). Yes, true, but there is an awful lot more than just the 'rational' for us to explore. Professionals cannot fully crawl through the glass. They can still explore the wide and rather perplexing other side of reflection: turn their world inside out and back to front, not just think about it rationally.

Reflective practice: a political and social responsibility

Reflective practice can fall into the trap of becoming only confession. Confession can be a conforming mechanism, despite sounding liberating, freeing from a burden of doubt, guilt and anxiety (Bleakley 2000b). Confessing has a seductive quality because it passes responsibility to others. Practitioners need to take responsibility for their actions and values, and their share of responsibility for the political and social situations within which they live and work. The desire to hold an audience with a 'glittering eye' (Coleridge 1834) is strong. Jennifer Nias, a researcher into the experience of women teachers (Nias and Aspinwall 1992), noted with surprise that all her potential interviewees were keen to tell their autobiographies at length. People always are: but they do not want their stories questioned; this is the role of reflective practice.

Reflective practice is more than an examination of personal experience; it is located in the political and social structures which are increasingly hemming professionals in (Goodson 2004). Their right to make moral and professional judgements is being eroded; they are being reduced to technicians, their skills to mere technical competencies. In order to retain political and social awarenesses and activity, professional development work needs to be rooted in the public and the political as well as the private and the personal.

To this end, examinations of practice need to be undertaken alongside open discussions with peers on pertinent issues, an examination of texts from the larger field of work and politics, and discussions with colleagues from outside the practitioners' own milieu. Reflective practice work can then become politically, socially as well as psychologically useful, rather than a mere *quietist* navel-gazing exercise. It supports, demands even, practitioners thinking about values:

> If we had asked people to talk about their values in abstract terms, we would have received generalised responses. By asking them to tell [write] stories about important experiences, we were able to see something of how values reveal themselves in a complex, varied and shifting way in practice.
>
> Pattison et al. 1999b, p. 6

Values which underpin practice are rarely analysed or questioned. Through reflexive practice professionals realise dissonance, or dissatisfaction with their own values in practice, or those of their organisation, leading them to make dynamic change. This might not be easy, particularly if they realise an action has been against their own ethical code, or that they are in an untenable but unalterable situation (Rowland 2000). Examining such fundamental areas requires a supportive, confidential, carefully facilitated environment.

Goodson creates a distinction between *life stories* and *life history*. The latter is the former plus appropriate and challenging data from a wide range of sources, and evidence of vital discussion with colleagues. 'The life history pushes the question of whether private issues are also public matters. The life story individualises and personalises; the life history contextualises and politicises' (1998, p. 11). Noel Gough (1998) uses a similar method with postgraduate students in education. He says he *plays* with the method, which he calls *currere* – a term coined by Pinar (1975) and Grumet (1981).

Gomez et al. (2000, p. 744) found how education students' reflection was unchallenging and non-risk-taking, because they only wrote personal narratives of their classroom teaching, from their own point of view. 'The nature of personal stories as ones that people actually lived limited the ways in which they could be interrogated. Questioning the viewpoint resulting from an event in someone's life was tantamount to challenging her overall integrity.' Future student narratives will be written from multiple perspectives, enabling challenge and insight.

Cartoons in another study offered a 'playfully ironic dimension for intensifying the process of critical reflexivity' (Cavallaro-Johnson 2004, p. 423). Visual images, which allow subtexts to appear unwittingly, prevented the autobiographical stories from being uncritical and confessional. I would argue that a range of different forms of text, such as from different points of view, can similarly offer layers of unwitting subtext.

Re-view

A film or story is a dynamic fresh look through the eyes of more than one actor. Replaying back what 'actually' happened is impossible: any retelling will inevitably be affected by the view of the person doing the retelling. Effective reflective practice enables the exploration of a range of viewpoints and possibilities:

Stories are a lens through which I view the world to make sense of my experiences and those of my colleagues and patients. In writing some of these stories I am able to focus on complex issues that have previously appeared distorted by time and emotions. Metaphors shed light on subjects that I had been unaware of before, patterns stand out in ways that I had not hitherto understood.

Mark Purvis

Reflective practice is learning and developing through examining what we think happened on any occasion, and how we think others perceived the event and us, opening our practice to scrutiny by others, and studying texts from the wider sphere. Reflexivity is finding strategies for looking at our own thought processes, values, prejudices and habitual actions, as if we were onlookers. It is a focusing closer and closer. In the film *Blow-up* the only evidence for a murder is a small, insignificant-seeming detail in a photograph. This tiny detail is blown up and up until the evidence is clear. No detail is potentially too trivial or insignificant to write, think and talk about. These vital details might have gone unnoticed at the time, as in *Blow-up*.

Many professions facilitate others to understand their lives and themselves better, and hopefully improve things thereby. A practitioner cannot support another in this way if they are not aware and open themselves (Murray 1982). Bringing the personal into the professional can increase empathy between client and professional (Smyth 1996). Aesthetic experience (such as writing) can leap over the seeming gap between the personal and the professional self, and the seemingly impossible gap between the safe and rehearsed story and possibly dangerous new stories. This can only bring greater unity and wholeness of experience to the practitioner or educator, and greater empathy between them and their client. Job satisfaction will increase, and work-related stress decrease:

Perhaps the most accessible form of freedom, the most subjectively enjoyed, and the most useful to human society consists of being good at your job and therefore taking pleasure in doing it – I really believe that to live happily you have to have something to do, but it shouldn't be too easy, or else something to wish for, but not just any old wish; something there's a hope of achieving.

Levi 1988, p. 139

Writing stories and sharing them in a trusted, confidential, facilitated forum of peers, or within supervision, is a way of increasing job satisfaction and effectiveness, and is the process offered by this book. Explorative and expressive writing is pivotal: the writing of a story or poem is a first-order activity. The writing, the essential discussions and the writing of additional stories from different angles with the support of the group, is a creative explorative process in its own right –

not a tool in professional reflection. Course participants do not think and *then* write, the writing is the vehicle for the reflection: reflection *in* writing. Not only does writing enable the most appropriate reflection, but also, as a participant commented, 'one of the values of writing is that you can freeze the film: reflect upon one frame or a short series, then run the film backwards and review a previous scene in the light of reflections upon a later one. This would be difficult to do in talking: it wouldn't make sense; impossible to do during action.'

> I consider writing as a *method of inquiry*, a way of finding out about yourself and your topic. Although we usually think about writing as a mode of 'telling' about the social world, writing is not just a mopping-up activity . . . Writing is also a way of 'knowing' – a method of discovery and analysis. By writing in different ways, we discover new aspects of our topic and our relationship to it. Form and content are inseparable.
>
> Richardson 2000, p. 345

The psychologist Oliver Sacks studied people who were missing, or effectively missing, part of their brain, and the bizarre things this led to. In his essay *The Man who Mistook his Wife for a Hat*, he studies 'Dr P.' who could see, but had lost 'visual perception, visual imagination and memory, the fundamental powers of visual representation . . . insofar as they pertained to the personal, the familiar, the concrete'. Sacks concludes:

> Our mental processes, which constitute our being and life, are not just abstract and mechanical, but personal as well – and as such involve not just classifying and categorising, but continual judging and feeling also. If this is missing, we become computer-like, as Dr P. was. And by the same token, if we delete feeling and judging, the personal, from the cognitive sciences, we reduce *them* to something as defective as Dr P. – and we reduce *our* apprehension of the concrete and real . . . Our cognitive sciences are themselves suffering from an agnosia essentially similar to Dr P.'s. Dr P. may therefore serve as a warning and parable – of what happens to a science which eschews the judgmental, the particular, the personal, and becomes entirely abstract and computational.
>
> Sacks 1985, p. 19

Reflective practice can learn from Sacks's 'warning and parable', and be open to as much of ourselves as is possible. A reflective practice suffering from agnosia will not get us terribly far.

Effective reflective practice encourages the seeking of understanding and interpretation of principles, justifications and meanings (Morrison 1996). It involves interrogating both our *explicit* knowledge, such as known and quantifiable evidence-based knowledge, and *implicit* knowledge – 'a collection of information, intuitions and interpretation' (Epstein 1999, p. 834) based on experience and prior knowledge (for further analysis of types of knowledge, see Eraut 1994; Belenky et al. 1997). Implicit knowledge is tried and tested, gained initially from experience, observation, or study. Intimately known, its appropriate application is intuitive. This does not necessarily mean that it is right, any more than knowledge gained from randomised control trial research (explicit) is.

Such re-viewing of knowledge and experience can lead practitioners to perceive a need for change in their world, their relation and attitude to it, and the attitudes of others. One of my students stated: 'this is not an academic module, but an assertiveness training course'. Asserting yourself inevitably involves challenging social structures.

One of the greatest benefits to a student in a learning situation, or a client with a practitioner, is the sense of their relatedness to the professional: that they are interested, involved, and care. In medicine this has been called the *placebo effect* of the physician as *healer*: 'the attitude of the doctor can make an appreciable difference to the psychological response of the patient who feels the need to be understood and listened to empathically' (Dixon et al. 1999, p. 310). To give the people we work with confidence in us as professionals, we have to be secure and happy enough ourselves in our roles, and not anxious or inhibited.

How can that happen in overworked, overstressed professions, which are getting less appreciated daily? One of the ways of being an empathetic, effective practitioner is to be reflexive as well as reflective.

Reflection is an in-depth consideration of events or situations outside of oneself: solitarily, or with critical support. The reflector attempts to work out what happened, what they thought or felt about it, why, who was involved and when, and what these others might have experienced and thought and felt about it. It is looking at whole scenarios from as many angles as possible: people, relationships, situation, place, timing, chronology, causality, connections, and so on, to make situations and people more comprehensible. This involves reviewing or reliving the experience to bring it into focus. Seemingly innocent details might prove to be key; seemingly vital details may be irrelevant.

Reflection involves reliving and rerendering: who said and did what, how, when, where, and why. Reflection might lead to insight about something not noticed in time, pinpointing perhaps when the detail was missed.

Reflexivity

A reflexive-minded practitioner will then ask themselves, why did this pass me by: where was my attention directed at that time? Reflexivity is: 'what are the mental, emotional and value structures which allowed me to lose attention and make that error?' This deep questioning is missed out if the practitioner merely undertakes reflection as practical problem-solving: what happened, why, what did I think and feel about it, how can I do it better next time?

Reflexivity is making aspects of the self strange: focusing close attention upon *one's own* actions, thoughts, feelings, values, identity, and their effect upon others, situations, and professional and social structures. The reflexive thinker has to stand back from belief and value systems, habitual ways of thinking and relating to others, structures of understanding themselves and their relationship to the world, and their assumptions about the way that the world impinges upon them. This can only be done by somehow becoming separate in order to look at it as if from the outside: not part of habitual experience processing, and not easy. Strategies are required, and the support of others. This critical focus upon beliefs, values, professional identities, and how they affect and are affected by the surrounding cultural structures, is a highly responsible social and political activity.

Reflexivity involves coming as close as possible to an awareness of the way I am experienced and perceived by others. It is being able to stay with personal uncertainty, critically informed curiosity as to how others perceive things as well as how I do, and flexibility to consider changing deeply held ways of being. The role of a trusted other, such as a supervisor or peer-reader of an account, is vital.

Mindfulness is an invaluable approach. A conscious exclusion of other elements of life, apart from that which is being attended to (Johns 2004), is achieved when senses and awarenesses are tuned into present action: the opposite of multitasking (Epstein 1999). Being mindfully aware develops communication, ability to use implicit knowledge in association with explicit knowledge, and insight into others' perceptions. Frank speaks of *practical wisdom*, from Aristotle: '*Phronesis* is the opposite of acting on the basis of scripts and protocols; those are for beginners, and continuing reliance on them can doom actors to remain beginners' (2004, p. 221).

The observation skills and awarenesses required of a reflective writer develop mindfulness, and are developed by it. Both require an acute and aware focusing upon what is happening at any time. Doctor-writer Verghese exhorts: 'We should be ministers for healing [and educating], storytellers, storymakers, and players in the greatest drama of all: the story of our patients' [and students'] lives as well as our own' (2001, p. 1016).

An example: Sam, a midwife, brought a furious account of an angry mother she had attended as an NHS midwife: 'stupid, hostile upper-middle class bitch who felt she had the right to boss me around, tell me what to do'. The birth had been exhausting and disastrous for both mother and midwife: Sam still felt bitter twenty-five years later. The reflective practice group offered insight and comparative cases, and suggested Sam wrote an account from the mother's perspective.

The following week saw a very different Sam: 'I don't know exactly what was wrong, but I do know, having relived it from this mother's point of view, that she was upset and confused. Because I saw her as a stupid, middle-class bitch who thought she could have everything she wanted her way, I never listened to her properly. I think I'll see demanding mothers in a different way in future.'

Telling the truth?

The narratives we tell and write are perspectival. Looking in through a window at experience to reflect on it from outside is impossible. Professionals, however open about themselves and their practice, can only perceive and understand from their own viewpoint, broad and empathic as that might be. To be objective is to be 'not influenced by personal feelings or opinions in considering or representing facts; impartial, detached' (*OED*). Yet, 'We don't see things as they are, we see them as we are' (Nin, quoted in Epstein 1999, p. 834).

Individual perspectives and values can be widened and deepened. One can look on the glass and only see one's self reflected, or through it as in George Herbert's hymn: 'A man that looks on glass, / on it may stay his eye; / or, if he pleaseth, through it pass, / and then the heav'n espy.' Lewis Carroll's Alice does even better: she crawls right through the looking-glass, leaving her stuffy Victorian rule-bound world, entering a world in which everything 'was as different as possible', things are 'all alive', where dynamic connections are made between divergent elements.

A creative leap is required to support widening and deepening of perspective, and the ability to mix tacit knowledge with evidence-based or explicit knowledge effectively. The professional arena can be opened up to observations and reflections through the lens of artistic scrutiny. We are still anchored to our own perspective, but these perspectives will be artistically and critically enhanced. We cannot pass through the mirror's silvering, and can inevitably reflect only upon ourselves, our own thoughts and experiences. Artistic processes such as writing can, however, enable a harnessing of, for example, material such as memories which we do not know we remember, and greater access into the possible thoughts and experiences of others. The perspectival nature of such writing is acknowledged (i.e. they do not purport to be objective or true), and the many skills used are those of literature.

Professional writers are being heard clearly, both students (DasGupta and Charon 2004; Hatem and Ferrara 2001; Gomez et al. 2000) and practitioners (Clough 2002; Loughran 2004; Bolton 1999b; 2003a; see also the *Annals of Internal Medicine: Physician-Writers Reflection* series, e.g. Shem 2002). Samuel Shem says fiction writing has been an essential way for him of humanising medicine (2002).

Writers acutely observe small details and subtle nuances of behaviour and situations. A teacher- or clinician-writer observes details missed by good observant teachers or clinicians (see Charon 2004). Try it. Observe a student or client walking into your practice place. Capture on paper how they hold themselves, breathe, move their limbs, their characteristic gestures and sayings. What do they remind you of – a cat?, a big soft armchair?, a locked filing cabinet?

A writer has the unparalleled privilege also of entering into the life of another. That this person is a character on a page does not make it any less of a privilege. Deep understandings can be gained by entering (virtually) another's feeling, thinking, perception and memories. This is writing beyond what you know, and has to be: if you know where writing is going to take you, start at that known point, and write on into the unknown. Try it. Take the person you have just described. Write the conversation they might have had on returning home that night. Remember this is an artistic exercise: don't think about it, let your hand do the writing, free of the police officer of your mind. If you add in something about how they got home, where they live or drink, you really are allowing your imagination to take you through the glass. You tap into latent understandings which have possibly not been so fully exercised before.

This is fiction; the writing has been invented imaginatively: it removes the straitjacket of *what really happened*. Writers are therefore free to draw deeply upon their imagination and aesthetic sense, and their intuitive knowledge of social and human areas such as relationships, motives, perspective, cause and effect, ethical issues and values.

It matters not a jot that you do not depict what actually happened, or what your student or client really thought. What does matter is that you have brought what you understand and think about this person into the forefront of your mind. Medical students write patients' illness stories in the voice and vernacular of the patient, imaginatively and vicariously entering patients' contexts. They 'become the other' through creative writing (Engel et al. 2002, p. 32). It is not quiddity we seek – the real nature or essence of a thing – but our experience of it.

Sharing this writing with a colleague can offer effective reflection upon understandings. Rewrite with the fresh insight gained. And perhaps a colleague, also present at the encounter with the patient, might write an account. Reading each other's account will offer the different perspectives from which you unwittingly work.

This method of reflection does not jeopardise professional accuracy of perception (Mattingley 2000). Neither does it impose distorted interpretations about patients (Garro and Mattingley 2000) because its purpose is to explore and express what is already there in clinicians' and educators' understanding and perception. It brings this to the fore to be reflected upon critically and effectively. It also brings to the forefront of attention the perspectival nature of our perception. No one can know *what really happened* in any situation. Perhaps it might become clear that the doctor understood the patient very differently from the nurse, or the teacher might think and write one thing today, reflect upon it perhaps with peer(s), and write something different tomorrow, their perception enhanced by the writing and discussions. Such a collection of stories can build up a composite picture, and what was thought and felt – getting as close as possible to *what really happened*.

Kevin Marsden, a special-school teacher, and Masters in Education reflective practice student tells a classroom story:

Malcolm

One morning we were doing number work. Malcolm was struggling to recognise sets of two. He was troubled by the book in front of him and sat slumped on an elbow.

I had one of those 'bright ideas' teachers tend to get. Let's make it more practical. 'Malcolm,' I said. 'Look at Darren. How many eyes has he got?'

Malcolm looked at Darren. Pointing with his finger he slowly counted in his deep voice, 'one . . . two'.

'Good, well done,' I said. 'Now look at Debbie, how many eyes has she got?'

Pointing carefully again Malcolm intoned slowly, 'one . . . two'.

'That's great, Malcolm, now look at Tony, count his eyes.'

'One . . . two.' Let's take this a step further, I said smugly to myself.

'Now Malcolm, look at Matthew. Without counting can you tell me how many eyes he has got?'

Malcolm looked at me as if I had gone mad. 'OK that's fine Malcolm, you just count them like you did the others.'

Relieved he slowly repeated his methodical counting: 'one . . . two'.

There is a magical moment in teaching, when the penny drops, the light goes on, the doors open. Success is achieved. I was starting to worry. We weren't getting there!

'Malcolm, how many eyes has Naheeda got?' Malcolm counted slowly, as if it was the first pair of eyes he had ever seen. 'One . . . two'.

'Good, you're doing really well.'

We carried on round the class. Eager faces looked up to have their eyes counted. I was growing desperate as we ran out of children. Was I leading Malcolm on an educational wild-goose chase? Were we pursuing an idea that was not yet ready to be caught?

The last pair of eyes was counted. 'One . . . two.' The finger carefully went from eye to eye. There was only me left. 'Malcolm,' I said, trying to hide my desperation, 'how many eyes have I got?' Malcolm studied my face carefully. He looked long and hard at my eyes. I waited expectantly in the silence. His brow furrowed. Finally he spoke.

'Take your glasses off.'

Kevin Marsden

Kevin read this to his established sub-group of five teachers. They trusted and felt confidence and respect for each other's professional abilities and views. Kevin was able to share his frustrations and sense of failure; the group learned about the methods, joys and problems of special-school teaching. They were able to explore the probability that Malcolm had had a different understanding of his task than did Kevin. Possibly Malcolm thought he was to count the eyes, rather than 'guess' how many each had. To do this he would have had to ask for spectacles to be removed so he could see clearly. The situation of a mismatch between a teacher's intentions and a child's understanding must happen so often.

Why reflective practice now?

The grand stories of patriarchy/patriotism, religion, family and community no longer bind society. We look to counsellors, psychologists, teachers, clerics, life partners, GPs or social workers for essential support. Marriages founder and professionals increasingly experience stress as they now have the burden previously carried by a nexus of local and family community.

Faith in that great god science has also been shaken: 'Science, in my view, is now at the end of certainty' (Prigogine 1999, p. 26). There has been a powerful frontier (boundary) between science (and scientific professions like medicine) and the arts since the Enlightenment. A blinkered view of what constitutes knowledge and experience cannot be held for much longer.

> If any of us are out of touch with any part of ourselves we are in an impoverished state. The dominant culture is scientific, but the scientist who concentrates on this side of themselves exclusively is as impoverished as is the musician or writer who concentrates only on the artistic.
>
> Paul Robertson (Director of Medici String Quartet), 1999

The age of post-Newtonian belief in our ability to order ('master' even) our world is going. It led to a mess: the rise of clinical depression and the spread of the deserts, for example. The assumptions that an objective view of the world (Kantian) is 'grown-up', that we should shed our subjective view along with sand and water play, are being questioned (see also Sacks 1985, pp. 1–21).

An ethnographer can no longer stand on a mountain top from which authoritatively to map human ways of life (Clifford 1986). Practitioners cannot confidently diagnose and dictate from an objective professional or scientific standpoint; teachers do not know answers. The enmeshment of culture and environment is total: no one is objective.

'Since the seventeenth century, Western science has excluded certain expressive modes from its legitimate repertoire: rhetoric (in the name of "plain" transparent signification), fiction (in the name of fact), and subjectivity (in the name of objectivity). The qualities eliminated from science were localised in the category of "literature"' (Clifford 1986, p. 102). These categories have returned from that 300-year marginal position, to be embedded alongside the scientific approach.

Holistic coherent understandings which might support us out of our alienated mess are increasingly entertained. 'We now see the world as *our* world, rather than *the* world' (Reason 1988). Complementary healing considers our wholeness, not just within ourselves, but also within our environment and community. 'We seek a knowing-in-action (and thinking-in-action) which encompasses as much of our experience as possible' (Reason, ibid.).

Ideal professionals, gathering data on which to base their pedagogy, diagnosis or care, are like social anthropologists. Geertz suggested that successful ethnographers create a 'thick description': a web of 'sort of piled-up structures of inference and implication through which the ethnographer is continually trying to pick his way' (Geertz 1973, p. 7). The reflective practice writer who explores and experiments with different writing approaches, using whatever seems appropriate at the time, is like Lévi-Strauss's *bricoleur* (1966). This knotted nexus has then to be understood and interpreted to some degree: 'a good interpretation of anything – a poem, a person, a history, a ritual, an institution, a society – takes us into the heart of that of which it is the interpretation' (Geertz [1973] 1993, p. 7). An effective reflective practitioner attempts to understand the heart of their practice. Understandings gained in this way, however, are always partial; the deeper the enquiry, the enquirer realises the less they know and understand: *the more you know, the more you know you don't know*. Geertz also stresses that it is vital not to generalise across cases but within them. Having got somewhere near the heart of clients' or students' stories and poetry, practitioners can begin to act upon this understanding.

Professionals writing about their work, sharing it with colleagues in order to offer insight, and relating this to a wider field professionally and politically, are together engaged in an activity rather like Reason's *co-operative enquiry method*, in which researcher and subject collaborate in all the stages of research, including reflecting on the experience and making sense of it (Reason 1988). The practitioner takes a full share of responsibility. All too often professionals act in the mould of traditional researcher; acting *on* people: collecting data, and coming to conclusions in camera. There is a similarity with heuristic research (Moustakas 1990; Etherington 2004)

'In this way, it may be possible to avoid providing care which is dry, barren and – perhaps the greatest sin of all – unimaginative' (Smyth 1996, p. 937). Effective reflective practice can enable care or education which is alert and alive to the client's or student's needs and wants, whether professed or not. It can enable the practitioner to use their skill, knowledge and experience creatively and lovingly, and look forward with a greater confidence.

Angela Mohtashemi, a management consultant, shares her experience of reflective writing in organisations:

As I help organisations become more effective through better communication and engagement with their employees, I introduce reflective writing wherever I can as a tool for teamwork, learning and development and coaching. The workplace is a tough, manipulative environment where people are often expected to comply without challenge, to 'live the company's values', to 'display the right behaviours' and even to adopt the corporate language. One's sense of self can become fragile and this limits potential. Whenever I have used writing with groups or individuals they have commented on the sense of liberation and the feeling that they are getting to the heart of things.

Sometimes I have run workshops or team sessions specifically to explore reflective writing, sometimes incorporate it into other situations. A writing activity, such as writing about your name, can be a great icebreaker. I recently ran a session on writing for personal and organisational development as part of a leadership course my firm runs jointly with a university business school. The session incorporated learning theory, my own experience, principles of reflective writing and practical activities. These activities were typical of the techniques I use and included free writing and using unfamiliar imagery to look at the daily work experience.

Free writing, although very simple, fulfils many purposes and is often a revelation to people. A number of participants went to their action learning sets keen to use free writing to explore organisational issues before discussing them with the group. They were excited about the patterns that emerged and about the honesty of a conversation with one's self. I encourage people in action learning sets to reflect about the experience afterwards. One wrote to me later:

> I spent almost 2hrs writing up how I felt during our discussion and how I intended to change my behaviour as a result. It was tremendously therapeutic and enjoyable, which I found surprising, as I have, until now, been avoiding writing down anything about how I feel – so Thank You!

Sue Smith wrote:

> Bringing the issue was like opening a door and seeing a crack of light – and seeing a very small slither [sic] of a room. Once the door was opened fully – which happened when I started to look at the amount of change I'd undergone – I could see the room in its entirety – and appreciate how full and intricate the things in there were.

Sue Smith has a tremendous opportunity to change people's lives. Writing helps her find a way to pause and reflect, to argue with herself until she believes what she says and can then find the voice to persuade others. In that way, writing can be a powerful force for change.

When I first began this work I feared the response would be cynicism and doubts about its relevance. After all, most workplaces are based on rational and 'scientific' management practices: plans, budgets, facts, timelines, blueprints etc. There is little place for emotion and individual expression. My fears were wrong. Every time the response has been very positive and unleashed the power people can have when they bring their whole selves to work. One team member said the writing was 'one of the most exciting, interesting and engaging things I've done since I've been with the firm'.

Angela Mohtashemi

Reflective practice and reflexivity according to the principles and practice outlined here is a valuable developmental process for any teacher, social worker, clinician or student. It can take its non-judgemental camera down to any aspect of practice, with patients, colleagues, administrative and other staff, the interface of home and work, and the impact of experiences in the past on present actions. No feeling, thought or action is too small or too big for this zoom or wide-angle lens.

2

NARRATIVE-BASED PRACTICE

There are in our existence spots of time / . . . whence . . . our minds
Are nourished and invisibly repaired; / . . . Such moments
Are scattered everywhere.

Wordsworth [1880] 2004, p. 208

How can we know the dancer from the dance?

Yeats 1962, p. 128

You are watching a film. One of those arty ones starting with a scene taken with a wide-angle lens – a hawk's eye view – of a city. From this height cars and buildings look like toys, and the grid of streets and fields are a pattern: pretty but with little human meaning. People are too small to be seen.

The camera zooms: into focus comes one particular street – people walking and talking, everyday interchanges taking place. The camera comes closer and closer: up to one building, and one window of that building. We pass through the glass and into the staffroom of a big secondary school.

Effective reflective practice is the focusing upon detailed stories of practice and life, and upon the thoughts and feelings associated with the actions in them. These stories are imaginative creations drawn from experience. Seen as a set of interlocking plots, the problems, anguishes, and joys of practice become comprehensible: to be dealt with creatively and developmentally. The use of the aesthetic imagination in creating this material provides a screen as wide as life itself, drawing upon all of a practitioner's faculties. Attempting to reflect only upon 'what actually happened', and then to subject such an account to rational questions such as 'how might I have done it better?', unnecessarily restricts what might be explored.

A film of professional practice

The camera has entered the big secondary school staffroom. The atmosphere is stiff and almost silent; only one staff member, the head of maths, is humming to himself, the rest look anxious and jumpy. The headteacher enters the room and the quiet deepens; she invites the hummer to her room to discuss something of importance. He follows her out, and the tension shifts, although, does it not lessen, but staff are enabled to talk, albeit in low voices. This tension has been building up for months: since the biology teacher began to suspect the head of maths of a sexual relationship with a pupil.

The camera pans out, circles at hawk level again, zooms. This time it focuses on a small terraced house in a narrow street where the houses have no front gardens and tiny backyards. We are in the front room, a distraught mother has run out, thrusting her dead baby into the health visitor's arms. The tiny body is cold – so cold. The little girl wants to play with the 'dolly', and thinks the nurse might be kind and let her, Mummy wouldn't. The health visitor is in anguish as she knows the baby has had an autopsy – a horrifying sight unclothed.

The third time the camera takes us to a high-rise block of flats deep in London's East End. It is one of those utterly confusing ones with walkways, where the lifts work sporadically and jerkily, and flat numbers have been assigned by a dyslexic infant. A grey-haired social worker confusedly studies number after number as the wind whistles round the corners, blowing crisp packets to reveal a pile of hypodermic needles. She jumps as heavy footsteps interrupt the sound of the wind, her heart missing a beat as a very dark shape looms round the corner.

What do the practitioners in our films do with the distress, guilt, anxiety, horror, anger, humiliation – which they cannot, or do not express at work? How do they prevent these powerful feelings from draining energy, disabling them from effective practice? How do they learn from their own feelings, turn all those negative energies into positive? How do they learn from each other's mistakes and successes, each other's ideas, experience and wisdom? How do they learn to empathise with another through experiences which they will never know? A man will never know childbirth, for example; how does he learn the compassion and understanding needed to support a mother in travail?

Our films zoomed in from the distant and impersonal to the close and intensely human. This close-up focus on the 'rag and bone shop of the heart' (Yeats 1962, p. 201) is what effective reflection can do. We move from the grand ideals of our practice, to the precise story of a small handful of people who cry and laugh, shout and tremble silently, and are involved with people at the thresholds of life and death, at periods of intense change and development.

Our professional heroines and heroes come to terms with their own powerful emotions, learn from their own and others' mistakes and successes, and develop empathy – through reflection – in writing, in discussions about those writings and rewritings.

This book is about how practitioners can examine their own stories closely, look at themselves as heroines and heroes in their own real-life films, and look at the people with whom they work as heroes and heroines also. They take themselves – their problems, griefs and anxieties, as well as joys – seriously.

Vital details of practice

All of those film plots are stories of experience, written about and brought to groups by practitioners. They reflected upon them in the writing, and we discussed them further together.

The story of the departmental head who was having an affair with a pupil very greatly distressed the teacher who wrote about it. She was closely involved with all parties: pupil, family, teaching colleagues, the community. She felt deeply entwined with the whole drama, as did many of the other staff, but of course confidentiality decreed it could not be discussed. A confidential reflective practice group was an ideal forum. She started writing the story as a romantic love story, following a suggestion from me about genre writing (see Chapter 12). I think perhaps this distance and strong set structure enabled her to begin. Her small Masters in Education sub-group became agog to hear each episode. Her writing was so important to her that it became powerful hearing; the discussion and group support was invaluable to them all, so much so that they continued as a special study module in the next semester.

The health visitor did, of course, prevent the toddler from unwrapping the 'dolly' dead baby at her bereavement visit; but she was distressed that she had not handled it sensitively enough for it to be a growing experience for the child. The group were able to help her unpick it, see it through the eyes of the child, and consider carefully how she might have acted rather than just anxiously ward off the toddler.

The black man who approached the social worker in the East End high-rise block courteously asked if he could help her find her way. The group helped her out of just feeling intense shame at her assumptions, and enabled her to consider her habitual state of mind on home visits.

Why practice as screenplay?

Sharing stories with each other must be one of the best ways of exploring and understanding experience. That is, if Winter is right that what we want and need to say is not just *stored*, but held in our minds as *story* (Winter 1988), and if Goodson is right about their import:

> Stories do social and political work. A story is never just a story – it is a statement of belief, of morality, it speaks about value.
>
> Goodson 1998, p. 12

Narrative telling is a vital part of our lives – in the nurses' station, the staffroom, and in our own kitchens. Narrative is a 'source of consolation' (Eagleton 1983, p. 185). Stories offer the fictive comfort of structure with some sort of beginning, middle and end, and of the closure of our desire. We are involved in an endless search for something lost – God, Lacan's Imaginary, Freud's pre-Oedipal stage, Sartre's 'Being-in-itself', a unity with the mother's body, a sought-after haven where the signified has a direct innate correlation with the signifier:

Something must be lost or absent in any narrative for it to unfold: if everything stayed in one place there'd be no story to tell. This loss is distressing
but exciting as well: desire is stimulated by what we cannot quite possess.

Eagleton 1983, p. 185

We relate to the loss or lack in every story because we want the good characters
to gain their just hearts' desires, and the bad to founder. We share their joys and
tragedies vicariously. The story has the effect of reinforcing our assumptions
about what we might desire and what fear; it affirms our sense of moral, emotional, spiritual, or physical right. We follow Odysseus past the Sirens holding our
breath, and when a fair wind brings him back to Penelope, we will him to shoot
his arrow straight to prove he is really her husband; and we help Dorothy kill the
wicked witch of the West. When Tony Archer's son was on trial for political activity (BBC Radio 4, *The Archers*, autumn 1999), that was what people were talking
about in my village, rather than the latest news or the football, until they were
satisfied the jury had found him 'not guilty'.

Listeners' roles are just as important as writers': 'It is the joint effort of author
and reader which brings upon the scene that concrete and imaginary object
which is the work of the mind. There is no art except for and by others' (Sartre
[1948] 1950, pp. 29–30). And:

so there is an art of listening . . . Every narrator is aware from experience
that to every narration the listener makes a decisive contribution: a
distracted or hostile audience can unnerve any teacher or lecturer: a friendly
public sustains. But the individual listener also shares responsibility for that
work of art that every narration is: you realise this when you tell something
over the telephone, and you freeze, because you miss the visible reactions of
the listener . . . This is also the chief reason why writers, those who must
narrate to a disembodied public, are few.

Levi 1988, p. 35

Reflective practice writers write for *embodied* readers: group, supervisor or
mentor. My practitioner students say how *re-storying* with colleagues is as essential as initial writing.

Reflective practice allows practitioners to see relationships with students,
clients, patients or colleagues within a range of possible roles. The whole person
of the professional relates to the whole person with whom they work.
Professionals do not leave their personalities, their souls, their sense of humour,
their fragilities outside the classroom, consulting room or client's front door; and
they take on different roles at different times, just as in personal lives.

The possible roles for both professional and client could be seen to be: *I, you,*
and *her/him*. The client as 'I' is at the centre of the drama – the subject, the hero/
heroine – the story told from their point of view. The client as 'you' is the other in
the script – the whole person in relationship with the professional, and the

professional is the teller of the story: whether telling it as 'I' (first person narrative) or 'he/she' (third person narrative). The client as 'her or him' becomes an object: an appropriate role in some circumstances such as research trials when the patient is only a statistic.

This poem explores a family doctor's awareness of the way her patients can see themselves *centre stage*, as 'I', and the way she handles that:

Performance

This is your stage.
Sit down, compose your face.
Lines rehearsed in the waiting room.
Family can't hear you—
'Leave mum she has a headache.'

Headache.
Muscle ache.
Spirit ache.
Tired all the time.
Tired of the time.
Too much time.

Let me perform for you.
Let me touch you,
measure your blood pressure,
measure your worth.
You are worth my time.
When you get home, they'll ask what I said.
Rehearse the lines.

This is your chance.
This is your stage.

Jo Cannon

What about a practitioner's relationship with her- or himself? A professional wrote in evaluation: 'Writing weaves connections between my work and the rest of my life, between my inner and outer selves, between the left and the right sides of my brain, between the past and the present.' A trainee said: 'This kind of writing has to have material about who we are and what we stand for.' A GP wrote: 'I'd considered resigning because I'd been struggling with being a doctor and who it turned me into. Creative writing has helped me see what was happening – share it with others and begin to find a way through.' Storying and re-storying our lives helps us to keep pace with the way we change and develop over time. 'Who I am' does not and cannot remain stable:

It is important to view the self as an emergent and changing 'project' not a stable and fixed entity. Over time our view of our self changes, and so, therefore, do the stories we tell about ourselves. In this sense, it is useful to view self-definition as an ongoing narrative project.

Goodson 1998, p. 11

And 'how it is' is neither stable nor definite either: an ongoing narrative project.

Why reflective practice?

Our stories are inextricably intertwined – with themselves and with those of others. We tell and retell, affirming and reaffirming ourselves in our own and each other's eyes (and ears). The accounts slip and merge as we tell, developing new twists and losing ones that have served their turn. This urge to recount and recreate each day is strong; but it is only too easy to devalue our own stories because they are unimportant compared with those of powerful others such as pop stars, surgeons, politicians: we have lost trust in ourselves, and ownership of our stories.

Reflective practice writing is a way of expressing and exploring our own and others' stories: crafting and shaping to aid understanding and development. These stories are data banks of skill, knowledge and experience: much of our knowing is in our doing. We can learn from our own and each other's mistakes and successes, each other's ideas, experience and wisdom, and tackle and come to terms with our own problem areas. Although practice is continually aired – over coffee with a colleague – we do not tell each other or ourselves the things at our cutting edge of difficulty.

Sharing reflective writings and discussing them in depth enables practice development because the outcomes of reflection are taken back into practice, improving and developing (Kolb 1984). Reflection reaches the stage, as Aeschylus said: 'Words can do no more . . . / Nothing remains but the act' (trans. 1999, p. 115). This gives a 'different way of being', or as another course participant put it: 'It seems like a new country, one which we've all been peering into for a long time.' This insight facilitates developmental change; Davidson reports using a reflective writing approach within an eating disorders unit:

Through reflection and writing, we can struggle to get a conceptual grip on the situation. With a leap of faith we can open ourselves to honestly experiencing what is going on in our relationships. Even if the resultant understanding and experience is partial, it should yield a point of leverage where something that we can *do* is revealed. And if it transpires what we do does not have the desired result, then at least we have new information with which to enhance our experience and aid further reflection.

Davidson 1999, p. 122

Rita Charon (2000c), general internist and medical professor, reports how sharing reflective writings about patients with them deepened and clarified understandings between them; some responded by writing also.

> I have realised that we have to make the day-to-day parts of our work more enjoyable and varied. Writing, and the reflection it allows, has brought me a real pleasure – that's why I used to smile and now I can keep that joy and even the intimacy by writing what I've felt or seen and its ironies too.
>
> Clare

Reflective practice can facilitate and enhance:

- acceptance of, and increased confidence with, the essential complexity and uncertainty of professional life;
- reflexive critical awareness of personal values, ethics, prejudices, assumptions of professional identity, decision-making processes;
- reflexive critical awareness of the professional milieu: its values, ethics, assumptions about roles and identity;
- acceptance of, and willingness to explore, the interrelatedness of the professional and the personal;
- sensitive, fruitful review of 'forgotten' areas of practice;
- analysis of hesitations, skill and knowledge gaps;
- constructive awareness of collegial relationships;
- relief of stress by facing problematic or painful episodes;
- identification of learning needs;
- dissemination of experience and expertise to and from colleagues;
- increased confidence in professional practice.

Hoping for answers to the conundrums of practice is like searching for a babyhood security-blanket. Reflective practice leads to more searching questions, the opening of fascinating avenues to explore, but few secure answers. Questions like: 'What should I have done?' become minor. More questions are thrown up, such as: 'Why did the maths teacher take so little care to hide his relationship with the pupil?' 'Perhaps I could have told the toddler a story about the dead baby in order to help her to understand; what story would have been right?' The East End walkway story was capped by another who recounted how she turned to face a gang of threatening young people and asked the way (although she knew it): the frightening 'gang' immediately became kids who communicated with her as a person. This supported the social worker to reassess her attitude to seemingly threatening people.

A paradox concerns effective practice not being certain. We all know colleagues who can't say 'I don't know'. Their effectiveness is diminished by their inflexible need to know. In order to acquire confidence, effective practitioners:

- let go of certainty, in a safe enough environment;
- look for something without knowing what it is;
- begin to act without knowing how they should act.

The essential uncertainty associated with effective reflective practice and reflexivity make it hard for many. 'Certainty goes down as experiential knowledge goes up. . . Pre-service teachers want answers and methods. They want to be certain. They want to know. In pre-service teacher education, working towards habits of uncertainty and puzzlement needs to be undertaken with modest expectations' (Phillion and Connelly 2004, p. 468).

> The goal of education, if we are to survive, is the *facilitation of change and learning*. The only person who is educated is the person who has learned how to learn; the person who has learned how to adapt and change; the person who has realised that no knowledge is secure, that only the process of seeking knowledge gives a basis for security. Changingness, a reliance on process rather than on static knowledge is the only thing that makes any sense as a goal for education in the modern world.
>
> Rogers 1969, p. 152

Experienced effective practice is about a willingness to have faith in your own knowledge, skills and experience; to trust the process you are engaged in (reflective practice writing, doctoring, teaching, etc.); to relate to the student, client or patient with respect and unconditional positive regard (Rogers 1969).

It is also about a willingness to subject every action and thought both to reflection *in action* and self-respectful effective reflection *upon action* (Schon 1983). Reflection *in action* is the hawk in your mind constantly circling over your head watching and advising on your actions – while you are practising. Reflection *upon action* is the process with which this book is primarily concerned: a considering of events afterwards so that practice can effectively be enhanced (Schon 1983, see also 1987). Self-respect is needed, while opening up to close observation, uncertainty and questioning areas which previously had been taken for granted:

- *actions*: what you and others did;
- *ideas*: what you thought; what others might have thought;
- *feelings*: what you felt, and what others might have felt.

We live in deeds not years; in thoughts, not breaths;
In feelings, not in figures on a dial.
We should count time by heart throbs. He most lives
Who thinks most – feels the noblest – acts the best.

P. J. Bailey (1816–1902) Festus

Sophocles has been translated as saying: 'Between feeling and action there is thought' (trans 1982). Our actions are effective if they arise from both feelings and thoughts. Emotions can too easily be marginalised in professional life:

> There is something rather odd about trying to get help from health workers who have not worked out their own feelings, or who deny them to themselves and others. Where do all those spontaneous feelings go and who is to say what damage they might be doing to the delicate internal workings of our minds if we continue to repress and suppress them . . . The key insights and changes in the way I view myself and my professional work have come through self-reflective work.

Heller 1996, pp. 365, 368

Uncomfortable emotions to reflect upon

Powerful emotions sometimes arise within practice and within reflection upon practice. Very strong emotion can initially appear to inhibit the ability to reflect and understand, however, as Andrew Eastaugh (1998a) found in his research into co-tutoring; he also found it well worth persevering:

> The idea that my emotions are a source of understanding has an exciting and novel ring for me. Exciting because it opens up the possibility . . . that the emotional part of me has a value outside my own personal attachment to it. . . . It is novel because my experience of the world of learning has been that emotions are, at best, merely the icing on top of the cake, for decoration, self-indulgence and treats, but not the real substance. Too much will make you sick and is unnecessary. At their worst they are a serious barrier to the real business of life – should be pushed aside and ignored.

Eastaugh 1998a, p. 48

Anger can prove to be a useful if uncomfortable focus for reflection. Here is a senior medical Masters student reflecting later upon the effect of his reflective practice story writing and work:

> As a result of reflecting upon these incidents I now understand much better how I have been dealing with anger and the effect it was having on me. I felt unable to express anger because I was afraid of making a fool of myself,

afraid of losing control and because I want to be well thought of. I feel that if I get angry with someone they will not like me. I want to be liked. I therefore tend to push my anger down inside. I have not been consciously aware of doing this and therefore have not been aware of how much anger I have been carrying. I have therefore not been able to explain the unpleasant feelings I have had when it has begun to rise to the surface.

I now know that it is not possible (or necessarily good) to please everybody all the time. I know the difference between telling someone I am angry and expressing the anger itself. I am able to recognise when I am angry, when I am suppressing it and the feelings that this causes. I feel more able to tell people when I am angry with them and that I can do this articulately.

Rod

And a doctor wrote a vehement and dramatic long-term 'diary' about his relationship with his health authority; when he reflected upon it later, he wrote: 'I am much less emotionally reactive in all these management meetings I have to go to, and certainly not as nervous!' Lindsay Buckell's 'expression of my passionate hatred of the current climate of fear and blame' (Chapter 4) is another.

Keith Collett, a GP (family practitioner) trainer, and supervisor for applications to fellowship of the British Royal College of General Practitioners, encourages the writing of drafts of medical reports, responses to complaints and so on, so that they can be discussed, reflected upon and redrafted:

This is incredibly useful to prevent registrars overstating support or condemnation for a patient . . . They have a chance to reflect on how it will be received by the patient, their relatives, or their solicitor . . . I encourage the first splenic draft to be written as I feel it has a healing and calming effect, and offers an opportunity for reflection. Too often dictaphones are used and the resultant text signed and sent without reflective reading.

Keith Collett

Anger is often seen to be an inappropriate professional emotion – beyond the professional boundary. Reflective practice is an appropriate locus for exploring it, and the other seemingly dangerous emotions.

Discussing each other's work, our focus moves naturally between personal development, professional development and writing technique. We work intensely, sometimes sharing deep emotions, but I rarely experience any tension or sense of effort.

Maggie

I wrote bits of verse which expressed conflicts of loyalty and fears for the future. I read them out and wept, and the silence of our group carried my emotions.

Clare

Paula Salvio supports teachers in *empathetic enquiry*, a deeper understanding of ethnic minority students. She says teachers must 'travel into our own worlds' in order to 'travel to those of others', and gain empathetic understanding. This process must include involvement with the emotions, as 'emotional whiteout' will disable this travel into both our own worlds and those of others (1998, p. 49). This kind of writing, involving the emotions, is what Cixous described as feminine:

All the feminine texts I've read are very close to the voice, very close to the flesh of language, much more so than masculine texts . . . perhaps because there's something in them that's freely given, perhaps because they don't rush into meaning, but are straightway at the threshold of feeling. There's tactility in the feminine text, there's touch, and this touch passes through the ear.

Cixous 1995, p. 175

Focus on reflection

Mark Purvis and the Death of Simon

The grown-ups stand around watching.
Grown-ups know what to do.
The grown-ups stand around watching.

Is that Simon lying on the pavement?
He has got blondie hair like Simon's.
The grown-ups stand around watching.

A boy has been run over, another kid says.
Is that Simon lying on the pavement? He *was* walking in front of me.
The grown-ups stand around watching.

Mrs Bailey puts a blanket over him – but I can still see his blondie hair.
She looks at me but before she can turn quickly to the other grown-ups,
I can see she's scared.
'Send Mark away.'
What have I done wrong?

The grown-ups know what to do.
They send me away.

I run ahead alone.
Trying to find Simon.
I might not recognise him.
Pulling kids by their shoulders – no that's not him.
I speed up when I hear the ambulance siren.

'Simon's been run over.' Pete Williams said.
I run away, trying hard not to believe him.

How can Pete Williams tell who is lying there,
anyhow I saw *him* looking for *his* brother too.
Surely I would have recognised my own brother.

My teacher says 'Simon will be in his classroom'.
But he isn't, so she smiles and cuddles me, warm and soft.
'It's alright Mark, they call ambulances for sprained ankles these days.'

When he came into the classroom everyone stopped and looked.
He didn't have to tell me.
I said 'Simon's dead,' and he nodded, unable to speak.

Mark Purvis

Mark's poem concerns his brother's death when they were both small. Mark (a GP trainer) needed to write about it in a professional development situation to free himself from the way the unexplored memory inhibited his ability as a doctor to cope with child deaths. After he had read the poem to the group and we had discussed it, he said this:

I had never before in detail talked about what I was feeling at the time when Simon died. Now I have written about it I can and do talk about it.

Simon and I had had an argument about a fortnight before he died. I'd asked Simon not to walk with me to school. You know what it's like, an older brother wants to be with his own friends and doesn't want to be seen taking care of his little brother. Until I did this writing I felt guilty about Simon's death – that it was my fault for not allowing him to walk with me.

In the past my feeling about Simon's death disabled me for dealing with the death of child patients. Everyone finds it difficult; but for me they used to bring all sorts of things to the surface. I remember one child who died, I was totally disabled and unable to cope with consultations with the parents. I cried with them, and told them about Simon and that I was crying for him.

The writing has made me feel completely different about Simon's death, has made me deal with it in a different way. I can now see I wasn't responsible; though my mother still feels very guilty that she didn't drive him to school that day. The time was right for me to write.

I didn't know I was carrying so much guilt. Now I know I don't need to carry it. I will cope differently now when a child patient dies.

Mark Purvis

Mark Purvis created the character of 9-year-old Mark in his poem. He was then able to visit that so-painful scene as the observer of this bewildered little boy. The poem seems so authentic: the voice of the child so consistently, movingly clear, drawing forth empathy in readers. Yet it is fiction, written by a senior and well-respected doctor, not a 9-year-old. Can you imagine Mark being able to *talk* about Simon with anything like this power? Writing enabled a private quiet space for this memory to be revisited.

Poetic form is a further enabling device. A poem is a further remove from 'real life', is clearly not 'true' even when it tells of life events (as poems usually do, one way or another). Poetry draws on a range of devices – such as repetition ('grown-ups'), and cutting away unnecessary words, as in the taut final stanza – which enable deeply painful events to be communicated.

Film-makers use similar devices, such as holding the camera at child height. The reflective practitioner has to be able to reinhabit their own skin at whatever time in their lives the event upon which they are reflecting happened; during training perhaps, or even earlier. They also need to experiment with seeing the world through the eyes of another – a student perhaps. The funny thing is that one *can* re-experience an event, or experience another's vicariously. 'The past is [not] a foreign country. They do [not] do things differently there' (Hartley 1953, p. 1). My son used to think that everything in the past was black and white, and people walked jerkily, because they did in old films. Listen to Cocteau holding his own camera at child height:

> I thought of going along the street from the Rue Blanche to number 45, closing my eyes and letting my right hand trail along the houses and the lamp-posts as I always used to do when I came back from school. The experience did not yield very much and I realised that at that time I was small and that now my hand was placed higher and no longer encountered the same shapes. I began the manoeuvre again.
>
> Thanks to a mere difference of level, and through a phenomenon similar to that whereby a needle rubs against the grooves of a gramophone record, I obtained the music of memory and I discovered everything again: my cape, my leather satchel, the name of the friend who accompanied me, and the name of our teacher, some precise phrases I had said, the marbled cover of my note-book, the timbre of my grand-father's voice, the smell of his beard and the material of the dresses worn by my sister and mother, who were At Home on Tuesdays.
>
> Cocteau [1930] 1968, p. 137

Making sense of experience

Life does not really have a beginning, a middle and an end (Sartre [1938]): that is
the prerogative of literature. Writing and telling our stories is not straightforward;
but if we can have sufficient faith in ourselves, trust in the process, and respectful
unconditional positive regard (Rogers 1969) for the people with whom we work
to create a beginning, the rest might well follow.

A closely observed event (Wordsworth's 'spot of time'), written about, reflected
upon, discussed critically, and re-explored through further writings stands
metonymically for the whole of that professional's practice. Stories and poems
are slices, metonymically revealing the whole of life (metonym = part standing
for whole, the pen is mightier than the sword: pen and sword stand graphically
and metonymically for huge social, political and cultural areas: literature and
war). Here is a reflective practice group evaluation:

> a different way of seeing: many insights, many views
> a sense of wonder at the creativity of so many people I had seen
> only as professional colleagues
> I am challenged to see others I meet with new eyes.
>
> a different way of hearing: many voices, many themes
> I have been moved by the quality of our listening and by the careful
> and gentle hearing of my own emerging voice.
>
> a different way of being: many persons, an experience shared.
> I have found a sense of integration in allowing the creative part of
> myself which I had stifled to energise my life and work.
> there is empowerment for deeper living in the shared silence,
> laughter and tears.
>
> Sheena

The camera focuses upon a drained doctor at the end of a long week. She reaches
into her lowest desk drawer and takes out something which will enable her to
cope, to continue to see her profession as growing and worthwhile. It is not a
bottle, hypodermic syringe, or pills, but a pad of yellow paper and a pen. She
starts to write . . .

3

THROUGH THE LOOKING-GLASS

Alice was through the glass, and had jumped lightly down into the Looking-Glass room . . . Then she began looking around and noticed that what could be seen from the old room was quite common and uninteresting, but that all the rest was as different as possible. For instance, the pictures on the wall next the fire seemed to be all alive.

Carroll [1865] 1954, pp. 122–3

The sage offered her disciple tea, but did not stop pouring. 'Master, the cup is full!' 'You are just like this cup: overflowing,' the sage replied, 'there is no space for you to learn.'

Story from Chuang Tsu

Effective reflection and reflexivity make the ordinary of one's experience seem extraordinary, 'as different as possible'. And it makes the extraordinary, the foreign, of another's experience more comprehensible, and close. Paying close attention to the stories which form our understanding of professional and personal life enables this to happen. Actions, interactions, professional episodes, memories even from long ago, spiritual elements, thoughts, ideas and feelings *are*, or are about to become, 'all alive' – both to the writer and their audience. Appropriate developmental change becomes apparent. This chapter discusses the *through-the-looking-glass* processes of reflection, and reflexivity, and the role of stories and fiction.

Practitioners open themselves to relating to a wide range, within both their own experience and that of others, through this dynamic process. They recognise many different ways of knowing, all of them valid. Nothing is irrelevant, however insignificant or personal it might appear to be: assumptions as to what is relevant or significant thwart the process.

When I realised my mother's cancer was terminal I considered resigning my job to help care for her. Realising that wasn't possible I then had to consider how to survive over the next few months. I'd considered resigning because I'd been struggling with being a doctor and who it had turned me into. Creative writing has helped me see what was happening, share it with others and begin to find a way through. I discovered that I could barely engage with my own emotions and fears any more. I had developed a protective shell through which I couldn't feel but which allowed me to keep going. The reality of a very significant loss in my life meant I had to feel it and understand my self again.

Clare

All aspects of ourselves are interrelated; practice is not undertaken with one part, and personal life another. They might be linked in surprising ways, moreover, by irrelevant-seeming factors. The insignificant-seeming incident, appearing seemingly out of nowhere in reflective practice writing, may be central.

Through-the-looking-glass processes can enable developmental, aesthetic and creative access to layers of reflective and reflexive material.

Professionals need to engage in 'that willing suspension of disbelief' (Coleridge, quoted by Schon 1983, pp. 296, 363), to open themselves to uncertainty as to learning needs and possibilities. This uncertainty, or knowledge of lack of knowledge, is an educative space for insight, intuition and credulity, leading to knowledge of what was already unwittingly known. Alice was instructed by the White Queen in 'living backwards', and told to practise believing up to six impossible things before breakfast every day (Carroll [1865] 1954, p. 173). I congratulated a novelist friend on having made me believe in impossibly extraordinary characters (Glaister 1999); she responded: 'the more you can believe the better'.

Three foundations

- certain uncertainty;
- serious playfulness;
- unquestioning questioning.

Certain uncertainty: the one certainty is uncertainty. In a reflexive, reflective process you begin to act when you do not know how you should act. Any interim goals are constructed in the light of material arising from the process, rather than there being a predetermined goal: a creative, dynamic situation, though perhaps less comfortable than having a clear road mapped out ahead. Students or supervisees, who are used to the certainty of a provided structure, may feel they have a 'right' to such a structure. The responsibility of uncertainty is uncomfortable, until confidence in the excitement of discovery is acquired. Students and supervisees often feel tutors should take responsibility: a non-developmental attitude.

A confident, effective practitioner responds flexibly and creatively to a range of influences, needs and wants of clients, colleagues, situations and forces. A practitioner who thinks they know the right answers all the time is bound to be wrong. To people willing to 'not know' all the time, all sorts of things are possible.

Serious playfulness: a playful attitude, and willingness to experiment, makes uncertainty a positive force, makes the fear of adventure safe enough to venture forth. It is looking for something when you do not know what it is, discovering some pertinent questions. An adventurous spirit leads onto that trackless moorland which education has come to be, rather than a walled or hedged field (Usher et al. 1997, p. 3). Sacred positions are not taken seriously: anything and everything is brought into question, even ourselves, leaving no room for self-importance. There is, however, only so much we can do to alter our own situation, that of others, and the wider political one, by reflexivity, reflection, or education: our power is *unlimitedly limited*. This playfulness is essentially serious: we are talking professional and personal development, not Ludo.

Unquestioning questioning: we accept, unquestioningly, the questioning spirit. Questions determine directions across the moorland, and therefore what we are likely to find along the way. These findings beget more questions. Reflective practice lays open to question our own and others' daily actions, and those of the organisations in which we work: a willingness 'to risk abandoning previous "truths" and sit with *not knowing*' (Gerber 1994, p. 290). This 'not knowing' is active and enquiring – rather like the small child's iconoclastic eternal *why*?

Paradoxically, the way to find out about ourselves is through forgetting ourselves. It is letting go of everyday assumptions about who we are, in order to be open to the discovery of other possible selves – the myselves of whom I am not habitually aware, the myself I might be, and the selves I am becoming. Only when 'the cup is empty' can the professional receive, hear what is being said, perceive what is happening.

These oxymorons underpin an aesthetic (Schon's 'artistry', 1983) and ethical approach rather than a logical or instrumental one. It is a way of telling and retelling one's story, in relation to the stories of others and that of the situation in which the writers of these stories find themselves. Socrates' pedagogic method was based on just such oxymorons; here is Meno struggling with Socrates' ruthless method of enquiry into the nature of 'virtue':

Meno:	Socrates, even before I met you they told me that in plain truth you are a perplexed man yourself and reduce others to perplexity . . .
Socrates:	It isn't that knowing the answers myself, I perplex other people. The truth is rather that I infect them also with the perplexity I feel myself . . . So with virtue now. I don't know what it is. You may have known before you came into contact with me, but now you look as if you don't. Nevertheless I am ready to carry out, together with you, a joint investigation and inquiry into what it is.
Meno:	But how will you look for something when you don't in the least know what it is? How on earth are you going to set up something you don't know as the object of your search? To put it another way, even if you come right up against it, how will you know that what you have found is the thing you didn't know?

Plato trans. 1958, pp. 127–8.

Facilitating effective reflective practice

Facilitating reflective practice is also uncertain: like handling a box of unpredictable fireworks. They will probably go off when the blue touchpaper is lit; but the direction or how they will explode into colour, light and sound is unknown.

Reflective practice facilitators stay with this uncertainty with their participants. Together they commit themselves to perceiving key stories which shape their existence, take responsibility for their own part in these narratives, and do what they can to develop and alter things constructively. It is not possible to set tidy session plans and learning objectives. The only achievable learning objective there can be is that practitioners have engaged actively and dynamically.

A safe-enough closed environment, an agreed way of behaving, and a time limit are required. A safe-enough boundaried confidential space can facilitate openness, willingness and courage. Course members have said such as: 'I have been able to be *me!*', 'I have been able to say what I really *think!*', in evaluation. Perhaps even more pertinently: 'I have been able to express what I *feel!*'

Courses constrain professionals, or professionals-in-training, to behave in certain ways for a certain time, in a specific place. This has the paradoxical effect of giving them permission to be freer in other dimensions, like exploring and questioning the stories by which they function. Losing responsibility for everyday issues enables them to take responsibility for more fundamental issues in their lives, such as values and professional identity.

Dialogue is required, rather than debate, or didactic discussion. In debate people construct intellectual arguments in order to win points; participants in dialogue attempt to express what they think, feel and experience, in order to gain access to deeper understandings.

Most training and post-experience courses include elements of reflective practice. There is a danger that it is only undertaken because it is the thing to do, or part of a course or continuing professional development. By its nature such an attitude cannot support reflection and reflexivity.

Fear of going through the looking-glass

Self-protectiveness against exploring the unknown of oneself arises from a fear of uncovering unpalatable things. Hence, Dr Jekyll becoming wicked grotesque Mr Hyde (Stevenson 1886), Dorian Gray with his mirror portrait ageing before his eyes (Wilde 1891), Hesse's *Steppenwolf* (1927), and 'The student of Prague', whose reflection stepped out of the glass and committed terrible crimes in his name (1929 Conrad Veidt film).

Freud built on this fear with theories of *ego, superego* and *id*. *Id* has been seen as 'animal instinct': potentially ungovernable, and in need of control by conscious *egos*. If *superego* – conscience – fails to direct *ego* appropriately, devil *id* might take over. Pat Barker (1991) studied this with reference to shell-shock and fugue in the First World War.

Through-the-looking-glass reflective practice can seem to the newcomer transgressive of psychological boundaries. An examination of our taken for granted psychological and social structures does not, however, let out ungovernable demons, though the uncertainty it occasions can make it feel as though it might. Crossing boundaries is a marginal activity to be undertaken with caution. When facilitators know what they doing, this is a *safe fear*. Perceiving that previously accepted situations and relationships are untenable and need to be altered can be as troubling and unrestful as unquestioning lack of change can be boring and depressing. But handled properly as reflective and reflexive thinking it is psychologically unbalancing. When dynamic change *has* to take place, due to the developed understanding of the reflective practitioner, it becomes inevitable and exciting: the energy and commitment to change is generated by the reflective and reflexive process.

Expressive and explorative writing is a trustworthy, paced reflexive and reflective process, if allied with carefully facilitated group or paired work. Participants get what they pay for: those willing to pay by expressing and exploring deeply will receive the most. Practitioners involve themselves in the process according to their strengths, wants and needs. Those not so ready only go as far as they can and need. There are often those who I wish could have taken themselves further: the choice is theirs, whether conscious or not.

Courageously adventuring through the glass, rather than merely gazing on its surface, is personally demanding. It enables practitioners to view their practice with unprecedented width. It can offer insight into the motives, thoughts and feelings of others, and suggest a range of possible actions which could never have been envisaged before. This is likely to change practice, and the relationship of the practitioner to their practice, dynamically – a politically and socially unsettling process. But it can not *transform* practice with the wave of a *hey presto* magic wand, without a deep personal investment. No education can offer definitive answers, and betterment is never unalloyed. The wish for *transformation* in this way can be as uncritical as Midas's wish that everything he touched might turn to gold. Here is the voice of Midas's unenchanted wife:

Look we all have wishes; granted.
But who has wishes granted? Him. Do you know about gold?
It feeds no one: aurum. Soft, untarnishable; slakes
no thirst. He tried to light a cigarette: I gazed entranced,
as the blue flame played on its luteous stem. At least,
I said, you'll be able to give up smoking for good.

Duffy 1999, p. 12

Even if magic wands were to hand the gains would prove non-developmental, based as they would be on uncritical, un-thought-through assumptions. Myth tells us to take full responsibility for our own lives and learning, to have our eyes clearly open to the drawbacks as well as advantages, to errors and blunders as well as successes of our educational journey.

Leslie Boydell (associate director), and Anne McMurray (organisational development consultant) reflect on leadership development:

The Institute of Public Health in Ireland (North and South) launched its first leadership development programme in January 2002 with twenty-two participants. The overall aim is to build a network of leaders across the island working collaboratively and creatively to reduce health inequalities and improve health and well-being during and beyond the life of the two-year programme.

The programme design is based on the model provided by Kolb's learning cycle (Kolb 1984). Leadership development requires assessment both of oneself as an individual as well as of the challenges faced in providing leadership. Action is based on assessment. Reflection enables learning from experience so that what has been learnt can be integrated into practice.

Writing as a means of reflective practice by professionals providing clinical care for patients with chronic disease provides a parallel for public health practitioners dealing with the intractable problems of improving the health of populations. We saw its potential for enabling those working in public health to reflect on their leadership, both to make sense of the challenges they face and to reflect on their actions taken. Participants worked in learning sets which had been formed at the start of the programme and participants had formed strong relationships of trust.

Following this workshop participants were asked to make a commitment to write regularly about their progress with their leadership challenges, what was happening, what they thought about it and what they felt. It was suggested that they write about how they brought leadership to their challenge and to consider how their leadership was developing as a result of the experience of dealing with their challenge. They identified partners within the group with whom they could share their writing prior to the next workshop three months later. Logistically this was a challenge as participants were dispersed throughout Ireland. At the next event they were asked to share some of the writing done during the intervening period and to do some further writing from a new perspective. A third workshop took place three months later following a similar format.

The group formed the idea they would like to produce a book, based on excerpts of their writing. At a final workshop, Gillie provided individual writing consultations to help people develop their reflections into publishable pieces for an audience interested to learn more about what it means to provide leadership in public health at this time in Ireland, North and South. The book [Denyer et al. 2003, see Chapter 8] provides a very personal and powerful account of the participants' views and experience of leadership, their development journey, the practice and the dilemmas faced. Writings are essays, short prose, poetry and metaphor.

While most of the participants embraced this approach, it does not suit everyone's learning style. Some found it a valuable learning technique, writing to find out what they think about situations where they do not know how to act or where they have already acted and need to make sense of what has happened. For others, a more interactive style of reflection may be more suitable, as writing is regarded as being a solitary activity (although sharing the writing is an important part of the process). A key leadership activity is to find some way to 'get on the balcony' and find perspective in the middle of action (Heifetz and Linsky 2002, p. 54). As Gillie suggests, reflective practice entails embracing uncertainty. Some people may be more comfortable with this than others.

Subsequent leadership groups have been offered this technique at different stages on the programme and have engaged in it to varying degrees. Two years later, participants from both of the groups who were introduced to the technique report they continue to use the approach as an invaluable tool to reflection, thinking and planning. The approach has been used to deal with conflict, power and leadership, explore complexity, come to terms with grief, and to unlock organisational and relationship impasses. It provides a way to develop the leadership discipline of thinking things through.

Leslie Boydell, Anne McMurray

Seeing through glass walls

The philosopher Zerubavel writes that we live within very tightly confined mental glass boxes. The world is perceived through the glass walls, leading us to imagine we are free of bias and preconception. Only when we try to get up and move to another mental space do we bump into walls, and become aware of their existence (Bell 1992).

Jill Bell reflected thus when she learned to read, write and speak Chinese: 'it simply never occurred to me that in attempting a new literacy, I might be entering a new way of looking at education . . . I never questioned whether for instance [the Chinese] notion of progress might be different from mine.' She had to learn also that 'the form of a text is inextricably linked to the content'; that 'balance and concentration' are essential mental and physical prerequisites to the learning of the language. Bell effectively (and surprisedly) saw the walls of her own 'cultural box', and the outlines of another (1992).

Reflective practice could lead to too much introspection, to pushing the practitioner more firmly and unquestioningly *into* the box of their cultural position. Reflexivity's role is to problematise self and identity: professionally, socially and politically. The support of a critical group (or co-mentor) of peers, and the searching out of material (professional, political and social texts) from as wide a sphere as possible will enable the reflexive process. Effective reflection and reflexivity examine emotions, experiences, thoughts and actions both of the self and of trusted confidential peers as embedded within the global situation.

Teams can usefully examine themselves as well as individuals (see Chapter 5). Barry et al. (1999) have persuasively written of their use of reflective writings in developing their team researching doctor-patient communication. The *patchwork text* reflective course assessment process aids team development (Illes 2003).

This letting go of our everyday assumptions about who we are enables us to be open to the discovery of other possible selves – the myselves of whom I am not habitually aware, the myself I might be, and the selves I am becoming, the team in development. Listening creatively to the voices within us, and those without, and responding creatively is effective reflective practice.

Synthesis, as well as analysis

Writing a story or poem is organic, synthesising elements from the muddle of experience, weaving them to create a coherent artefact which communicates a seemingly single strand. Sharing this text with peers, and writing new accounts about the same incident from different angles or different points of views in ways suggested by these peers, can enable both writer and reader to perceive the core experience or incident as a synthesis of a multiplicity of stories and potential stories. If this is associated with a reading and discussion of significant related material from their larger professional, social and political world (journal papers, more popular material such as magazines or television programmes, views and opinions of colleagues), then the experience will be deepened. This perception takes place because the professional experience is not only examined across a range of levels of reflection (as in Mezirow 1981) but, more importantly, refracted through different lenses, in different lights, and with different senses predominating, as well as material considered from psychological, social, political and spiritual arenas. This process is, then, a critical-synthetic one, rather than a critical-analytic one.

Kant used 'synthesis' to indicate the process by which the two sources from which our knowledge is drawn are combined. 'Judgement requires what Kant calls a "synthesis" of concept and intuition, and only in this synthesis is true experience (as opposed to mere intuition) generated' (Scruton 1982, p. 25). Kant argued that imagination has a central role in this 'synthesis'.

The synthetic process in reflective writing is between cognitive understandings of events (the rational discourse of Mezirow 1981, quoted above) and intuitive perceptions (sensibilities), between what appear to be facts and our feelings about them. Feelings and ideas are multifaceted, complex. Writers cannot *know* others' feelings, ideas, experiences: they can, however, create imaginative understandings by writing fictionally from their perspective. Writers' own feelings and ideas can be explored further by writing fictions in which the events are altered in some specific way (such as a happy instead of a bad ending). The wider field of knowledge and opinion can be drawn upon through reading and discussion. There will then be a multiplicity of stories and themes perceived within a single incident.

Writing fictionally is one way of gaining a sight of this complexity, of being aware of the embeddedness of so much knowing in experience. We know things in so many different ways. Marshall and Reason report a Ph.D. student responding to her supervisors' anxiety that her thesis did not have 'a sufficiently wide-ranging exploration of literature'. The student:

> told us forcibly. 'There is a lot of theory in this, and you will find it integrated throughout the text. But more importantly, what I have written here is known through my body, my imagination and my practice. The quality of my work is in its integration with my whole being, not simply in academic theory.' We accepted her argument, as did the external examiner.
>
> Marshall and Reason 1997, p. 240

Writing as if the student, or rewriting with some of the genders switched, can give tremendous insight and release of emotion. An allied approach is to collect written stories from all the actors in a situation, as Mavis Kirkham (1997) has with a series of births (mother, midwife, doctor, etc.).

Reflective writers will be faced with no single answer to such questions as 'How could I have done better?' In place of answers yet more questions arise, such as 'If I had done this, which I think would have been better, what would the patient/doctor have felt?' As Masters student Ann commented: 'no wonder it all takes so much time!'

Exploring issues in depth and width can take time. On the other hand, enlightenment can arrive after a fifteen-minute writing session. Rereading written experiences can help enable the writer-reader to 'own' depicted experiences, recognise them and begin to accept and work on them.

> [Professionals] who learn on courses to take more responsibility for their successes, weaknesses, actions and feelings, and to relate their course functioning to their work context are in fact developing competencies that are readily available for transfer to their work settings. At worst, staff thus empowered may offer a challenge too threatening to be coped with by an unempowered organisation and management structure. At best, they can become a stimulating and thoughtful resource for their agencies.
>
> Hughes and Pengelly 1995, p. 170

Or at very best they thoroughly shake up their organisation, or seek a new and much more dynamic post.

Guidance or control?

Where you start from, and what pedagogical principles you use, affects where you will get to in learning. The old chestnut is apposite: when asked 'How do I get to Dalston', the Londoner in Holborn scratched his head: 'If I wanted to get there I wouldn't start from here!'

Just as there are severe drawbacks in *structuring* practitioners' reflection for them, so too there are inherent potential problems in *guiding* it. Reflective practice is most effective when undertaken with a discussion group (or pair) of peers, with knowledgeable and skilful *facilitation*. Open discussion can widen the experience of the reflection and reflexivity politically and socially. *Guidance* of this discussion is inappropriate: to be reflective and reflexive effectively, practitioners must question and be brought up against political and social aspects rather than, or as well as, being subject to the interpretation and direction of a superior.

An examination of daily practice undertaken under guidance may well transform practice by creating a more effective and self-satisfied workforce. But this workforce may be regulated from outside (by the supervisor and line manager) as well as from the inside. The practitioner internalises the instruction of the supervisor relative to the practice as discussed. The practice which was once private and formed by their own ethical and professional judgements is now public – open to scrutiny and guidance. The professional is controlled from without *and* from within.

Authority

An effective reflective practitioner has authority for their own learning. Careful support by facilitator or mentor is useful to help them be brave enough to stay with uncertainties, and feel they are strong and intelligent enough to develop their own questions.

If we always think we know what we know, or know the foundations or parameters for what we know, or the type of thing we want to learn about, there will be no room for development – no room for the 'aha moment', the 'epiphany', the 'dropping of the penny', the sunlight to come through the window. Similarly, wanting safe, understood structures for our learning leaves no scope for effective learning. As you read further chapters in this book you will meet practitioners who say such as this in evaluation:

> I felt to begin with that the course was slightly wacky and flaky – surreal . . . I felt uncomfortable and a bit insecure at first . . . But now I feel this process is empowering. I was initially afraid it was too self-indulgent.

This senior professional's criticism at the beginning might have been 'lack of structure and analysis'. These assumptions, however, did not close her off from throwing herself into having a go. I have often found that articulate participants, those used to telling other people what to do, will try to prevent us getting to the most uncertain stages because of their fear of insecurity in believing unbelievable things, and questioning givens. Nine senior doctors resembled a class of naughty infant lads recently, using delaying and warding-off tactics. They thought they wanted structure, to be told what to do and think. We did get somewhere in the end: but it was exhausting.

In the more didactic nursing and education literature, practice is problema-tised, and teachers or nurses are asked to isolate small areas of experience to be described and then dismembered for answers to such questions as: 'What did I do right here?' and 'What could I have done better?' (Atkins and Murphy 1994; Tripp 1995a). In these texts, as in other such structured work, the practitioner is even sometimes given a fictitious situation on which to reflect.

Yet, 'Argyris and Schon remind us that the ego-protecting function, as well as the relative implicitness of some theories-in-use, might make their access through reflective exercises very difficult indeed' (Greenwood 1995). So these exercises are likely to occasion musing, or anecdote telling: largely reviewing obvious points. It can also be merely a reiteration and strengthening of attitude and per-spective, which might be prejudice.

Such reflective practice, furthermore, takes apart incidents in order to reflect upon them. This is essentially necrophylic: taking an organic entity apart will nec-essarily kill it; only a dead creature can be dissected.

There is an assumption in much reflective practice literature that material for reflection is accessible, such as: 'practitioners must first select what aspects of the situation to attend to' (Greenwood 1995). If practitioners are 'selecting' in this conscious way, they will not be able to stand outside their own actions and view them creatively. In fact, how can they 'select' in this way when, as she also asserts: 'the problems of practice do not present themselves ready labelled for solution; the knotty problems of practice inhere in messy indeterminate situations of uncertainty, instability, uniqueness and value-conflict'? A muddle in the model, I fear. Another problem with reflection, as reported in the literature, is lack of clar-ity about how it can be facilitated:

> [I have sought] out again some of the literature on reflective practice. I realise now how varied this is in quality, scope and depth. On one level some people talk about reflective practice as if it was just a chat about an incident over a cup of coffee.
>
> Ann

Levels of reflection

Reflective stories, additional stories, journal writings, discussions and wider researches can be undertaken without set questions, such as, 'Why did I inter-vene as I did?' (Atkins and Murphy 1994), reference to levels or stages of reflection (e.g. Mezirow 1981), or writing guidelines (e.g. Tripp 1995a, b) other than the writing and group-work support. A reliance on the writer's inherent abil-ity to create working stories to critique their own practice makes the writing process organically synthetic, and close to the *writing of the body* of the feminist post-structuralist writers (Flax 1990; Moi 1985). Reflective writers can follow the train of their own deep knowledge, experience and understanding leading to professional and personal cognitive, affective and spiritual insights.

Research by Baernstein and Fryer-Edwards (2003) showed critical incident reports (CIRs) to be less effective than reflective interviews without writing. This is hardly surprising as the CIRs would have been a shallow response to guiding questions.

Analysis of reflective practice can clarify understanding of reflective and reflexive processes, once deep reflection has been established. Van Manen has reported Dewey's five steps (van Manen 1995). Keith Morrison has derived a four-stage process of reflective practice from Habermas (Morrison 1996). Tripp uses an extensive list of items for the creation and analysis of *critical incidents* (Tripp 1995a, b). Johns has developed Barbara Carper's four ways of knowing: empirical, ethical, personal and aesthetic (Johns 1995). And then of course there is Kolb's learning cycle (1984). In her final journal entry, Ann asserted:

> Looking at the discussion of the previous week and thinking of the Mezirow stages finally made the whole thing click into place for me. What is hard about the reflection is that it is so multi-layered. Analysis is of the actions, motivations, perceptions, etc. of the individual players in the story along with making links to other situations in the players' own past histories. But connections are also made at a more political and theoretic level of analysis which makes you then re-look at the original incident from another angle. No wonder it all takes so much time.
>
> Ann

And no wonder it all takes so much trust in the group, as well as a degree of self-confidence and faith in the professional self. These also all take time and nurture.

Is reflective practice for all?

People naturally reflect in different ways and in different times and spaces: some feel happier getting on with the job and leaving the thinking to others. But this inevitable variation is *not* like blue or brown eyes, as the learning styles' approach seems to suggest (Reynolds 1997). Some children find it hard to learn to share, or not to be aggressive: this might be genetic or socialised. Teachers never conclude: 'Oh Tom's a non-sharer', instead, they develop appropriate strategies for supporting Tom to perceive life from others' perspectives.

Copeland et al. found that teachers are reflective to very different depths at different stages of their lives and careers and feel this should be catered for in education and training. They also mourn that 'opportunity, time and assistance from others are often lacking in typical teacher education programmes' (Copeland et al. 1993, p. 357). Truscott and Walker found, however, that 'despite the opportunity for critical reflection, student teachers appear to focus on technical skills' (1998, p. 291). Ferry and Ross-Gordon give a comparison of those teachers who do reflect, and those who do not (1998).

Tutors of reflective practice report very different levels of success, and different experiences. I imagine this difference relates to the way the process is introduced, facilitated and supervised. Clarke (1998) found student teachers write reflectively on *themes* rather than on *incidents* or single events. I find asking people to write about *a time when* . . . focuses them upon an event. I do also find that journal work lends itself to the kind of in-depth longitudinal thematic musing to which he refers.

Reflective writing portfolios (including such material as poems and 'free writes') for pre-service science teachers have been found to be very useful for 'encouraging positive attitudes towards science, developing an understanding of science concepts, providing embedded diagnostic information and creating "natural" opportunities for curriculum integration'. In addition, it 'seems to help students become aware of their own growth and beliefs regarding science' (Deal 1998, p. 244).

School students are encouraged to write reflectively too. Caroline Keys encourages science students to write creatively and expressively (writing to learn) 'to help acquire a personal ownership of ideas conveyed in lectures and textbooks . . . [which] promotes the production of new knowledge by creating a unique reflective environment for learners engaged in scientific investigation' (Keys 1999, pp. 117, 119). Phye (1997) reports school students similarly writing reflective portfolios. Kim (1999) reports a highly supported model: nurses write and share descriptive narratives in interview with a researcher, developing depth of description and reflexive and reflective critique.

Strawson asserts that not everyone stories their lives (2004a, b), that encouraging professionals to do so has no positive results. The perception that medical students need to develop narrative competence, he maintains, is only another way of saying doctors should listen to their patients better. He misses the imperative need for educative strategies to enable such communication. Professionals need to listen both to themselves and to others: this can be developed by reflection, reflexivity and dialogue.

Ann Williams: professional and personal world collision

My professional and personal worlds collided when my eight-week grandson, Luke died a cot death. For many weeks I lived a double life working as a health visitor and lecturer, and grieving. I had a role to play, of grieving grandmother, with professional colleagues who knew that grief follows a structured model, and were willing and able to support me through the stages. It kept the pain at bay, but it was not where the grief resolved. My personal world of grief was chaotic. There was no sense to be found, the pain and despair were unpredictable.

When the pain became unbearable I jotted down notes: a safe place to record my feelings before they were lost and somewhere to store the sadness until it could be faced. There were so many adjustments to make, the loss of Luke himself, of my new identity as a grandmother and all that meant to me, and finding that for the first time I had nothing to offer others in resolving their own grief.

Letting go of Luke was difficult. Eight weeks is such a short life. There were so few memories, every one precious. Why did he come if he could not stay? In place of memories, I created a life for Luke, imagined him at 3 months, smiling, guzzling his milk. I needed a story of Luke before I could let him go. The dissonance between my public grief, where the goal of acceptance held sway and the wish to hold on to him in private, to deny his absence, became wider.

I have used reflection professionally to manage difficult situations. As I became stronger I was able to look at my jottings and the story they told, not of Luke but of me. I wanted not just to create an account of my experiences but to share it. This was a way to validate not only Luke's short life, but my commitment to him. I submitted an abstract to a Medical Humanities Conference a few months away, the first step in reconciling the two worlds. This also gave me a breathing space. I did not have to reflect on my experiences quite yet.

Presenting a personal account in a professional arena raises all sorts of doubts. My personal account was far removed from the tidy, professional model of grief. Would I be acceptable as a professional if I shared the world I had created behind closed eyelids? Would others accept my account of private denial as a positive way of managing overwhelming emotions?

The conference was my chance to peep out from behind barriers grief had helped me build. Creating the story, and reading it with tears running down my face, was powerful but emotional. Although I think that experience is helping me professionally, this is where it is most difficult to separate the personal and the professional. Luke's death has made such a difference to me in all aspects of my life but I have found that I can be more myself professionally than before the conference. I have become aware that I had fairly strong ideas about what was acceptable. Now I take more risks with letting clients and colleagues see a more authentic version. It makes life easier for me but whether it makes me a better professional I don't know. The conference really was like setting down a heavy burden.

Ann Williams

4

WRITING AS A REFLECTIVE PRACTITIONER

We write before knowing what to say and how to say it, and in order to find out, if possible.

Lyotard 1992, p. 119

Roland Barthes . . . said an *ecrivante* is someone who uses language only as an instrument, an instrument through which a message . . . can be transmitted. And an *ecrivain*, a writer, is someone who uses language as an end in itself, as something that in itself has justification.

Llosa 1991, pp. 114–15

[Writing] is a bit like looking at the world through a kaleidoscope. You can look at the same scene but find it different every time you turn the viewer.

Diski 2005, p. 31

Writing for reflective practice is a first-order activity, rather than recording what has been thought, it *is* the reflective mode. 'Writing no longer merely "captures" reality, it helps "construct" it' (Plummer 2001, p. 171). Writing, discussing, and associated text writing (such as from different perspectives) is creative exploration in its own right. Reflection in writing facilitates a wider view from a distance, a close acute perspective, and authority over practice.

Reflective writing can create informative, descriptive material from the mass of ideas, hopes, anxieties, fears, memories and images provoked by everyday working life. Window-shoppers focus out unwanted reflections by restricting light sources: cupping their eyes against the glass. A reflective practitioner uses writing methods to focus clearly and minutely. Paula (2003) described writing-à-la Bolton as being like self-supervision, like watching the self on video. This requires high concentration: one likened it to a long refreshing swim, another to a deeply dreaming sleep. I remember someone whispering 'disgusting': scribbling hunched over her page, we had all disappeared from her consciousness. Writers interact with and respond to drafts, subjecting them to interpretation and analysis, clarifying and extending understanding, deepening their involvement in the text.

'The only time I know that something is true is at the moment I discover it in the act of writing' (Jean Malaquais, quoted in Exley 1991, p. 64). Reflective practitioners say: 'I didn't know I thought/knew/remembered that until I wrote it'; one said: 'it is an opportunity to inhabit the unknown'. Laurel Richardson advises a range of writing activities in order to acquire writing confidence and skills, such as joining a creative writing group (2000, pp. 363–6). Elbasch-Lewis runs such courses to enable enquiry, re-storying, appreciation of diversity of voices in education. A student said: 'a useful everyday tool enabling me to continually examine assumptions and patterns of living and to maintain a dynamic of ongoing change . . . to confront, understand and study ourselves, what we were, what we are now, how we got here . . . we didn't expect these to appear in such a significant and lucid way in our stories' (Elbasch-Lewis 2002, pp. 425–6). A study in medicine concluded: 'we observed that doctors felt the process of writing and talking about the stories was both profound and helpful' (Horowitz et al. 2003, p. 774).

To write is to open oneself up to chance, to free oneself from the compulsive linking up of 'meaning, concept, time and truth' that has dominated Western philosophic discourse. Writing involves risk, play, loss of sense and meaning. (Flax 1990, p. 192).

> In everyday life I am sceptical of many things, and scornful of superstition. Writing fiction has taught me to respect what seems to be random, or coincidental; to have faith in small beginnings, and faith that the process of writing has its own alchemy . . . in writing the sense of touching something both beyond and within myself which I can do in no other way. Only through solitude, the tap of the keys, the discovery of some connection between inner and outer, intellect and emotion, body and spirit – feeling aspects of all these, and of the smallest and most everyday events, fall into place in silence and stillness, striving towards a whole.
>
> Sue Gee (see also 2002)

Taking responsibility

Reflective practitioners write about their own experience for specific others (group or mentor) with whom they are read, discussed and developed. There is full interplay of story, teller and audience, or text, interpretation and intentionality, without alienation (Tyler 1986).

> For me, the group is not about using the writing to analyse my work as a general practitioner. It is about discovering, through the medium of writing, something about my personal and professional relationships – with patients, family, the world, the past etc. Constructing or crafting a piece of writing is part of the discovery process, and reading it is the final act of legitimacy.
>
> Becky

Writing is increasingly introduced into professional courses (Reifler 1996; Montgomery et al. 2003; Hatem and Farrara 2001). Davidson (1999) comments how, on introducing colleagues to reflective writing, they 'say how it helped their writing to know it was acceptable to write in forms of their own creation, and as a way of expressing their experience. The [reflective practice] norm seems more often a feeling of intimidation at the prospect of using a foreign tool with stuffy rules.'

If meanings are formed by language, if signs do not have innate meaning but are in an endless interplay or diffusion of signification, and if writing is more important than the spoken word, then undertaking a conscious process of self-examination through writing must develop awareness of language and meanings.

Many of life's constraints are constructed around us and by us, rather than being an imposed situation whose bars we can only beat against. Responsibility for actions lies with all of us, not an inhuman, inhumane system out there. Sartre suggested that unperceived choices face us all the time, although we rarely perceive our freedom to choose. The philosophy or theory is embedded, as in Sartre's novel *Nausea* (1938).

If control can be exerted over everyday elements, then, metonymically some control will have been taken over the larger structures. In deciding to write, tell and take ownership of some of our stories we positively and enjoyably exercise choice. Self-expression in writing and critical reading is vital. Paolo Freire (1972) asserted that illiteracy spells oppression. The boundaries of our under-standing and communication need to be pushed beyond what have for so long been considered its limits. 'In the struggle to reassert feminine values, feminine writing which draws on the unconscious is a key site for bringing about change' (Weedon 1987).

The confidence acquired in reflective practice writing can spill over. A Masters student described one of her 'benefits and achievements' as 'learning to write with freedom'; I would add: with confidence and authority.

The discipline of writing

Writing goes beyond the emotions of the moment, taking on more universality, yet at the same time drawing upon deep experience. It distances (puts out there, onto the paper), but also creates closer contact with emotions, thoughts and experiences. Some of the dynamic, immediate properties of speech can seem to be lost in writing, which can appear to freeze or embalm experiences. Explorative and expressive writing, however, is as dynamic as speech, if not more so.

> The imaginative structuring of experience, then, is not only an intellectual structuring but a response to an emotional challenge – a sort of emotional discipline.
>
> Winter et al. 1999, p. 204

Writers have paradoxically to allow, 'circumstances in which it is safe to be absent-minded (i.e. for conscious logic and reason to be absent from one's mind)' (Freud 1950, p. xiii). Writers surrender to 'safe' 'circumstances' of creative 'discipline'. The Church of England Book of Common Prayer offers a similar oxymoron: [Thy] service is perfect freedom. The discipline of creative writing allows greater freedom of exploration and expression than can be obtained without it. A carefully boundaried space is created in workshops, secure and confident enough to enable surrender to the structured discipline of writing. I encourage people to develop safe-enough writing situations in their own space and time. Creating such a 'safe-enough', disciplined environment is fundamental.

> One of the reasons people seem able to open themselves up in these sessions is that Gillie imposes nothing of herself when she suggests the writing. The suggestions for writing and introductory words are very open and opening, with no way of doing it suggested, nor definite subjects, etc.
>
> A student

Surrendering to creative discipline is neither simple nor straightforward. Understandings created by expressive exploration can be dynamically unsettling: 'One leaves a piece of one's flesh in the inkpot each time one dips one's pen' (Tolstoy, quoted Exley 1991, p. 25). And 'The progress of any writer is marked by those moments when he manages to outwit his own inner police system. Writers have invented all kinds of *games* to get past their own censorship' (Hughes 1982, p. 7). My methods, such as *six minutes writing without thinking*, are *games*.

> It's happening – that thing where I dismiss my own thoughts: *No, not that. You'll get stuck if you go with that. That's so dull, you'll bore yourself stupid. Not that, not that, not that*. It makes it so imposssible to get started and then to follow through. It's the Thought Police, as Gillie said Ted Hughes said. I have a whole battalion of them – bobbies on the beat, sergeants in the office, sharp-eyed interrogating inspectors – loads of them. And then there's the Crown Persecution[*] Service complete with judge and jury and some hopeless, depressed woman from Victim Support as my only ally.
>
> Is it experience that tells me, *Don't go there, it'll be dull?* Not just dull – something more like, *It won't get born. It'll be a messy miscarriage, a deformed foetus that'll die shortly after it slips into the world*. Is it experience? In fact, experience tells me, *Focus, write, give yourself over to it and whatever comes out will be healthy, with full lungs and kicking limbs*.
>
> [*]This is what I actually wrote instead of *Prosecution*
>
> Chris Banks

One reflective writer described it pleasurably: 'everybody writing alone yet together'. But many find it difficult to go on to create discipline, or permission, in their own space and time.

Penny wrote effectively in the group, but could write nothing at home for the second session. I suggested she try somewhere else, other than in her home, or with carefully chosen material she liked, or at a different sort of time. Penny then wrote two pieces, clearly gaining great benefit from writing and group sharing. She wrote the first in a café, having bought a shocking pink folder, a new pad and a bright pink pen.

Some find it hard even to begin to think of writing. One new participant looked startled, rummaging in her bag, saying: 'I've only got lipstick.' Many professionals find it difficult to find the time, though are very glad when they do:

> All of us lead busy lives, and a lot of the actual writing is done like naughty children's homework, at the last minute, yet it is also clear that the stories come into being in the context of our lives, though they may only be written down in haste under a Sunday morning deadline. I think this may be what gives some of our efforts an immediacy and seriousness which is occasionally beautiful, and always interesting.
>
> Seth

Many find writing on their own easier, finding the structured discipline of group writing time problematic. And there are those who cannot start at all:

> I know this small group now in a deeper way than I could ever have done in a whole course worth of sessions. You [a colleague] look different now. You have become a person for me. I'm so glad. I had been so nervous of writing when we started, feeling I can't write what comes into my head; I really can't. And Gillie said 'fine, we must all write in the way that suits us, you do whatever that is'. But having heard all your pieces I can now see how I can do it; I'm going to rewrite mine with all my feelings, thoughts, ideas and other things – some of them really personal.

Finding the writer's voice

People are often nervous about beginning to write, not realising expressive ability in writing is as innate as speech. They gain confidence as they learn trust in the writing processes, faith in themselves (that they can do it), and a desire and determination to write. Positive encouragement is facilitative. However inexpressive, imitative or inauthentic a beginner's writing is, they will progress, offered positive encouragement.

> Finding a voice means that you can get your own feeling into your own words and that your words have the feel of you about them . . . A voice is like a fingerprint, possessing a constant and unique signature that can, like a fingerprint, be recorded and employed for identification.
>
> Heaney 1980a, p. 43

Heaney's *writer's voice* is found when the pen dodges brain *police officers*. 'That willing suspension of disbelief for the moment, which constitutes poetic faith' (Coleridge 1817). Ted Hughes likened it to silent, still night-watching for foxes: 'Till, with a sudden sharp hot stink of fox / It enters the dark hole of the head' (1967, pp. 19–20). These passive approaches suggest writers need specific states of mind for inspiration to arrive. Seamus Heaney's metaphors are active: 'Between my finger and my thumb / The squat pen rests. / I'll dig with it.' (1980b, pp. 10–11). And:

> Usually you begin by dropping the bucket half way down the shaft and wind-ing up a taking of air. You are missing the real thing until one day the chain draws unexpectedly tight and you have dipped into water that will continue to entice you back. You'll have broken the skin of the pool of yourself.
>
> Heaney 1980a, p. 47

Hélène Cixous becomes a jewellery thief: 'These pearls, these diamonds, these signifiers that flash with a thousand meanings, I admit it, I have often filched them from my unconscious. The jewellery box . . . Furtively, I arrive, a little break-in, just once, I rummage, ah! The secrets!' (1991, p. 46).

Writing stories rather than abstractions

Writing stories or poems about remembered events, or fiction from depth of experience, enables people to grapple with everyday issues at the same time as abstract feelings (e.g. a sense of alienation). Writing an abstract and generalised piece about mistakes without it being related to a particular mistake offers no access to deeper levels of meaning and understanding. Memorable poems and stories are all about events and people, their thoughts and doings: never abstract philosophising. The philosophy, or theory, is embedded. Sartre's philosophy (see pp. 115–6) from his novel *Nausea* (1938) is part of the story, spoken by a charac-ter; making the theory memorable and comprehensible.

> We got so much further than I could have thought we might in one short session. We slipped between theory and story in the discussions about the writ-ing. Somehow the stories seemed to open us up to the theory and to clarify it.
>
> Brian

> Writing about an incident clarifies thought. Instead of a rambling account that moves back and forth in time (which I'm particularly prone to, as I don't have the facility for precise language) writing tends to make one create a sequential story. In doing so, various particulars, or gaps may stand out as one tries to present a story that makes sense. 'The process of writing inevitably leads to a reformulation, added clarity and ideas for further analy-sis' (Miles and Huberman 1994).
>
> Jane

William Carlos Williams said 'no ideas but in things' (Williams 1951, p. 231): in effective writing, 'things', events, experiences carry or infer 'ideas' and feelings, abstractions are not expressed directly. Writers are exhorted to *show don't tell*: readers learn from characters, place and actions, rather than from the authorial voice. Don't tell me she's pregnant, show me her ungainly movements, swelling belly, hand to her back as she stops to get breath.

Writing in abstractions is self-protective. Beginning poets often need to be gentled out of it. Such pieces are sometimes clever, and groups do not realise they have had no discussion, just exclaim 'I wish I could write like that'. Thus engendered authorial pride tends to prevent more seemingly simple, but much more effective and deep, direct accounts of practice. Writers need to be encouraged out of being *clever* and into being open.

The following abstract writing was wonderfully useful to the group because it followed a pair of reflective stories. It exemplifies how abstraction can be fruitfully reflective when related directly to previous writings.

So at the end of this I know where I started, and that is being a good creative confident practitioner is about love not fear. It's about looking at what we do and others do with honesty and loving criticism and not with a big stick. It's about learning from the good and bad bits even if it's painful sometimes. It's about the excitement and satisfaction of doing the job a bit better.

Leaving aside the issues of resources, behind a lot of bad practice is fear. Fear of getting it wrong, fear of patients' strong feelings, fear of our own strong feelings, fear of the demons inside us, of change, of saying 'I don't know', of our own inadequacies, of being out of control.

In making more and more rules and edicts perhaps we are in danger of making the fears more powerful. We build the rules, the threats, the edicts into huge castle walls to keep the fears at bay. What if we took the walls down stone by stone and invited the fears to come in? For within our castle walls are the good fairies, the kind caring fairies who have to live alongside the fears. If we dismantle the walls and let the fears come in they wouldn't go away because they are real, and many of them are necessary but they might mingle a bit better with the good fairies. The fears might spice us up a bit and the good fairies – care, compassion, love and laughter – would maybe be able to stretch their wings and fly about a bit better.

What if, in taking down our castle walls, we started with a piece of paper and a pen?

Lindsay Buckell

Lindsay said: 'When I wrote it, it didn't feel like an abstract piece at all, more an expression of my passionate hatred of the current climate of fear and blame.' Hatred, fear and blame are all abstract, but here they have a strong effective meaning for Lindsay and her readers because she is writing not about hatred, fear and blame in general, but specifically related to the incident which brought these emotions out so forcefully; which she had written previously.

It is a summer's day and I am looking after Simon. He lies, poor young thing, deeply unconscious, the machinery puffs and blows, whirrs and chugs. I am concerned that all the machinery, which is keeping Simon alive, is working right; and yet I love this young man, not sexually or romantically but from somewhere in my middle. I am not accepting that he is as ill as he is, I am not denying it either. I do not believe in a miracle cure, I am simply not engaging with it. I am concerned, at this moment, with looking after him and his machines.

The door opens and the ward sister comes in. She has trust in me that I can nurse her patient. She asks if I would like her to help me turn him. It is a question, not an order, in the way she says it she acknowledges that today Simon is my patient and she is simply offering to help me. She is cheery and competent, not cheery which might suggest avoidance of the situation, she is just present but lightly so. She says 'wouldn't he have hated this'. She is right – he is a diffident and intensely private young man. His mother died of the same disease. He has that depth in people whom personal tragedy has robbed of that illusion we all carry that life is essentially benign. He is quiet and shy, but laughs and chats with the other patients who are all much older than he.

Now he lies, totally dependent, his body exposed to anybody. She is right: he would have hated this. As we turn him she is very careful with the body which is on loan to us, because he can't protect it himself at present, careful to protect his dignity. We talk to him, not across him. In this care of this young man is our understanding that he is still a person with right to care and dignity, whether he knows or not.

In that moment I learned the truth of empathy; I received permission to have empathy with my patients, to believe in their rights as individuals, to allow myself to love them, but as a professional, not as a friend. She didn't talk about it, she didn't analyse it, she simply modelled it and all I'd heard about not getting involved which had never made sense inside me fell away. I understood something profound about the nature of being truly involved in a professional relationship with my patients.

Lindsay Buckell

Story and fiction

Lindsay's piece is undeniably a story. But is it fiction? In a way any writing about a situation is inevitably fiction, in so far as it reconstructs or recreates the event: it cannot be a factual or true carbon copy. It is certainly perspectival, relying on Lindsay's perception: the ward sister or patient would write it differently.

Lindsay may, furthermore, have embroidered certain bits, and downplayed others, to make her point persuasively, interestingly, and confidentially. My suggested writing theme was 'an aha moment, an epiphany of understanding'; her personal theme, emerging as she wrote, was 'the time I learned about empathy'. All stories could thus be said to be fictions, however much based on memories of actual events. The distinction between fiction or fact (true or false) is one of those artificial binaries which beset modern living. A story is a creative construct, whatever material is drawn upon. All reflective writing is from a practitioner's depth of experience, knowledge and skill, as true as you can get in the way a straight line is true.

A story can recreate a telling situation with powerful re-presentations of interpersonal relationships. A writer can draw unconsciously on deep professional and personal experience to convey nuances of gesture, speech, intention, memory, thought and feeling. Rereading such an account therefore offers insight to writer and readers. The audience can share their insights with the writer, thus expanding their knowledge gain.

Stories and the transmission of culture

Such stories can re-present a picture of unwritten social and professional rules and codes as well as an implicit comment upon them:

> Fiction not only legitimizes emotions and aspirations, it also, again particularly since the appearance of the novel with its devotion to the minutiae of personal relationships, gives models and patterns of acceptable and unacceptable behaviour. I have certainly noticed that those who never read, or have never read, fiction, tend to be obtuse and insensitive in personal relationships. It does really seem as if the consumption of fiction is a part of the necessary education of modern people in the fine points of human relationships. So many examples are given of how people are, how they may be expected to react, and what the harvest is likely to be.
>
> Rockwell 1974, p. 81

A clash of codes is embedded in Lindsay's sentence: *We talk to him, not across him.* Aha, think non-nurse reader I, some nurses would treat this nearly inanimate body as an object; perhaps until this point, Lindsay had only experienced nurses who did exactly that. She responded to my guesses:

> I like what you wrote about it except that the bit that was so unusual and liberating for me was her comment about 'wouldn't he have hated this?' I had, in fact, met many nurses who would treat unconscious patients well – in not talking across them, and so on. What was so unusual was this indication of her deep understanding of him as an individual in that sentence. It joined up with all the other things I wrote about her in her ability to treat patients

as individual people, therefore with empathy, rather than as a collective noun patients: i.e. part of the institution and all alike to be worked round as if they were all identikit and those who wouldn't play ball being labelled difficult or manipulative.

Lindsay Buckell

This issue, and its corollary, has also been reflected upon through reflexive journal writing and discussion by a student palliative care nurse: 'patients must be seen as real people not just patients. Patients need to see nurses as people . . . not mere nurses doing their job' (Durgahee 1997, p. 141).

Stories can tell how we might or ought to act, think and feel. Think of the writings informing your thinking: the unloving stupidity of King Lear (Shakespeare); the selfishness of Henry James's Isobel (*Portrait of a Lady*); Agamemnon's monomaniacal stealing of Achilles' girl, Briseis (Homer). The same is true of reflective story writing, such as Lindsay's (see also Winter et al. 1999).

Stories enable us to perceive and question

A story not only presents a comprehensible set of possible ways of being, it always leaves questions. Stories offer understandings, but also lead the reader on to want to find out more about such behaviour, situations, emotions.

The truest respect which you can pay to the reader's understanding is to . . . leave him something to imagine, in his turn, as well as yourself.

Sterne [1760] 1980, p. 77

Story writing allows writers to explore experience roundedly. Insights often hinge upon small details, such as the sister relating to the patient as a person rather than just another patient. These insightful details often appear unplanned: like the opening of an inner eye. Awareness of detail, inculcated by writing and discussing, increasingly slips into daily practice, making it more aware and reflective:

This course helped me, encouraging me to be more aware of each day, and making me more observant.

Brimacombe 1996, p. 15

Novelist Lesley Glaister, whose ideas come from 'my eyes, ears and gut feelings', would advise writers to 'stare, eavesdrop, never stop wondering'. Such awareness inevitably benefits practice. Some professionals do not fully perceive their students, clients, colleagues and environment, but only what they themselves think, just as Virginia Woolf depicted Orlando:

He opened his eyes, which had been wide open all the time, but had seen only thoughts.

Woolf [1928] 1992, p. 101

Carefully observed, detailed descriptions of events are a sophisticated reflective form because 'we theorise every time we look at the world' (Goethe 1998). Picasso said 'we must not discriminate between things. Where things are concerned there are no class distinctions.' Awareness of details can enable insight, pushing away assumptions and habitual perspectives and modes of understanding. 'God is in the details' (Verghese 2001, p. 1013). A closely observed event, however small, written about, reflected upon, discussed critically, and re-explored through further writings, stands metonymically for the whole of that reflective writer's practice. A short story or poem is a slice of life, metonymically revealing the whole of life (metonym = part standing for a whole, as in *the pen* is mightier than *the sword* – *pen* and *sword* stand graphically and metonymically for huge social, political and cultural areas: *literature* and *war*).

Acute observation is required: not the narrowly focused observation skills required by practice, but the detached and impartial detailed observation of a writer. Reflective writers I have trained are amazed at vital details previously missed.

Careful description can create dynamic re-looking, re-observing and re-understanding: e.g. what impinged on whom, when, where. 'Writing of narratives in itself is analytical in the sense that practitioners become engaged in conscious efforts to view themselves and their actions with a certain degree of detachment and suspension' (Kim 1999, pp. 1207–8). Why and how naturally follow from, for example, the precise recollection of a colleague's expression. Take Mark Purvis's simple, but acutely observed rerendering of his little brother's death (Chapter 2). A forgotten memory until the poem was written without forethought, the writing and the subsequent discussions enabled a wealth and depth of insight and learning. This is working with stories rather than about them (Frank 1995, p. 23).

Such a reflective approach has to be learned experientially. Professionals or students have to be trusted to observe and write with all their faculties wide open. Facilitation of discussions about their writings is key to the development of professional observation, reflective and reflexive skills. This is counter to the view that 'description only serves the process of reflection, covering issues for reflection and noting their context' (Moon 2003, p. 216), and 'is not reflective at all, but merely reports events' (Hatton and Smith 1995, p. 40).

Writing from varying perspectives

Stories are fragmentary texts offering narrow experiential slices. Reflective practice writing widens this. Associated writings deepen the learning for both writers and readers. Lindsay's abstract reflective passage, above, shows her working out what she meant, and enables us further to grasp messages from her story. Bev (whose stories appear in Chapter 10) wrote from her own point of view, and then wrote from the other protagonist's perspective. This enabled her to begin to grasp the kind of forces at work upon them both. Readers not only gain from the learning contained in the story, but can relate it to their own experience. A window of understanding opens not only into Bev's incident, but also into their own parallel experiences.

Some reflective writers readily create stories from alternative points of view, or fictions based on their own experience. Others find it less easy. Telling the same story through different characters' eyes is currently common in novels. Jane Rogers's *Mr Wroe's Virgins* (1991), the story of an eighteenth-century religious fanatic, is written through the voice of four of the virgins he abuses. This multi-voiced approach gives the text a depth and roundedness which could be achieved in no other way. Frankenstein (Shelley 1820) and Dracula (Stoker 1897) are both also written with the 'I' being taken in turn.

A range of reflective stories and writings are possible around a core story. Professionals with whom I have worked have been imaginative in devising additional texts. One doctor wrote from the perspective of the sofa on which his patient sat day in and day out: it had quite a story to tell. There are many other ways in which practitioners might write associated texts to further their insights from their core story (see Chapter 10), such as in genre (see Chapter 12). A butterfly's eye is really a myriad of tiny eyes, each one recording an image from a slightly different angle. Bodies of reflective writings offer a similar texture of images.

Rose Flint: writer in healthcare

I have learned that when a group or an individual engages with their inner world they are bringing forth something previously *unnamed*. It may have been known, perhaps in a subconscious sense; it may be very subtle, not even necessarily in the words we work with, but its power may affect every-one in the group, including myself.

A non-group leader aspect of my self – the vulnerable part with its history of emotional experience – is present, watching, listening, feeling. The relationship of group and leader contains many nuances; the shadows of other relationships may hover around, or mirrors may be held up at unexpected times, sometimes with shocking effect. The huge emotions that some groups contain – fury, despair, terror – can leap and burn with extraordinary unpredictably. This burning can be cathartic, as it is named and written and worked through.

There are times when I go home feeling grey and heavy although I'm not sure why. I often experience a dread of even opening my notebook and it sits with all the presence of an unexploded bomb. But this is when I most need to practice reflective writing because something in the work has hit some deep note in me, perhaps memory, or an ongoing fear. I am not made of stone, not elevated above the reality of the flesh and spirit of the people I work with. I care: and their lives touch mine. Good, grounding supervision helps me to keep my balance, but sometimes I'm frail enough to be overturned.

Writing at this time is often very difficult. The dread I feel may be made of unnamed pain: perhaps partly theirs, partly mine. Working in the Spinal

Unit how could I not be affected by the young men who were so suddenly traumatised by accident? How frightening the idea of the consequences of these terrible accidents: to me and mine? For months I wrote notes, typed up scribed poems, but I could not write from my own centre, I felt myself utterly gagged – helpless – paralysed . . .

Then someone started talking about the way a paralysed body hears sound differently. I was intrigued and that night, after the notes I started to write.

The poem came very quickly and received very little editing. It's the only reflective writing poem I wrote from the Spinal Unit work, but for me, it was a mending, a separating out. It held the awe and the anger that had dumbed me for months. And of course – it was about facing fear.

. . .

What is a body when it discovers itself as a drum
the world tuned to a new acoustic, centred in new space

What is a body that echoes, resonates, re-locates —
makes stereophonic initiation: a seedling sense pushing
out from breakage and decay. Raw at first, in discord
noise scrapes harsh, vibrates fire along the unknown tension
of a timbrel-skin inside the self and sometimes dins
tinnitus ringing through the lymph and blood as if
all arbitrary sound came now with a collected purpose:
to beat into the body, to strike *this this this* primal note —
insistent, purposeful, stridently, determinedly alive

What is the body beyond its sack and pieces, beyond
its secret, aching diffusion, its inchoate random knowledge?

Rose Flint

Other ways of writing reflexively

There are many different ways to write exploratively and expressively. Autoethnography is a 'blend of ethnography and autobiographical writing that incorporates elements of one's own experience when writing about others' (Scott-Hoy 2002, p. 276). It involves critically examining one's own stories with a view to rewriting them, and challenging the accepted surrounding stories (Sparkes 2002, 2003; Ellis and Bochner 2000; Etherington 2004; Richardson 2001).

Experience of, and potential for online work is tremendous; a whole book is needed. I have run online postgraduate continuing professional development courses for medical practitioners, each compiling a portfolio of reflective writings, reflections upon the writings, responses from other group members, and evidence of discussions with colleagues (such as team members), and research undertaken. All communication is electronic in a closed email group; each member writes accounts which are read and commented upon by the others, who also make research suggestions. This mode of communication inevitably has distinct advantages and disadvantages; it is particularly appropriate for busy, reasonably articulate clinicians, but requires careful facilitation. Email communication is very different from any other. A group member reflected how it 'enables you to *meet* colleagues you would probably never meet otherwise'.

Julie Hughes uses virtual learning environments in teacher education for post-compulsory education:

> Virtual groups are built into tutor group activities with overwhelmingly positive responses: 'teaching and learning like a disco ball – multi-reflective' (student metaphor). Eportfolio allows for multiple asynchronous conversations. What changes is the role of the tutor: as ementor you are 'differently' available, and have a different role in the dialogue so it sort of deconstructs the idea of a personal tutor as once-a-semester contact. The eportfolio allows students to input whatever they like into their chosen pebbles. Within each *pebble* is a structure to support reflection based quite simply on a cyclical model as it's aimed at undergraduates. My postgrads are using it in a more developed and sophisticated fashion I think.
>
> Teacher Education for the post-compulsory sector has long been committed to promoting and embedding reflective practice and action planning for professional development and is therefore positioned to engage reflexively with the PDP community and with traditional assessment mechanisms. The standard, summatively assessed, paper-based 'teaching-practice portfolio' may be viewed as a static assessment product whose shelf-life is limited and it may be argued of little relevance to the new teacher following its compilation. The eportfolio's emphasis upon dialogue and reflexive patchwork writing (Winter 2003) offers the opportunity to explore the eportfolio as a social practice and situated literacy (Street 1995). The patchwork eportfolio offers unlimited peer and tutor 'talkback' (Lillis 2001) spaces as opposed to institutional summative feedback 'spaces for telling'. Eportfolio dialogue is not a one-off, its discoursal features are forward-looking and exploratory and it is concerned with the process-making nature of academic texts and literacies.
>
> The use of eportfolio will be considered in research as a driver for action planning and critically reflective thinking linked to the development of professional practice with a pilot group of students in the School of Education and report on this teaching community's response to the dialogue opportunities of eportfolio and the extent to which the technology supports the creation of embodied audiences. It is hoped that this research will contribute to developing a vocabulary; a philosophy; a theory, and a practice of eportfolio.
>
> Julie Hughes

Fictional dialogue with either characters, or with the *internal critic*, or *internal supervisor* is fruitful. Dialogues are written like drama script, the hand being allowed to write in the voice of the other alternately with the writer's own habitual voice.

Reflective writing can be similar to the *internal supervisor*, recommended by Casement (1990). The silence of writing is relatively undemanding, as there is no listening other, and no time limit. Writing can provide a *safe* present in which to reflect upon unsafe things:

> Writing is a disinhibition strategy, as it anchors people to a safe present while they re-experience a past event, providing optimum distance possibilities and hence cathartic reset.
>
> Evison 2001, p. 256

Linda Garbutt, a therapist in a GP (family medicine) practice, engages in, and is researching the *internal supervisor* in reflective writing. Here is a dialogue extract from her journal:

Me: Kay is a vibrant young woman engaging in counselling in depth and with much thought. As she tells me her story, I listen carefully. I can see her struggling with her own path forward.

Internal supervisor: It sounds to me as if you are doing some person-centred therapy here, Linda. You are accepting Kay and her story in a way which allows her to accept aspects of her past that she now finds unacceptable. She is valuing herself as a person: possible as you 'prize' her. You are being genuine, I know, using self-disclosure suitably. And, staying empathic, being in her frame of reference, reflecting her feelings, using advanced empathy when she does not articulate some powerful thought or feeling. This is facilitating her process within this trusting counselling relationship.

Me: Right, that has put the theoretical framework in place. Now I can acknowledge and value this work. This is not 'just listening'; it's deeply person-centred practice which can make such a difference to a young person's life. I am encouraging Kay to write. She may journal or actually use reflective writing in this way.

I feel that is useful and helpful. I think I shall show Kay this writing, gain her permission to use it.

Me, reflecting on the dialogue: 'Vibrant' captures the essence of Kay bringing to the forefront a positive picture to help balance her story – one of negativity and destruction which is captured in my reflective writing.

My reflective description of this young person indicates a strong liking. This has several implications for counselling. 'Taking to' a client contributes to establishing a trusting relationship, creating the arena for openness. This also raises the issue of whether a counselling relationship can be established with a client who is not liked. Further, within my reflection, I can see the potential for major therapeutic movement or boundaries being crossed if I become over-involved with Kay, creating difficulties for the counselling relationship such as dependency. This reminds me of the need to watch out for this pattern both in clients and in myself.

Another example of deeper understanding is the succinct account of Rogers's person-centred therapy, noting that the 'core conditions' of unconditional positive regard, empathy and genuineness, communicated through counselling skills, are necessary and sufficient for desired change to happen within a trusting relationship. Having the essential principles of my approach affirmed in this way is encouraging and links to insight that acknowledging the person-centred work reveals how my acceptance of Kay has helped her move towards self-acceptance.

I have found I gain increased self-awareness through reflective writing. For example, in this case my own awareness of my own self-esteem issues helps me to keep in suspension my own material and to hear what Kay says about herself which has a resonance for me.

Linda Garbutt

Trainee cognitive therapists reported a 'deeper sense of knowing' of cognitive therapy (CT) as a result of reflective practice writing involving 'self-practice, and self-reflection: SP/SR [in which] trainees practice CT techniques on themselves (SP), either from workbooks on their own or "co-therapy" with a training partner. Then they reflect in writing on the sessions (SR), looking at the implications for themselves, for their clients, and for cognitive theory' (Bennett-Levy et al. 2003, p. 145). 'The written reflections are, in my view, crucial to the process, enabling trainees to look in depth at the implications for themselves, for their clients, and for cognitive theory' (p. 205). In a further study with experienced psychologists and cognitive therapists 'designed to assess the experience and impact of SP/SR on practitioner development . . . CT practitioners report an enhancement of their therapeutic skills in specific areas . . . SP/SR participants appear to develop a more "lived theory" of CT and a more elaborated "theory of the client", and "theory of the therapist" '(p. 152; see also Bennett-Levy et al. 2001).

Metaphors are powerful elements to examine (see Chapter 8).

We ask [participants] to describe education as a pudding, then to write up their luxury version. Much of this activity is light-hearted, as we aim to keep a distance from personalistic accounts, heavy by definition, but nevertheless, startling, surreal images abound, aesthetically subverting the humdrum world of everyday practice.

Kemp 2001, p. 350

Visualisation can be harnessed to extend the reflexive and reflective power of description. 'Over the next two weeks we immerse ourselves in writing. We ask participants to write about a landscape they know really well, then to describe their actual classrooms in the language of landscape, then their imaginary classrooms. We then ask them to populate them' (Kemp 2001, p. 350) (see also Chapter 8).

Susan Kersley: reflective writing at a time management workshop

Time management is about managing your life in its entirety not only in relation to work; professionals already know how to manage time effectively, but don't implement it. I guided them on a visualisation exercise of walking along a corridor with many doors. When they went through one door they saw the person they are now and their life. I asked them to notice with all their senses: what do you look like? What are you saying? How do you feel? What do other people notice about you? What is the room like?

Next I asked them to cross the corridor into the room opposite where life was how they would like it to be. Then I brought them back along the corridor and into the present.

They wrote about this experience and discussed their vivid descriptions of 'good rooms' and 'bad rooms', and how they might move from one to the other.

At the end, they wrote a poem or statement about how they felt about their lives and how they might be different. In just ten minutes several amazing poems were written – one in French. Here is an example.

Lynn a GP educationalist: Thank you for such an inspiring workshop! It was fantastic on a personal level and has given me a real push in the educational direction I need to go in.

> *Away from the critic*
> *Into the delicious timeless place*
> *Where movement melts into movement*
> *Each entirely as it was meant to be –*
> *Imminent and unknown until it arises.*
>
> Susan Kersley, Life Coach

Writing and anxiety

Reflective writing can help reduce anxiety and stress. Writing has an evidence base for alleviating the symptoms of anxiety and depression. A report of a randomised control trial (Smyth et al. 1999) shows how writing about the most stressful event of their lives can create clinically relevant symptom reduction in asthmatic and rheumatoid arthritis patients. The journal's editorial opinion was:

'Were the authors to have provided similar outcome evidence about a new drug, it likely would be in widespread use within a short time' (Spiegel 1999, p. 1328).

Lepore reported a trial where subjects who engaged in expressive and explorative writing about 'deepest thoughts and feelings' about a stressful event 'exhibited a significant decline in depressive symptoms' (Lepore 1997, p. 1030). These trials follow on from a wide range (e.g. Pennebaker et al. 1988; Lepore and Smyth 2002; Bloom 1999), all demonstrating significant health benefits from disclosure writing.

Research into expressive and explorative writing has shown that benefits 'appear to require translating experiences into language . . . the act of changing emotion and images into words changes the way that the person organizes and thinks about the trauma' (Pennebaker 2000, p. 8). The words matter: those venting anger by writing large numbers of expletives benefited less than those who used such language moderately. Those who used significantly few expressive words benefited less also, presumably because they were insufficiently involved.

Not only are words the best route, but 'building a narrative seemed to be critical in reaching understanding. Those people who started the study with a coherent story that explained some past experience did not benefit from writing' (Pennebaker 2000, p. 10), whereas those who came with an unsupportive story to tell, benefited from writing a new one. The value was found to be the same whether people wrote fiction or about a remembered event. 'Once a complex event is put into comprehensible story form, it is simplified' (Pennebaker 2000, p. 12).

Men may benefit more than women, because women have more socially acceptable outlets for such expression and exploration (Pennebaker 2000). Such writing is a recognised form: 'Montaigne [wrote] to heal himself, and those who attend to his *Essays*, of the pain and fear of dying' (Heitsch 2000, p. 105).

Bloom discusses the implications of similar findings on the understanding of trauma and the unique processes of writing in psychotherapy (Bloom 1999). A study of palliative care nurses involved in verbal group reflection (von Klitzing 1999) concluded that over time they reflected less about themselves and more about patients. This might have been because they withdrew and protected themselves in response to increasing stress. I wonder if they might have been able to tackle that stress directly and reflectively had they *written* as well as discussed.

Many texts explicate the personal development power of writing (e.g. Bolton 1999a; Hunt and Sampson 1998; Schneider and Killick 1998; Mazza 2003; Bolton et al. 2004). Many also tell of the professional and personal development impact of writing story and poetry about professional practice (e.g. Borkan et al. 1999; Belli and Coulehan 1998; Campo 1997; Williams 1951; Hilfiker 1985; Anderson and MacCurdy 2000; Verghese 2001; Helman 2003; Davis and Schaefer 2003). Shem uses fiction writing as a resistance against the inhumanity of medicine (2002).

Is reflective writing an art?

Art has always questioned the boundaries of existence. Artists and certain ethnographers and philosophers put themselves in situations in which conventional orderliness of everyday systems of thinking are suspended. Artists cross dangerous mental and social barriers to create images that jolt or shock audiences into reassessment. Brecht, for example, used the form of his work to set viewers questioning taken-for-granted structures. 'There is no such thing as a literature which is "really" great or "really" anything independently of the ways in which that writing is treated within specific forms of social and institutional life' (Eagleton 1983, p. 202).

The belief that only writers can write, that art is a God-given capacity is erroneous. Poets do not lie around (either luxuriously or starving in garrets) waiting for the muse. Writing is 1 per cent inspiration and 99 per cent perspiration. 'I rewrote the ending of *Farewell to Arms* thirty-nine times before I was satisfied' (Ernest Hemingway, quoted in Exley 1991, p. 13).

We believe we have no power: that it is located in father, God, government, philosophers. Academic literary criticism is such an authority: policing acceptable language and writing as either literary or non-literary, what form it should take, and who is allowed to create and take part in the discourse (Eagleton 1983). We must overthrow these gods and listen to the quiet voices within ourselves and our colleagues. Expressive and explorative writing develops confidence, co-operation and collaboration, encourages skills sharing, the development of team-building, and enhances ability to deal with conflict in an artistic, aesthetic process.

Writing, an ancient power

Writing is first known in the Near East in 3300 BC. A hieratic papyrus from Thebes from about 1850 BC, the teaching of Ptahhotep, says: 'It is good to speak to the future the future will listen.' And we can listen to what was written all those years ago, such as Butehamen writing to his dead wife *c.* 1075 BC: 'there is no one who stays alive. We will all follow you. If I can be heard where you are, tell the Lords of Eternity to let me, your beloved, come to you.'

Writing was considered to belong to the gods, because of this power to enshrine text. Thoth, the ancient Egyptian god of writing, 'knows the mysteries and sets the gods' utterances firm . . . proclaims all that is forgotten'. Egyptian hieroglyphs were called 'gods' words', were considered to have numinous power and were used as amulets. Stelae were inscribed with magical texts for water to be poured over and drunk to ingest the magic of the texts. 'Damnatio memoriae' was attacking a dead enemy by damaging or erasing their written name: destroying a written name was to deprive its owner of identity and existence. Reflective practice writers gain power over their practice by naming it in writing.

Endnote

Theorising is a practice of writing. One writes about the meanings in practice and through writing creates the meanings of practice. Practice is itself always changing hence there are always new meanings to be written about. At the same time, through writing, the meaning of practice is re-created, always cast anew.

Usher 1993, p. 100

I even enjoy the physical holding of the pen, the shaping of the words, and I like the way it unfolds before you, like thought unravelling. The rest of the book is blank; I wonder what the next chapter will be?

Jenny

5

PRINCIPLES OF REFLECTIVE PRACTICE

We teach and write to become what and who we are . . . The function [of pedagogy] is to invent the conditions of invention.

Wen-Song Hwu 1998, p. 37

A disciple became frustrated at never knowing how long meditation would last. The master always rang a bell: sometimes after five minutes, sometimes five hours. The disciple became so infuriated that one day she grabbed and rang the bell when *she* wanted meditation to end. The master bowed to her. She had learned.

Ancient Zen story

Reflective practice is an educative process, often undertaken with a tutor. Tutors and students relate to each other within a particular paradigm, or model of teaching and learning, whether they are aware of it or not. This chapter examines and critiques a range of such models, and offers one which seems to work for reflective practice. An understanding of the foundation principles of any course or teaching and learning situation is essential. A muddle in the models will lead to muddled dissatisfied non-learning students. If the through-the-looking-glass method is used within a wider course, the principles of both must be sufficiently consonant.

The vital relationship between tutor and student is also addressed. At times the educational process is supported either individually or in a group. At times the practitioner is reflecting alone in their journal. This chapter addresses educational relationships, and finally the contexts in which teaching and learning take place and some ways in which this can be understood and handled.

Alice did not stop to study her reflection before she went through the looking-glass. Had she done so her reflection would merely have been a back-to-front image of her accustomed self. Having crawled right through the glass she encountered a world where everything 'was as different as possible' (Carroll [1865] 1954, p. 122). She learned a great deal from the way familiar things and situations being so different ensured she could not take anything for granted. For example, when she wanted to reach an attractive small hill, she bumped into the house again every time. She learned to walk away from anything she wanted to reach, trusting looking-glass methods to get her there (pp. 132–6).

Effective reflection and reflexivity does not allow anything to be taken for granted. We need to walk away from things in order for them to come into focus. Why?, how?, what?, who?, where?, when? need to be asked of everything – all the time. Alice had to ask these questions because nothing worked as she expected; professionals have to push themselves into this state of incredulity.

Through-the-looking-glass education requires self-respect in both learners and tutors; willingness and ability to work either autonomously or in collaboration, with whomever – as appropriate; and the confidence to ask questions which might lead anywhere. It tends towards the aesthetic rather than the purely functional. The very questioning playfulness, rooted in uncertainty as to where the process will lead, is essentially non-goal-directed (however valuable outcomes might be). Physical (rather than purely cognitive), passionate (rather than purely intellectual), context-bound (rather than goal-driven), this artistic process requires flair, style and intuition. It is aesthetic; learners and tutors appreciate and explore the nuances in people's sense of themselves, their environment and experience. Winter has defined the imagination and the aesthetic in this context as: 'a universal capacity for the creative interpretation and representation of human experience' (Winter et al. 1999, p. 199).

We are all culture-bound – physically, socially, psychologically and spiritually. We might change that culture, but can never make ourselves culture free. Nor can we be fully uncertain, playful or questioning – our lives would fall apart. But we can do a great deal in that direction: in a game of *what if* . . .

This chapter looks at look at (a) the characters within the teaching and learning situation – the relationship between teacher and learner; and (b) the place in which they are working – the context. It then examines the educational situation at a *meta* level: that is, some of the assumptions both teachers and learners make about the processes in which they are engaged: the plot or storyline of education, which is being constructed with a certain set of characters in a particular place.

Educational relationships

> The role of the teacher is not to tell others what to do, not to issue edicts, nor to assist in the constitution of prophesies, promises, injunctions and programs. The task of the teacher is not to affirm prevailing general politics of teaching but to question critically the self-evident, disturb the habitual, dissipate the familiar and accepted, making the strange familiar and the familiar strange . . . The classroom is therefore a place of invention rather than reproduction.
>
> Wen-Song Hwu 1998, p. 33

Carl Rogers maintains it is the relationship which ensures the success or failure of a teaching and learning situation:

> The initiation of such learning rests not upon the teaching skills of the leader, not upon scholarly knowledge of the field, not upon curricular planning, not upon use of audiovisual aids, not upon the programmed learning

used, not upon lectures and presentations, not upon an abundance of books, though each of these might at one time or another be utilised as an important resource. No, the facilitation of significant learning rests upon certain attitudinal qualities that exist in the personal relationship between the facilitator and the learner.

Rogers 1969, p. 153

This opinion was borne out by a group of community nurses in training for reflective practitioner facilitation. One said 'the person of the teacher is the vehicle' for the learning, and another that it is the 'being' of the tutor which creates the success or failure of the teaching and learning situation. I had asked the group to tell each other, in pairs, about significant teaching and learning situations in their lives: both effective and dreadful. There was animated agreement about the underlying principles of good teaching; these were when the tutor:

- is able to create a relationship with each student which feels 'special' even when it is known to be one-way, i.e. the student knows the tutor does not feel specially about any particular student;

- 'gives of themselves', not just taking on the 'role' of tutor, but being a whole person;

- engenders confidence and respect;

- wishes to challenge both students and themselves as tutor, at the same time as valuing, being respectful of, being patient with, and offering praise to the students: an unconditional positive regard (Rogers 1969);

- makes the learning pleasurable, clear and significant; to do this they must love their subject.

The group turned to the qualities which they felt made for a destructive rather than a positive teaching and learning relationship. These cause students to close in on themselves and feel negatively about the subject, possibly lastingly. They were when the tutor:

- has no understanding of or interest in the student;

- bullies, humiliates or even abuses the student with personal intrusions, generally wields power negatively;

- has a set, inflexible agenda, a mission with no regard of the needs of the student;

- lacks confidence in the student as a person;

- transfers their own anxiety onto the student.

These lists were created by eight nurses in half-an-hour, demonstrating how effective teaching is known intuitively from bad, transcending any cognitive understanding or articulation of methodological models. The best teachers and practitioners are reflexive and reflective, qualities enhanced and fostered by education.

Fundamentally important issues for successful teaching and learning are the environment the tutor is able to create, and their relationship with the student: of trust, respect, openness, confidence and security both ways. This is a *good-enough* relationship: every tutor is human. If the foundations are there, then inevitable tutor errors and misjudgements are much more likely to be forgiven; and it might prove a learning situation for both. Peter Abbs laid greater emphasis on the role of the student than that of the tutor, but still stressed the same principles:

> Education is not primarily concerned with the accumulation of facts and techniques but rather with the expression and clarification of individual experience. The centre of education resides in the individual. If we are to achieve a genuinely human education we must return again and again to the person before us, the child, the adolescent, the adult, the individual who is ready, however dimly and in need of however much support, to adventure both further out into his experience and further into it, who is ready, in some part of himself, to risk himself in order to become more than he now is. The teacher, the tutor can provide the conditions and the support for such a journey – but the journey itself can only be made by the assenting and autonomous individual.
>
> Abbs 1974, p. 5

This resembles Rogers's view: wanting to 'return again and again to the . . . individual' is the kind of tutor my group wanted, and Rogers endorsed. In an in-service training reflexive (and reflective) session, my own Masters (Medical Science) tutors each drew how we viewed our role as educators. One drew a candle, educator lighting the darkness; one a map and compass, teacher as guide through rough places; one a church, initiating others into the holy of holies; and another a gardener watering a tree, the educator as *enlightened guide* nurtures, supports and initiates the weaker other. In my drawing I had outstretched arms inviting everyone to an exciting party. Alan Bleakley (see also 2000a) adds: 'I have always imagined my own teaching in terms of contemporary jazz (post-bop): opening theme with chorus – long improvisation – chorus – coda. I like the idea of strange harmonies, dissonances combined with resonances, melodies that lose themselves in improvisation but are echoed throughout, and then restated at the end of the piece.'

Modelling

Educators are role models (often unwittingly). The above lists show students do not forget model best and worst teachers, possibly spending professional lives unconsciously emulating (or trying not to be) these vital figures. My best teacher was humorous, matter of fact, straightforward, caring but not motherly: a biologist, I shall never forget her impassioned account of earthworms copulating under the moon. My worst teacher, a chalk and talk didact, made a fascinating subject boring with her flat instructive tone: we dared hardly move, cough or hiccup, let alone ask a question. I still think historical romances must be turgid, as she recommended them to widen our understanding. The influence of those two is probably clearly discernable in this book. Teachers are seen to be vital companions in education.

I now wish to turn to the terrain we explore together.

Landmarks on the syllabus moor

A country area with no paths can appear a confusion of walls, sheep-tracks and tors. The view from a helicopter would seem to make more sense: walls joining up to make comprehensible fields with a gate. Our walker would gain clarity of the whole walk from a light aircraft. Adult education has recently been likened to 'moorland', rather than a 'field' (Usher et al. 1997). The helicopter or light-aircraft view offered by a heuristic model, meta-understanding of the situation, can be useful here. Stephen Rowland (1999, 2000) has suggested that under all circumstances both tutor and students might understand their resources for learning as a triangle of three areas, as in Figure 5.1.

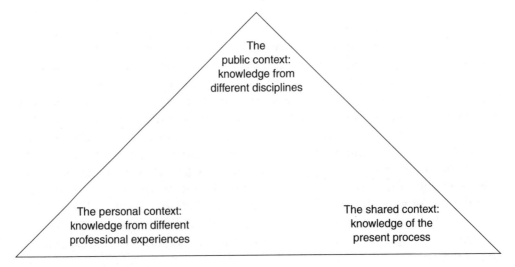

Figure 5.1 Resources for learning
Adapted from Rowland 2000, p. 61

The *public area of knowledge* is, in principle, open to everyone through public texts, whether government documents, or professional and academic papers and books. Interpretations of these may vary, and some professionals will be more knowledgeable in certain areas than others. If an area is disputed, the text can be referred to as arbiter. Reflective practice must be embedded within this public arena, to prevent it being merely personal confession.

The *personal area of knowledge* is private, known only to the individual. Much of the material of reflective practice belongs in this arena. Knowledge of the situation, people involved, and the thoughts and feelings involved, belong in individuals' minds. The process of examining this area might be the reflective one of laying any aspect of the situation open to question; or it may be reflexive: questioning one's own impulses, attitudes, assumptions and so on. The individual is the authority on these matters.

The *shared area of knowledge* is the 'process of the group's work', or that of the teaching and learning pair. Each individual within a group or duo has their own private set of stories of their own lives – personal and professional: this is the personal area of knowledge. In association with others a shared set of stories, assumptions, principles and so on is created. All those present remember how they struggled to grasp the difference between reflection and reflexivity; or when Sue shouted at Bob for assuming she was late because of childcare. They have their own tacitly understood group methods, such as sitting in silence reflecting deeply when appropriate rather than rushing to come up with immediate answers. This knowledge and understanding is available only to participants – and no member has more information or rights over it than another.

The *shared* area is often missed out for reflexive consideration. Yet addressing it, whether under supervision or in group, can be invaluable. People can only learn when they are confident, respected and valued, and to an extent control the process of learning. Exposing the educational process (including the role of the tutor) to scrutiny can enable participants to take a degree of control: say what they want out of a teaching and learning situation, and attempt to redress anything which they feel is going wrong. The tutor can be enabled to adapt their methods or syllabus to the needs and wants of their student(s). This can be an invaluable area for any reflexive and reflective practitioner to develop within their practice, enabling them to gain and act upon effective feedback from colleagues and clients/patients/students.

The focus on any one area will be different in different situations. Within reflective practice the focus is often the *personal arena*, though *public domain* material develops, extends and critiques ideas, and ensures participants' burgeoning understandings are embedded in the wider social, professional and political sphere. My reflective practice students pursue what they have realised are knowledge or theory gaps, such as about ethics. A reflexive examination of the *shared domain*, the educative process undertaken with the tutor (whether group or 1:1) models any teaching and learning process.

Aware tutors can harness and drive these three contexts to their own and their students' advantage. Students can use them to broaden their awareness within, and response to, learning situations. Awareness of different ways of functioning within the three contexts can further enhance understanding and ability to maximise teaching and learning efficacy and interest. Within the *public* context, *reason* comes to the fore. Within the *shared* and the *personal* contexts, actions, thoughts and feelings are all appropriate for consideration. Examining what was done, thought and felt about a specific situation helps explore dark corners in personal professional experience, shared group experiences, and in the political situations in which we work. 'We understand through feeling' (Shem 2002, p. 935). 'Reflective practice is the public recognition and interrogation of the *e*ffects of *a*ffect within action' [emphasis in original] (Usher et al. 1997, p. 220).

Ethics and patients, students or clients

Reflective practice raises serious ethical considerations concerning practitioners, the populations with whom they practise, and the organisation for whom they work. Ethical issues are properly aired in reflective practice. A practitioner's response to material thrown up by the reflective process may be unexpectedly emotive (angry or distressed, for example), or present them with unexpected issues to sort out. John, a Masters student, commented: 'this really made me realise the learner is not in control when exploring new ideas'. Inexperienced facilitators, furthermore, may find the content of a student's reflection raises issues or emotions of their own, which may otherwise have remained buried. Hargreaves has examined the ethics of requiring nurses to undertake this activity (1997, and see below). Effective facilitation of reflection can support practitioners in appropriately sorting out issues which arise.

Confidential material about the population with whom reflective practitioners work is exposed even when names and details are altered. Practitioners do all in their power to discuss cases with respect. Sometimes the need to release feelings overtakes: a group of doctors falling about with hilarity about a dropped corpse being unpickupable in snow and ice. No disrespect was intended, but the situation was too horrific to be countenanced until some emotion had been released. I understand paramedics and police officers respond in similar ways. Specific issues need to be addressed rather than generalities. As a user of services myself, I would rather think I was discussed among colleagues – in whatever way was appropriate – than feel I was treated by an unreflective practitioner.

Reflective practice is an appropriate arena for the discussion of ethical practice. Anne Hudson Jones describes how narratives of practice are used to teach 'narrative ethics', offering 'richer ethical discourse for all' (1998, p. 223). Ron Carson maintains that both the study of one's own stories of practice and the reading of literature are the best way of studying and maintaining ethical practice: 'literature shapes sensibility by giving form to feelings and by revealing the narrative structure of experiences of love, loss, loyalty and the like' (1994, p. 238). Reflective journals, and discussions upon them, have been used sensitively and carefully to support student palliative care nurses:

> The diary sessions are in-depth critical discussions and comparisons of clinical situations where logical and rigorous analysis of moral and ethical concepts takes place. Through this analytical process, assumptions made by health care professionals, patients and relatives are uncovered and examined. This leads to the revelation of attitudes, stereotyping, prejudices, preconceptions, philosophical ethics, frames of references, cultural influences, and the nurse's predisposition to act in a certain way: 'reflecting on clinical situations made me aware of my beliefs . . . and the assumptions I make . . . the uniqueness of people and their rights'.
>
> Durgahee 1997, p. 143

This is a fully rounded reflective process involving emotional responses and synthetic functions, not restricted to the 'logical and rigorous'. Ethical dilemmas may arise in reflection upon a colleague's faulty practice: should it be reported? What does the confidentiality of reflective practice mean? (see Cutcliffe et al. 1998). What would I have done had my teacher student (pp. 18–20) not made it clear her school was dealing with the colleague who was having a sexual relationship with a pupil? There can be no hard and fast generalised rules: careful one-to-one discussion is the starting point.

Practitioners bring their whole selves to reflective practice; and that whole person has vulnerabilities. Reflective practice, to be effective, does not shy away from emotional realisation of ethical problems.

Aspects of therapeutic theory and practice are therefore relevant to through-the-looking-glass work. Carl Rogers, a therapist, advocated this way of working in education (Rogers 1969); Jane Abercrombie, an academic biologist, brought therapeutic group work principles into higher education teaching in the 1960s (Abercrombie 1993). A basic tenet is respect and 'unconditional regard' (Rogers 1969) for the student.

Reflective practice facilitators are not therapists; but an understanding of therapeutic ways of working can offer greater powers of empathy and facilitation, and greater confidence in handling emotive situations. Therapeutic needs may arise through reflective processes; appropriate outside support must be sought. Pre-service students are considered by some to be more likely to uncover material needing therapeutic support. Young students (undergraduates, for example) in my experience tend to tumble in and out of being emotional in reflective practice; I have not experienced them as any more vulnerable, but yet have known extremely experienced doctors break down and need support. I have, though, noticed undergraduates making definite statements about themselves and each other; 'I'm the sort of person who . . .', 'that's just like you, you always . . .' Young adults are finding out who they are, and the location of their personal boundaries.

Checks and balances in reflective practice facilitation can help prevent distress. Facilitators need supervisors/mentors. Co-facilitating group sessions can enable one to be tutoring while the other observes, reporting back to co-facilitator in debriefing after the session. Group reflexivity and an awareness of Rowland's 'shared context' (2000) is invaluable. The group can be facilitated to take responsibility for its own processes; they will observe if a member needs extra support or to be handled sensitively and will alert the facilitator if necessary. Each member has responsibility for sharing any distress or anxiety before it becomes too big for the group to handle.

Clear and agreed ground rules of boundaries and confidentiality help. Ethical and power issues always need addressing in supervision, particularly if the supervisor is also in a position of authority over the practitioner, who may be justifiably cautious about what and how they will disclose. Differing assumptions concerning reflective practice and supervision cloud the area. Fowler and Chevannes stress 'there are potential disadvantages in making the assumption that reflective practice should be an integral part of all forms of clinical supervision' (1998, p. 379). Marrow et al., however, write of effective supervision, where the sister of a busy accident and emergency unit offered effective supervision to her staff focusing on reflective diaries, which she read (1997). And Judy Hildebrand describes deeply reflective and reflexive supervision of family therapist trainees (1995).

Janet Hargreaves: the ethics of reflection

Issues of confidentiality are a concern in recording reflections, which are often personal and may be controversial. There are also a small number of cases where a reflective diary has been used in a legal setting as 'evidence'. But once I really started to think about all this I realised that these were not the really important questions. They presuppose that reflection is given: they challenge some of the consequences of reflection, but not the act itself. The really important issue was why were we encouraging nurses to be reflective in the first place? What is it for? What does it achieve? Once I started asking these questions everything changed. Mezirow (1981) talks of paradigm transformation, and this is what happened to me here – a sudden realisation that if I looked at the same thing from a very slightly different angle – I would see a completely different picture. Reflection is not without moral significance, for example:

- Reflection is emotionally demanding for the person who is doing it. Can we insist they do it?

- On reflecting the reflector may feel more pressured to act to change a situation, thus disturbing the status quo.

- If you then share those reflections with others verbally then you expose a part of yourself, and divulge information about unsuspecting third parties.

- If you write down those reflections as part of an assessed course they are read by at least one other person, and are given into that third party's custody for safe keeping. Also in doing this there is an obligation to reveal part of yourself which may usually be private in order to gain academic credit, and to use the experiences of your (non-consenting) patients as the medium for your achievement.

In themselves none of these things is awfully shocking, but they are not without moral worth. Consequently to justify them there has to be some perceived gain. What is it? What can we clearly say has been achieved, or is achievable through reflection, what is the end that is gained via these means? The justification can be that it makes better nurses, or happier nurses, or better people generally – but all of that would be pretty difficult to prove. It leaves a need to reflect on the nature of the good nurse, and the lack of literature regarding the value of reflection.

Janet Hargreaves (see also Hargreaves 1997)

Forgiveness

Reflective practice can enable a shift in attitude to events, relationships and values in professional life, whether institutional or relative to clients. Forgiving others and oneself can be an element. A connectedness with ourselves, each other and our world tends to have been lost in obsession with measurement and evaluation, external success and appearance, and a belief that people can shape their world by making conscious plans. This connectedness has been replaced by anxiety around relationships, and a fear of each other evidenced by such phenomena as road rage.

Mercy has been marginalised as rather soppy and/or religious. Blake's description of mercy as having a 'human heart' (Blake 1958, p. 33) and Portia's powerful plea (Shakespeare's *Merchant of Venice*) have too often been forgotten. 'Given this situation it is no wonder that people are flocking to various mental health practitioners with chronic guilt, shame, resentment, disease, and feelings of estrangement' (Rowe and Halling 1998, p. 227). The goddess Athene says of forgiveness:

Let your rage pass into understanding
As into the coloured clouds of a sunset,
Promising a fair tomorrow.
Do not let it fall
As a rain of sterility and anguish.

Aeschylus trans. 1999, p. 184

'The failure to forgive . . . stands in the way of our development as persons who are free of unnecessary restraints from the past and illusions of human perfection' (Rowe et al. 1989, p. 233). Practitioners have found a capacity to forgive colleagues, clients and themselves through reflective practice, in my experience. This forgiveness is like the letting go of a weight which has been carried, often for years; it can come accompanied by grief (Bauer et al. 1992). Forgiveness of oneself and of others go hand in hand and both are vital; the letting go of remorse and hatred or anger with another cannot be planned for, nor directed by a facilitator, however.

Forgiveness is like a gift which comes with increased understanding. The example I shall always remember is the midwife who was still furious with a mother, years after the birth. She wrote the story – angrily – from her own point of view. The reflective practice group (Masters degree module) and I then suggested she wrote it from the perspective of the mother. When she returned the following week with her second story she said humbly: 'I don't feel angry any more. I don't know why she behaved so badly, but if it was like in my story she was as hurt as I was, if not more so.'

Risk

> I have come to realise through the process of writing about this incident that reflection is not a cosy process of quiet contemplation. It is an active, dynamic, often threatening process which demands total involvement of self and a commitment to action. In reflective practice there is nowhere to hide.

This kind of work comes with its own anxieties, doubts, fears and sense of risk. Those who gain from the process feel: nothing ventured, nothing gained. I would like to explore the issue of risk with reference to one reflective writing group: an educational principles and practice module on a Master in Medical Science course (see Bolton 1999c).

This group had been working together for some time, discussing and learning about education. But this was the first time they were to expose their thinking and understandings in writing with each other. It is one thing to say something tentatively in discussion, and then develop or alter it as the subject evolves and mutates. It is one thing to sit silent, or only venturing the odd expression while the more verbal and confident develop their ideas through discussion. It is quite another to put yourself on the line and stand by your written words. The group members knew I would be asking them to write very quickly without forethought – not merely as rational discourse (Mezirow 1991), but also to write from intuitive knowledge, understanding, and memory of experience.

One asked: 'Are we just going to sit here and write? How do I know which incident to choose?' I replied I would be facilitating the session; every step would be very carefully explained and agreed to. There was a sigh of relief: the facilitation itself would be strong and straightforward. The process of writing explorative and expressive texts, and sharing them (albeit in a well-formed and effectively performing group) needs, I feel, a supportive, clear, facilitative, interactive tutor, to offer confidence and trust. The growth and development of this kind of work can only too easily feel unsafe and confusing: as much safety as possible and as much respect for confused feelings and seeming muddliness needs to be facilitated. The members need to feel that whatever they write is the right thing for them at that time, and will be respected as such by the rest of the group, as will seeming contradictions and changes of mind. They need to feel that the confidentiality and possible privacy of writings are respected. During the ensuing week, I assured everyone, we would pull apart my facilitation style and skills, for the sake of their educational understandings – and we did – but that is not the story here.

The group understood this would be hot writing (improvised, rather than played coolly from pre-planned ideas). But they still needed me to explain how to allow words to flow from their pens; after all their heads were empty of ideas, or full of apprehension rather.

The students were asked to trust themselves to go back to the very first stages of writing. The stages of writing without thinking. Those initial stages are the breath of creative life to poets, novelists, playwrights, autobiographers, but are missed out by academic writers. Everyone wrote for six minutes without stopping, putting on the paper whatever was in their heads (like stream of consciousness). This was not for sharing (but could be if the writer so wished): it was to clear our heads; or capture whatever floating thoughts and ideas were there; and to get the pen flowing untroubled (or perhaps feverishly fast) over the page.

> [One group member] has just left the room, obviously upset, and I think that emphasises just how powerful this can be. How does this 'power' get dealt with without leaving more scars?
>
> Liz

This element of risk, which the students rightly discerned from the start, is of course, as Liz so rightly judges, the seat of the power of this kind of writing. It can seem like a tightrope to a beginning student. Having facilitated a very large number of such sessions, I know that writing these things, although so powerful, is also well paced, people do not normally write more than they are able to cope with at that time. It is important to give the writer sufficient time to read and acquaint themselves with their own writing before sharing anything with tutor or group. From Elaine's journal:

> The facilitation allowing the group to respond to the writings primarily and giving permission not to disclose any part of the writing made the group safe and gave responsibility to its members.

This is different from a talk-based discussion group when it is easy to blurt things out and then regret at leisure (Hulatt 1995). Sonya (NHS Senior Nurse Manager) commented in her journal on her own six-minute writing:

> this seemed to spring from nowhere and resulted in me actively seeking a new job!! All based on a few minutes' thought!

We then wrote about 'a time when I learned something vital at work'. Ann, (herself an experienced educator) wrote about a disastrous session with a group of young disadvantaged mothers which she had facilitated many years ago. From her final portfolio:

> When I began to write this critical incident I started with a series of descriptive words. They mostly related to emotions, both mine and those I had felt from the other people involved in the incident. Then I began to write the story. As I began to write I was unsure about why I had chosen this incident. It had happened some years ago and I felt that as I had discussed the incident with a number of people at the time, I had understood and analysed it sufficiently. Perhaps that was why I used it – perhaps I felt I had the answers ready to be neatly inserted into the story. Nevertheless, I had been instructed to write about the first incident which came to mind and this was the one. As I wrote, the situation was recreated before me. I could see the room, feel the atmosphere, although parts of the sequence of events were hazy in detail. What I did remember and what hit me again was the emotional force of feeling, both those of the women in that room on that day, but more particularly my own feelings. As I wrote I couldn't believe how much there was to put down. I had to force myself to stop after all the others had finished. When I read the piece to the group I was overwhelmed by the emotional force and couldn't complete the reading. All those emotions. And I thought I had 'dealt with' this incident.
>
> Ann

Writing in this way can enable practitioners to begin to listen properly to some of the different voices within themselves. This is risky because writers enter marginal states where certainties dissolve. These certainties resemble professional straitjackets, though they can feel comfortably secure. Within the marginal writing state, the writer loses clarity in a unitary self, begins to perceive alternative selves in the different retellings of the story. Narrators can become the narration, crossing over that threshold of certainty, of knowing how they should respond in given situations into the unknowingness of uncertainty. The feeling of riskiness lies in the possibility of facing issues previously buried as un-faceable, to begin to doubt their practice, become confused (how will I know who I am if I bring my basic practice into question?), need drastically to alter their practice, their world, even the worlds of others.

They do all these things: hopefully. Later they realise the exhilaration and increase in self-confidence and self-determination, though initially they only perceive dangerous uncertainty. Facilitators ensure this happens at a pace and depth, and with sufficiently created boundaries, so 'this "power" gets dealt with without leaving more scars' (Liz, above).

The next stage was to read and discuss writings. I wrote and read alongside the group, though I always make it clear I will keep my verbal contribution until everyone else has had a say. The discussion was not directed except to avoid mere anecdote-capping (unlikely with this group), and to support it towards deeper reflective levels. We worked within clear guidelines and boundaries set by the group.

Jessica's story concerned a knotty, ongoing work situation unflinchingly brought to the group. She took her fresh understandings back to the work situation, and implemented them immediately: 'I don't believe I could have done it without the learning opportunities I have been given.' Her stories can be read elsewhere (Bolton 1999a).

The group also worked in peer-mentoring pairs, as well as a whole group without their tutors. This enabled discussions which were additional to the ones with myself as facilitator. One commented that he could discuss issues with his peer-mentor which he would never have been able to expose to the whole group. Participants wrote additional stories and reflective passages alongside original core stories. Creative, original and deeply helpful suggestions were made for fresh writings.

> I surprised myself with both the subject of what I wrote and the power of emotions it provoked. I hadn't realised I had so many unresolved feelings about the incident despite having talked about it to others many times. On reflection I feel that Gillie is right: there is something in the writing that gives another dimension. Seeing the words on the page gives an added intensity to the power of the feelings. There was a lot of honesty in the group this week, although some people understandably chose to use a far less problematic incident than others. I feel I have learned a lot from hearing the others in the group talk through their incidents. What have I learned? . . . I have learned about the power of the written word. I have thought about trying to do sharing of critical incidents with primary health care teams and feel it could be very valuable. I'm sure every group finds its level of exposure.
>
> Ann

Ann felt the group were not sufficiently critical in the discussion, that they supported her too much to feel she had acted out of the best intentions. She wanted to face the possibility that having good intentions just was not enough. She noted six weeks later, however:

I can see that I had still not been able to put this incident behind me and therefore was cross with others for trying to help me to do that. I feel rather embarrassed now by my reactions to the group. It was, of course, not about them but about me . . . I can now forgive myself for this incident, understand it and accept that everyone gets it wrong sometimes.

Ann

She later noted impressions of discussions around our second story (on gender issues, a theme chosen by the group), commenting how we had had more time, and were more confident about what we were doing. She was more positive about the depth of reflection we reached. To me it seems no bad thing that a group starts off very sensitively and gingerly supportive when discussing such writings. Also Ann could not fully take into account, then, the effect her evident emotion had had on the group.

Liz rewrote her piece as a series of thought bubbles, thoughts which had not been expressed in the writing. Elaine wrote about a frustrating consultation with a client; she had felt anxious and responsible for things not going better. Her initial strong desire was to put the writing away, never read it again, nor think about that client. On the suggestion of the group, however, she rewrote the event twice fictionally; from the client's point of view; and as win:win, an occasion when both client and nurse felt in agreement about a positive outcome.

I was amazed at the reduction of anger when I wrote the win:win situation towards the client and myself. I was also struck by the lack of centrality of my position in the clinic compared to the wide complex circumstances of the client's life . . . Writing a win:win situation enormously reduced the overall anxiety and power which caused both myself and the client to OVERACT and OVER-REACT.

Elaine

Both Elaine and Liz stressed in their journals how the writing, rewriting and discussion helped them to become more objective about the incident, and to separate out responsibilities. Both realised they had taken on responsibility which really was not theirs, some of it belonging to the client. Elaine commented in her journal that the writing and discussion: 'helped change my emotional response to the situations and be more mentally open to all options rather than solving it in a specific way'.

What kind of education is this?
An unmuddling of models

Any involvement in education as teacher or learner can only be undertaken from within a particular approach or understanding of the processes, and end-products expected or hoped for. Sometimes the parties concerned are only too aware of their own image, metaphor or model of education; sometimes they accept a 'given' model without knowing what it is. In order to be involved in an effective, consistent educational process, I suggest it is invaluable to be aware of the model used.

Chalk and talk

A traditional model, recognisable from schooling and much university education, is called the banking model (Freire 1972), transfer or moulding theory (Fox 1983), or the didactic model (Rowland1999). This is when teachers who know the answers attempt to funnel them directly into the heads of students who do not know. Tutors retain control; learners are not considered with respect and are not expected to contribute creative ideas. A hierarchically determined system of knowledge and social status is reinforced, and the impact and body of knowledge is predetermined.

Rocky path

This has also been called the 'exploratory model' (Rowland 1993), or *fofo* way of teaching (f*** off and find out). Rowland quotes a DES document:

> The broad objectives of the work were discussed with the [students] but then they were put in a position of finding their own solutions.
> Department of Education and Science 1978, para 3

The student is respected (possibly) and given autonomy, but probably not enough guidance and support; the tutor is not primarily involved in the processes of learning.

Hey presto

We live, teach and learn in a consumer culture with a market orientation in which people, practitioners included, are constantly bombarded with new practices and new ways of being. A time of individuation, difference appears to be celebrated, yet conformity is fostered. We can choose to change and mould our lives (even our bodies) in ways never before possible: to fashion new identities for ourselves. Outward signs (packaging) are important: what things are called, what they look like. Market-place understandings dominate. We can buy 'care' these days, even 'love' according to adverts of an oncology nursing organisation as I write. And the word 'trust' is used of those who hold the purse strings. This has had a huge impact upon education. Organisations 'deliver' courses on the assumption that the commodity bought will directly improve their service, as if it were the latest fertiliser.

Competencies, skills, and fully developed reflective practice abilities all need to be acquired by practitioners. But in this system they are seen as products or commodities – *things* like bricks or vitamin tablets – to be bought with education currency without primary attention being paid to fundamental educational *processes* which enable their development, such as tutor-student relationships and the learning environment.

Teachers are assessed on the *value* they offer the consumer. The *objects* students consume are all too often *signs*, communicating social position and worth. *Who I am seen to be?*, and *What I can get as a result of this course?* (e.g. a better job) have become more important than the innate value of intellectual enquiry. A social worker's client bemoaned the fact that she could not take up jogging for her health, although she dearly wanted to, because she could not afford the gear. She had to be seen to be doing it right.

Giving students set pro formas, lists of prompts, questions or areas which must be covered in reflective practice will stultify, make for passivity and lack of respect. Professionals need to ask and attempt to answer their own questions. Otherwise their practice is being moulded towards the system's wants and needs.

Testing and checking up on students to see if they have acquired the required competencies further endorses this subordinate sense. Tutors saying 'I get the students to . . .' manipulate students in a semblance of 'choice', yet they only have to paint the right bits the right colours, join up the dots. The 'shopkeeper' delivering the 'package' gains a neat pile of pigeon-hole sized submissions with predetermined areas accounted for: evidence this, this and this has been 'learned': products which can then be consumed by both practitioner and assessor. It matters not that it is solely a paper exercise as there is no continuity between course and practice, no one to see practice has changed or developed; what matters is the product: the neatly ticked boxes look right. This has been called 'surface learning' (Prosser and Trigwell 1999; Rust 2002).

Our *problems* cannot be *solved*, however many *problem-solving* exercises we undertake. Problems, issues, relationships can all be aired and examined constructively, but to see the process as a straight line from *identification of need* to *problem solved* is effectively to prevent constructive learning. Learning is innately complex.

The values basis of this functional competence model is technical-rational, utilitarian and instrumental. Students are short-changed and manipulated. A full educational process has to be undergone, however painfully and expensively. There are no short cuts, no prestidigitation. But this next model, for all its wonderful features, is not The Answer either, for there is no Right Answer.

Path to freedom

Carl Rogers described *personal* liberation in education and psychotherapy (1969). Paolo Freire developed a model of effective education called *problem posing*: a liberating *political* process (1972) (it must be remembered that Freire was working in a politically revolutionary situation in the l960s):

> Authentic reflection considers neither abstract man [sic] nor the world without men, but men in their relations with the world . . . That which had been

perceived objectively but had not been perceived in its deeper implications (if indeed it was perceived at all) begins to 'stand out' assuming the character of a problem and therefore of challenge. Thus men begin to single out elements from their 'background awarenesses' and to reflect upon them. These elements are now objects of men's consideration, and, as such, objects of their action and cognition . . . The banking method emphasizes permanence and becomes reactionary; problem-posing education – which accepts neither a 'well-behaved' present nor a pre-determined future – roots itself in the dynamic present and becomes revolutionary.

Freire 1972, pp. 35–7

My students echoed this, calling their course 'consciousness raising'. Such reflective practice can lead to very real change – both to the individual and to the organisation or state upon which they might act. Freire was right that education should be rooted in the present, and should pose problems about our lives here and now: this is the stuff of reflective practice.

Effective reflective practice is critically active and dynamic in a wide sphere. Practitioners question and problematise themselves, their roles and those in authority over them, the political, social and professional situations in which they find themselves. They cannot again uncritically accept a situation, nor just moan about it. Reflective practice encourages *action*, and that means not just keeping the fridge in better order so the wrong injection is never given again, but questioning appropriate aspects of the system. One participant during her very first 'six minute' writing realised she had to change her job. She not only got one much more suited to her, but also one in which she could and did implement significant change for her staff.

Marx recommended a 'relentless criticism of all existing conditions, relentless in the sense that the criticism is not afraid of its own findings and just as little afraid of conflict with the powers that be' (1962, p. 212). Carr and Kemmis (1986) with their theory of critical social science and *praxis* of *action research* drew upon the work of Marx and Freire. Based on the work of the philosopher Habermas, this is a political-social understanding (critical theory) rather than the personal one developed by psychoanalysis or therapy (as in Rogers, for example):

The purpose of critique then is to provide a form of therapeutic self-knowledge which will liberate individuals from the irrational compulsions of their individual history through a process of critical self-reflection . . . Critique is aimed at revealing to individuals how their beliefs and attitudes may be ideological illusions that help to preserve a social order which is alien to their collective experience and needs. By demonstrating how ideological forces generate erroneous self-understandings, ideology critique aims to reveal their deceptive nature and so strip them of their power. . .

Action research is simply a form of self-reflective inquiry undertaken by participants in social situations in order to improve the rationality and justice of their own practice, their understanding of these practices, and the situations in which these practices are carried out.

Carr and Kemmis 1986, pp. 138–9, 162

Action research, as its name implies, is more research based than reflective practice, with a 'self-reflective spiral of cycles of planning, acting, observing and reflecting' (Carr and Kemmis 1986, p. 165), but it does offer a model for reflective practice.

So what is the problem? It seems an unwarranted certainty to consider that the 'compulsions of [participants'] individual history' *before* they begin on a 'process of critical self-reflection' are any more 'irrational' than those they will be enabled to arrive at *after* the process. It could also be said that *all* 'beliefs and attitudes may be ideological illusions that help to preserve a social order which is alien to their collective experience and needs', *however* they are acquired – through reflective practice or otherwise.

Freire was certain, in the political sphere, Carl Rogers in the personal (see below), and Carr and Kemmis in both, that progress is taking place towards a particular goal of personal or political productive change and development. This model asserts that reflective practice (or critical action research) automatically brings people from ignorance to knowledge, from political passivity to effective action. But this certainty is based on nothing more than an assumption that a greater understanding of ourselves or the world will make things better. In the personal sphere this model asserts that these can be *self-actualising* processes in which each practitioner will find the *real me*, the *me* they were intended to be.

The very notion of *me* is problematic, however: I am not a static entity, but in the process of being created every day as social and political forces impact upon me; I am a story I tell and retell every day, with fresh facets and new viewpoints each time. I am not so much a thing – static in shape, form and time – but more a verb – not *me* but *to me*.

Reflective practice has, contrariwise to the *path to freedom* model, been accused of encouraging practitioners to accept their lot, however bad: a form of quietism. People cannot be 'empowered' or 'given a voice' by a more powerful other (tutor, for example); they can only give it to themselves – *take it*, that is. According to this critique:

> We become active knowing subjects but now we subjectify ourselves rather than being subjected by others. We think we have mastered the power that imposes itself from 'outside' only to find that it is now 'inside'. We have the power, indeed the obligation, to exercise our 'freedom' but we are not thereby empowered to affect our social and political environment.
>
> Usher et al. 1997, p. 87

Practitioners can become trapped in controlling themselves to work according to the wants and needs of the system, rather than responding to exterior control. Power is a slippery, omnipresent thing, and does not necessarily do what it *appears* to do. Professionals, tutors and curriculum designers have to be sensitive to undercurrents and meta-levels in education: 'the most effective forms of power are those which are not recognised as powerful but as enabling or "em-powering". . . The drive for emancipation may itself become oppressive' (Usher et al. 1997, pp. 87, 190). And:

> Practices of 'freedom' or 'authenticity', or search for a 'real' self are in fact rule-bound examples of governance of self by self through self-surveillance. While advertised as a route to liberty or autonomy, [they] offer strictly coded forms of self-governance and regulation.
>
> Bleakley 2000b, p. 406

Carr called it 'essentially an enlightenment project' (1995, p. 121); such a project assumes a knowledge of what *rationality* is: we do not have this knowledge. The very notion of *enlightenment* maintains a confidence that the 'light' I am in now is any better than the 'dark' I was in previously, and that what my tutors tell me is 'light' is 'light' indeed for me. What is wrong with the dark anyway?

Reflective practice education is constant reflexive self-examination: actions, thoughts, feelings, motives, assumptions. In order to be critical of my own personal, social and political situation I have to be able to stand outside it to some extent. Of course I cannot do this fully, whatever contortions I attempt. No one can critique one paradigm while within it: no sailor can propel a yacht by blowing into the sails. We all wear culturally tinted lenses through which we view the world: emerald spectacles cannot be removed to see the world, our actions, and those of others as *they really are*. Alice was the only one who managed fully effective reflexivity and critical emancipation: by crawling right through the looking-glass and experiencing herself and her world from the other side: not an action we can imitate.

No tutor (facilitator or supervisor) can guide anyone else towards their own emancipation, no one can have this wisdom or power; nor can it be an aspect of the curriculum. There can be no specific way of working (however wonderful reflective practice may be) which supports another to 'free' themselves from their social, political and psychological constraints. Educative reflective practice can yet lead to greater agency, responsibility, self-understanding and self-confidence.

Through the looking-glass

The previous models made assumptions which, I have suggested, we need to shed, and missed out other vital elements. Effective education is based upon both tutor and learner being able to make as many aspects as they can of their situation, and themselves, strange and different – in order to study them.

In this approach learners are encouraged to be as reflexively aware and questioning as possible of social, political and psychological positions, as well as their environment. In this dynamic state, things will appear to be strange, back to front, and to operate in unusual ways: they should do so. A student called it 'making the ordinary extraordinary'. It is this very strange-seemingness or extraordinariness which will enable students to formulate their own questions about the situations in which they find themselves (reflective), and the self they find there (reflexive). These questions are almost bound to be different from the ones they thought they might ask. Spirited enquiry leads to specific, usefully appropriate and meaningful questioning. Interim answers will appear, but as markers along the way rather than finishing posts.

Learners are supported to find ways of discovering what they feel they need to know, from literature, from knowledgeable others whether other students or external authorities, from tutors. This can be as widely understood as the students wish – popular culture, as well as literature carries vital data.

Many elements of previous models come into play eclectically in through-the-looking-glass learning. There is no comfortable beginning, middle and end, and the *characters* and *places* are not clearly delineated and set. Individuals take on varied roles: tutor as didactic teacher at one point, and equal friend along the way at another; a colleague may be the enemy at one time and fascinating authority at another. Students may think they are well on the way to understanding something, and then realise they have to stand one step back and view the matter from a fresh standpoint and begin all over again with a new set of questions.

Student and tutor are both engaged in a process, and their roles are more equal than in the other models. Knowledge and understanding are seen as something they are constructing together according to the wants and needs of the student. Their relationship and their roles will constantly be under reflexive review.

Conclusion

Marilyn Pietroni gives a useful set of 'nature and aims of professional education' (1995):

- to provide a containing environment in which individual practitioners are given the opportunity of recovering or establishing creative individual thought;

- to offer partnerships in learning between educators and learners;

- to provide a learning environment in which the log-jams and messiness of day-to-day practice can be faced and scrutinised in detail;

- to provide continuous workshop environments (Schon's practicum) in which new ideas and approaches can be explored before and after their use (the double-feedback loop);

- to enable the nature of the organisational structures and defences that frame the work to be examined in relation to identified tasks;

- to educate for a context of continuous change in which professional categories and languages, and organisational structure, are constantly by definition under erasure.

Pietroni 1995, p. 48

This chapter has gone some way towards examining some of the underpinnings of educational situations: relationships, contexts, structures of assumptions. There is no one way of getting the education business right: eclecticism is a valuable approach. But attention to these vital areas, in particular to mutual respect and authority and a genuine openness as to end-product, are likely to enable effective reflective practice: professionals and students *ringing the bell themselves*.

6

PULLING TOGETHER: WRITING FOR PEERS; TEAM CREATION

Shape clay into a vessel;
It is the space within that makes it useful.

Lao Tsu trans. 1973, p. 11

Sunlight's a thing that needs a window
before it enters a dark room.
Windows don't happen.

Thomas 1986, p. 53

Reflective practice writing is undertaken for specific others, whether mentor or group. Such collaborative learning is deeply educative, and can be powerfully team-building. The writing and discussion processes facilitate an effective level of frankness and openness. A safe-enough environment can be created for elements of relationships and organisations to be faced and reconfigured. 'Doctors felt the process of writing and talking about the stories was both profound and helpful. The process stimulated clarification of personal values and priorities, created a context for peer support (which doctors often seem to resist), and fostered recognition of opportunities to make constructive changes in their professional lives . . . Amid so much discussion of what is wrong with medicine, the work-shops seemed to help them remember what is right' (Horowitz et al. 2003, p. 774). All the examples of reflective work in this book are of stand-alone courses or modules. Through-the-looking-glass work can be an invaluable element of longer courses as long as the overall principles of the course are consonant (see Chapter 5).

Tom Heller gives a riveting description of a reflective writing group, followed by my account of a social work team course (see Chapter 5 for further course descriptions); discussion of mentoring, co-mentoring, action research and Socratic dialogue follows.

Reflective writing in a group of doctors

Several years ago I wrote a story about Sheila, a drug addict whom I had been looking after for several years, and read it out to the reflective writing group. 'Sheila', not her real name of course, had deeply affected me. She was exactly the same age as me, and although she had lived a very different life to mine, including spells in prostitution, a time in prison for drug running and a serious opiate addiction, we really liked each other. The other members of the group remember other 'Sheilas' that they have met and how difficult they found them. But they start to gently probe why I may have chosen this particular story from all the others I could have chosen. What role does her age have in all this, might I have a special empathy with people who are exactly the same age as me? And what about the role of that big decision in Sheila's life: is her decision to run off with Jim reflected in any way by big decisions in my life? Is there an equivalent moment from my own past which, had it been different, would have changed my whole life? How does Sheila's experience relate to other things going on currently in my life? Well, this is the time that my own children are making choices for their own life's paths. Does Sheila, as a teenager, remind me of one of my own children and their current struggle for detachment from me and the family hearth? Does any of this give clues as to why I find it difficult to remain detached from Sheila and why I apparently became embroiled in her story-web?

By opening myself and my emotions to the group through the writing, I remained in control of what I disclosed and how deeply I wanted to take all this. The continued process of sharing the written work I prepared usually gets the whole procedure down to other levels which individual, personal reflection never approaches. The group immediately establishes its caring credentials for me and empathises with the difficulty that people like Sheila may present to doctors. I know that in general they are going to help me in my quest for further enlightenment, this is the pattern that has been established in the group. The doctors are not competitive or aggressive, they will not laugh at me for getting something wrong, or leave me feeling exposed when delicate emotions are touched on.

The group leader, Gillie, patrols the boundaries and asks the 'naive questions' that no one else dares to ask. She pretends that she knows little about the work of general practice and is an interested outsider in the process. The group does not make suggestions or proposals, there are no conclusions, diagnoses or certainties. Various things are considered, mulled over and the enquiry moves on. This is very different from the formal, often rather aggressive approach of bog-standard general practice, where the drive for evidence-based, cost-effective interventions and the like leaves little room for philosophical ruminations, experimentation, or the following of feelings or hunches.

After the group I felt that I really could understand at a greater depth both the way that Sheila's life has panned out for her, and what is happening in the interaction between her and me during the consultation. I felt that I learnt as much about myself during the group session as I did about Sheila, and this is useful, if not always comforting. It may have brought up quite disturbing things for me to think about and which may need resolution in other contexts and at other times. I recognised that it is not possible to get help at this level with every person who comes to see me, but that selective, intensive work of this nature does help me to understand at a general level what may be going on in the lives of people whom I have some responsibility to try to help. It is a valid and important form of training for all my work, not just a help for my work with Sheila. It might also help me in my way of being with other people (specifically my own children) at important times of decision in their lives.

Why write?

The act of writing down Sheila's story has helped me to empathise about her situation. It doesn't really matter that I was not clear about all the exact details, or the chronological precision of her life story. Indeed I had fantasised and embroidered about some events and had forgotten or changed other things to make it into a story rather than a case history. The important feature seems to be that I was able to see the world through her eyes for a while. The process of writing has clarified many things for me. What must it be like to live your entire life as Sheila has, with a major regret? How can that event have shaped everything else she did and the way she thought and felt about things thereafter? The feelings of guilt, self-loathing, remorse, hatred and despair were immediately transmitted through the written word from Sheila's own life in a very direct way into my consciousness. It is not that the written product is especially brilliant literature, it is just that it responds to the human dimensions of the situation.

By writing it down, I have acknowledged the importance of the story to me and started to consider the things that happen when these two human beings meet. The story has established a grid pattern to start to make Sheila's life understandable and accessible to me and to any others who take the trouble to read or hear the story.

In the group

We have started to develop a way of working together that looks at some of the institutional, structural and especially the personal strains involved in our jobs. When we sit down to write in the privacy of our own homes we focus naturally on events and situations that have affected us in some way. There is no point in writing about neutral events.

The process of writing gets me in touch, very directly, with my feelings, and I imagine it is the same for the others in the group. Writing, the flow of words and ideas, thoughts and inner feelings . . . and then the editing and rewriting, polishing as best I can for presentation to the group, is a ritual that I now know will help me sort out and organise my feelings about the subject which I am preparing. The next stage is to bring the contribution to the group. It has become less scary to bring these little private efforts and lay them bare before the others. The group seems to be able to accept each other's imperfections and are relieved and strengthened to find that many of them are shared . . . and that all of them are understood by the group.

The levels of discussion that follow the presentations are important also: acknowledge the human being within the professional concretions; discuss the feelings behind the descriptions; empathise with the situation; ask a few questions to get to the nub of the problem. Ease and joke as well to relieve some of the intensity. All these techniques seem to have been developed unselfconsciously as a group together and they have arrived at levels of intimacy which are indeed supportive.

When I next met with Sheila I felt that a warmth and understanding has developed and deepened since our last meeting. I felt emboldened to suggest things that might never have been tried if I had not felt the support of this group behind me. . .

Tom Heller

Teamwork

Alan Bleakley reports a research project:

The Theatre Team Resource Management project was established in December 2002 as a collaborative inquiry between a hospital operating staff and a research team (Bleakley et al. 2004). The process is congruent with reflective practice philosophy, but moves its usual concerns from the individual to the team process. While these practitioners reflect, they have little opportunity for formal critical interrogation of the process of reflection.

Writing is used as a medium for reflection only in the context of close-call reporting. We use a narrative reporting system for incidents that do not lead to harm to patients or staff, but could potentially do so. These reports reveal a variety of systems communications issues such as poor teamwork. Such reports are often descriptive and patently rhetorical. We encourage more reflexive narrative accounts (and reinforce this through educational support) as a means of identifying good teamwork practice that leads to better patient safety.

Reflection in teams and groups I have come to term 'refractive practice'. Just as a stick refracts or appears to bend when placed in water, so a new member of a team refracts when placed in the medium of the team. Reflection is here conceived as a shared or distributed activity (Bleakley 2002).

Where one enters a new community of practice and attempts to come to terms with its value system, as in a professional education, this can be described as 'refractive practice'. The values you bring to the community of practice are automatically refracted within the new community, and the extent of this refraction should be noted. Ironically, while Schon's model sets out to offer an alternative to technical-rational approaches to practice it has gained the status of a technical-rational 'tool'. For example, it is formally taught and learned as an educational technique.

Reflective practice can be used as a political football [in a professional team]. For example, Mantzoukas and Jasper (2004) describe how reflection amongst nurses working on a ward is stifled by the rhetorical strategies of doctors. Where medicine does not have a historical tradition of reflexive accounting, where nursing does, medicine can stifle the reflective practices of the nursing culture through invalidation based on a power hierarchy. This study then reminds us that reflective practice occurs in institutional contexts where climates exist that variously support or stifle both reflection-in-action and reflection-on-action. We need to study the refractive climate of such institutional structures to better understand how individual reflection may flourish or founder.

Alan Bleakley

The growth of a team

Six officers-in-charge of this and the nearby old people's homes were sitting on easy chairs when I entered the long, narrow huge-windowed room. Unlike me, they were used to the warm atmosphere, where old people moved slowly, one shuffle at a time with the aid of a stick or frame, between tea table and telly. They were all strangers to me; their area manager (my ex-Masters student) wanted a course for his staff which would be *for them*, and might bring these isolated professionals together into a collaborating supportive group. Chocolate buns, fresh from the oven, and piping hot coffee welcomed me after my long January drive over the moor.

My new colleagues, I was later to discover, were even more nervous than me and didn't know each other very well either. They later shared their initial perplexity. They asked me, as so many others have: 'Writing is so difficult, why can't we just discuss these issues with each other?' One member commented in her final evaluation:

> First day – not too keen. Did not know what to expect – wasn't going to be really clever – I am not an academic type person.

They were almost immediately plunged into the process. We picked up our pens and started to write. For six minutes we wrote whatever came into our heads in whatever jumbled order, without stopping. Since this writing was not to be shared, the morning's irritations, a shopping list, diatribes against an impossible colleague/family member, last night's unshareable nightmare were all possible subjects. Nobody ever has nothing in their head.

This *six minutes* put writing on the paper. It also allowed the busy business of everyday concerns to surface, be recorded, and hopefully put on one side; or perhaps a flash of insight to be recorded. We immediately wrote a story about *a time when something vital was learned*, for a further 10–20 minutes. This might be a personal thing from way back, such as discovering that Santa was only Mum; or something from yesterday; or a completely made-up event. Once more: no stopping to think; thinking can block inspiration and flow. We would share all or part of this writing with each other, if appropriate.

Resting aching wrists and fingers relievedly on their pads, all six realised they could write; pens had scribbled frantically. Reading both pieces of writing privately with attention, to acquaint ourselves with what we had written, and to look for previously unnoticed connections, was next.

Some boundaries

Before we read our pieces to each other we established initial ground rules to underpin the discussion. My suggestions were:

- We will be trying to tease out professional and possibly personal issues embedded within the stories, and draw out related, underlying themes that are of concern to the writer and the group.

- We will be doing this in a spirit of support and respect for each other.

- A thoughtful silence often arises after a piece has been read. As facilitator, I will never break this silence, as I could so easily do all the talking. The silence may be felt as supportive and reflective; but it may be experienced as unnerving to the waiting writer. Someone must take responsibility for breaking it.

- While you are listening, be formulating your discussion queries/points, which will probably be provisional and might take the form of a question, a suggestion, or a request for specific further information.

- When you read you may feel hesitant, but the group will not perceive the imperfections of your writing as you do. They will be interested and involved.

- Everyone's thoughts are of value: yours *and* theirs must be heard.

- These pieces are fictions, although they may seem to slide along what appears to be a fiction-faction-reality continuum. The extent of this is not our business; fiction preserves confidentiality. Writers may wish to share more during or after the session, but this is up to them.

- Confidentiality is essential: anything written or said in the group belongs to the group and cannot be spoken of outside without express permission.

The seven of us discussed fears and anxieties concerning the sharing of writings. One of our ground rules concerned careful timekeeping: everyone was to have their turn without transgressing beyond the agreed finish time. We felt no one should be under any pressure to contribute at any one time, whether in writing or discussion, and I suggested I should not take up group time by bringing my own writing to ensuing sessions. Everyone recognised the need to be warm and involved on the one hand, but cautious and incurious on the other; we laughed at ourselves: what a tightrope!

Everyone read out a snippet, a paragraph or all they had just written that morning. The discussion was wide-ranging and rewarding, if careful, after our boundary-creating session. Group members were generous in the personal information they shared, much of which related to how and why they became involved in such demanding and potentially stressful work. Most felt immensely relieved afterwards: this course is about something I can do, and I *think* I might even be going to enjoy it. The unanimously experienced shadow, felt then and expressed later, was: *everyone but myself is a brilliant writer*.

Time was running out. I had learned already that this is in short supply for these officers; they decided to keep journals. Everyone was to write and bring a new piece in any form, for the next session. I suggested a topic, but every ensuing one was evolved by the group in discussion. I suggested *A Clean Sheet*: literal or metaphorical.

Story within a story: a clean sheet

Here I am again on the laundry shelf, and it's lovely and warm in here with all my companions. Light goes on – just when I was feeling drowsy too – someone is picking me up – what rough hands she has got – I wish she wouldn't hold me close like that. Am being carried along – what's that tune she's humming, I'm sure I've heard it before.

Now I am being unfolded – what a shame to disturb my lovely creases and folds – up into the air. I hover – just for a second. The sun is shining through the window although it is frosty and misty outside; the world looks different today – an air of mystery surrounds the home. Funny how mist and mystery go together – sense of excitement but foreboding. Well, I've landed now on the bed, her rough hands are smoothing me out and tucking me in all around the mattress. Oh heck! Here comes the duvet, what a monstrosity – covering me up – suffocating me – oh well, I can't do anything about it – must grin and bear it.

Hours have passed and now someone is coming into the room – three people in fact but one of them is very frail. She is being undressed by the other two – now she is being washed – they are doing their best to converse with this old lady but she does not appear to understand what they are saying to her. They lose interest in talking to her and start to talk to each other about the day's happenings. What a pity they have not time to talk to this old lady.

She is now lying on top of me and is being covered by the duvet, one of them has at least taken the time to make sure she is comfortable and has kissed her goodnight.

All is quiet now, her breathing is slowing down and I can feel her relaxing as she is getting warm. What's that she is saying – she is now talking about bygone days – as though she is young again – and talking to a young soldier. She is walking with him down sunny lanes and is feeling really happy – now a tear falls from her cheek and lands on me – a salty stain spreads, albeit a small one – I am touched by this emotion – what can I do – what is she thinking about now?

She moves slowly with a slight moan, and then goes quiet – she is sleeping now.

The writer had felt extremely uncertain about her ability to write, but had managed to overcome her fears by setting her alarm and scribbling for fifteen minutes and no more. The group had many discussions about staff relationships with residents, being concerned that there should be grace and loving care. The *Clean Sheet* writer brought a wise yet humorous slant on all this, as her contributions always did.

More stories

All participants read their pieces: *like opening windows on themselves for each other*, I wrote afterwards. Headings for ensuing pieces included: 'dilemmas', 'leadership', 'changes', 'aspirations', 'perceptions', 'a conflict of loyalties' and 'a frustrating episode'.

As week succeeded week there never was enough time for sharing their immense range of work and work-related issues, which included very trying long-term difficulties despite supportive area managers. One participant thought fate had laid on a fortuitous series of calamitous events to create writing topics. We decided it was probably always so, but the course made them aware, and able to deal with them.

Time was found to write about some past, unsorted-out issues, such as the suicide of clients. This led to a long discussion about dealing with death in a dignified and loving way. I was impressed, as I was time and time again, by thoughtful and caring professional attitudes.

The six gained confidence exponentially in their abilities, and felt happier writing regular reports, etc. They never felt the course writing should be clever or literary, but an expression of things difficult or impossible to take elsewhere. Touching or searing material often took me off guard.

Trust and confidence was a vital outcome, leading to supportive relationships radically altering their working experience, particularly those fresh to it, or taking on role changes. Each had been struggling with daily problems with staff, equipment, inspections, disciplinaries, new rules from the top and so on and on, all of which they were now able to share.

The writing and discussions confirmed that writing, evaluating, sharing and therefore taking greater control over professional experience enhances freedom and self-respect. Thinking of life as a story, and having the opportunity and courage to tell that story oneself, offers some measure of control.

Evaluation

Brief formative evaluations in which members reviewed the ground rules, format and content concluded each session. On one occasion the old people's homes group arranged dates for further meetings: that was their evaluation. One wrote in summative evaluation:

> Coming each week has been a great source of strength and support to me. Sometimes I have come away feeling a more valued member of 'the team'.

Before the group there was no 'team', only a handful of people in the same area doing much the same job. One fear was: 'I hope we don't lose it all!' They did not need me in order to continue. Feedback since has been that they are still supporting each other through further problems and challenges.

Other teams

A community health project team invited me to work with them for two sessions to reflect upon their busy, stressful work with disadvantaged communities; we met in their big, bright animated room full of children's artwork. Derek Snaith, in his writing, focused upon feedback he received which gave him 'the realisation that I am doing something right within my work', and how that felt:

> She said that I was a *key worker* because I had helped start a social club for adults with learning difficulties in the area. What I had never realised in all my time here at Riverside was that my work was making a difference to people. I could tell from the passion in her voice that this initiative 'The Millennium Club' is something she and others have been looking for for years. And I still am shocked when positive feedback comes from those involved in helping to run the sessions and those who come along to enjoy it.
>
> This simple statement, and the subsequent realization of the impact of my work has helped me in my mind to be more confident in my own abilities and my own views. I think I will be able to be myself more at work and be

more assertive when it comes to dealing with people and groups who are there purely for self-interest or generally negative reasons.

Because I now know that I have made a difference to people who are in need of supporters to do things for them and alongside them, it means I can stick my neck out and say more of what I think clearly, rather than a watered down mish-mash that is often not understood.

Derek Snaith (Bolton 2003b, p. 19)

'We *never* normally *talk* to each other like this about what we *feel* and *think* about our work and the lives of the people with whom we work.' Many of the group shared feelings, hopes and anxieties, which surprised the others. They were amazed Derek needed feedback to assure him of the value of his work, and were able to reinforce it. One other staff member wrote about the way a negative encounter had knocked her confidence. Once more the group had not realised she was not as confident as she seemed, and were able to offer real support (adapted from Bolton 2003b).

Even a one-off session can positively affect later working relationships. I ran a single session with a large, wonderful, fascinating group from an academic medical department who wrote and discussed excitedly and excitingly. I later discovered they did not normally have smooth working relationships with each other, but more than one reported to me up to a year later how they could still sense the improved working relationship engendered that morning.

Mentors and co-mentors

The first mentor was a goddess. Telemachus, son of Odysseus and Penelope, is mentored by Pallas Athene in human form: ' "For you, I have some good advice, if only you will accept it" . . . "Oh stranger," heedful Telemechas replied, "indeed I will. You've counselled me with so much kindness now, like a father a son. I won't forget a word." ' (Homer trans. 1996 pp. 86–7.)

No mentor since then has been a god, although 'mentors are creations of our imagination, designed to fill a psychic space somewhere between lover and parent' (Daloz 1999, p. 18). Mentoring is usually a situation of a more experienced professional supporting a less experienced in a learning process, the offer of a supportive hand at its most informal.

The mentor helps the mentee step 'outside the box of his or her job and personal circumstances, so they can look in at it together. It is like standing in front of the mirror with someone else, who can help you see things about you that have become too familiar for you to notice' (Clutterbuck and Megginson 1999, p. 17). A mentor asks the questions one does not, or cannot, ask oneself.

A mentor can act as role model, enabler, teacher, encourager, counsellor, befriender, facilitator, coach, confidante, and supporter in 'unlearning' negative habits or attitudes (such as apologising for oneself, and a sense of lack of self-worth). These roles inevitably overlap, but research into helping to learn relationships shows that clarity of role expectations makes for greater effectiveness (Clutterbuck 1998). The pair need to be aware of whose interests are being pursued: a mentor or supervisor who is also a professional superior can be seen as (or can even be) controlling. It is also important for them to realise when a matter is beyond their relationship, and help should be sought from elsewhere.

Mentoring deals with the whole person of the mentee; the difference between this and counselling is that it is professionally based, concerning professional issues. Mentors offer empathy and non-judgemental critique, helping mentees examine and reflect upon the relationship between emotional, intellectual and behavioural content of issues. Mentors challenge: the behaviour not the person, their assumptions not their intellect, their perceptions not their judgement, their values not their value (Clutterbuck and Megginson 1999).

Mentoring is a relationship in which vital, often confidential issues can be shared: uncertainties, hopes and fears, anxieties and angsts, shame or guilt, wants and aversions, the influence of intense emotions – whether positive or negative, tentative suggestions for action, lack of or partial understandings, questions of role, personal or career ladder issues, repeated errors or inadequacies, and stories of success, failure or conflict. 'Mentoring for me is about personal investment, and I wouldn't/couldn't do it if I didn't give a bit of myself to all of them: equally I expect to see them investing in their students and each other – and Gillie – they do' (Julie Hughes, post-compulsory education lecturer). Everyone needs support, reassurance and challenge, even (or perhaps particularly) those at the very top:

> It's no disgrace for a man, even a wise man,
> to learn many things and not be too rigid.
> You've seen trees by a raging winter torrent,
> how many sway with the flood and salvage every twig,
> but not the stubborn – they're ripped out roots and all.
> Bend or break . . .
> it's best to learn from those with good advice.
>
> Sophocles trans. 1982, pp. 95–6

Nathan Field: the Scribble Society

I use writing in my supervision: I require the supervisee to write down from memory a verbatim account of one session, but include their own feelings, ideas, and bodily sensations in the process (counter-transference). I receive it by email before the session, so I have a chance to mull it over. They agree producing this written account is hard work but very rewarding in itself. What I haven't yet done is to review these process recordings to track the progress of a particular patient.

Nathan Field, www.scribblesociety.com

Angela Mohtashemi: management consultancy for team-building

An activity I have found very effective is writing group poems. I have done this with my own team. We started by listing on a flip chart all the words that came to mind when thinking about our team. Each individual then wrote a piece about how they felt as a member of the team while I composed some linking lines. The group was moved by the commonality of themes and echoes of words and yet the distance between the different individual paths, in terms of both content and form. One participant's writing revealed his struggle to 'fit in' to the work environment while hanging on to his identity.

Like the boat without a rudder,
I move from highs and lows
Kicked by the strength of the wind,
Carried away by the endless immensity of the ocean

I am learning to swim I told myself
For when the boat stops I can jump and
Make my own journey...

Angela Mohtashemi

Peer-mentoring

Effective and intensely deep reflective practice groupwork and teamwork can be supported by co-mentoring pairs of peers with no problem of payment, control, or god(dess) worship. Pairs of peer-mentors are created out of the whole group; these pairs meet to work together independently. They read and comment on each other's reflective journals and discuss matters which might or might not be brought to the whole group. This enables an initial tentative sharing of issues with one trusted other. Some shared issues are inappropriate to the group, and would therefore otherwise not be aired at all. Confidential pairs can cover more ground than a whole group, so each participant receives intensive feedback on their work, journal and portfolio (examples: Whewell, Chapter 11, McLaggan, Chapter 9). Paired working gives many people more confidence to use group discussion more effectively. I cannot sufficiently emphasise how valuable peer-mentoring is.

Courses, and support for practitioners, in co-tutoring in general practice (family medicine) are offered in Britain: 'a system of peer-supported learning based on a relationship of parity, whereby participants facilitate each other's thinking and reflection to enable them to address the problems that are pertinent to their individual situation'

Eastaugh 1998b, p. 2

My Masters students have always found peer-mentoring relationships support them through the challenge of the course and portfolio writing. Each pair creates a working contract – many read and comment on learning journals and assignments in progress, and discuss appropriate issues. The students also spend time together as a whole group without us, their tutors, in group co-mentoring activities. Professional students quite properly learn widely from each other; co-mentoring structures this effectively.

Carry Gorney, family therapist, and Joolz Mclay, art therapist, in an NHS child and family therapy team practised reflective writing together:

> We are interested in language, images, metaphor, poetry and stories. Our relationship evolved in our shared office: showing each other snippets of our work, reported scraps of dialogue and listened to each other's descriptions of eyes, faces, clothes and movements. We told stories of the process of our work, of our anxieties, our successes and our feelings of helplessness. The writing developed from these stolen moments in our working day. We agreed to meet every couple of weeks and to develop and explore some of these conversations through writing. We met in the art room after work and began to create a safe space. We experienced this 'peer supervision' as a confidential process, mirroring the therapeutic process.
>
> We agreed to write alone and meet together to read aloud. We listened to the words, the sentences and the spaces between words. We would reread each piece silently together and then put the paper aside. Conversations evolved around the children, the effect of the writing on each other and on our subsequent work. Then we wrote more.
>
> At first the writing we brought was stiff and professional, calmly and cognitively placing our practice within a context of intelligent observation. Then as we trusted each other more our writing began to flow from somewhere else. Sometimes it seemed to bypass our brains all together. It poured out of our hearts, our guts, our fingertips and our imaginations. It moved in a circle of unexpressed, previously unidentified responses to the children we saw.

Joolz:

For me, the process has been one of untangling the professional from the personal and private self. By writing without constraint, without fear of judgement about clinical practice I have begun to rediscover and to nurture the inner voices of my private self. These voices have been strengthened through writing, through being heard, and through conversation. They have engaged me in dialogues with neglected and forgotten parts. They have drawn attention to things overlooked, ignored and misplaced. They have made me laugh and cry and feel I am not alone.

A reader:

I am fascinated by the writing. It is very moving; I felt quite lonely reading it. Lonely, not because we are not doing this together but because I think there is no one with whom I might do it. And yet reading what you have both written has the effect of making me aware of what other ways of processing our work with our clients is not being accessed within me, although 'calmly and cognitively placing our practice within a context of intelligent observation'.

Carry:

I felt I was exposing a secret part of myself hidden under layers of professional convention and boundaries. In my role as systemic practitioner I often seem to be balancing many perspectives and many realities around the child. I feel responsible to act as a mediator for the child in his/her world. This leads me to talk as an adult in an adult world. Sometimes I feel that this talking swallows my energy. If I let it take me away from the child's fragile truth I fear I will become lost in a world of adult assumptions and expectations. This poem is from the perspective of a child patient.

Words

I tried to sit still; this woman was sat opposite me.
I couldn't understand what she was saying, too many words,
You see
Just a jumble of words.
They floated past.
I just sat there letting them come.

My Dad's words are different. They sort of hit me over the head,
A sharp pain running from my head to my heart, my Dad's words, when they hit me.

Words happen to me. I don't understand them.
Sometimes I think if everyone talked slow, I'd get it.
I'd get what everyone goes on about.
It would all make sense.

School – the words are bad there. They come thick and fast,
Sometimes I put my head down on the desk 'cos it hurts.
It does my head in.
Sometimes I just run out of class, or even school, too many words jumping at me,
Too many sounds they might catch me out. They might find out I don't know jackshit, Nothing, nada in my brain.
Rotten like my Dad says, a bad un – I got those words all right.
Words are enemies
I'm an alien.

Carry

Boy aflame

I know something is different the moment I set eyes on him. He holds my gaze just too long. Doesn't back down, lets me know he's looking right at me. He swaggers down the corridor, creating an impression of confidence, arrogance and power and images unfold rapidly in my mind's eye. I see a panther, a king, a boy aflame. He emits a raw animal energy that electrifies the air. I think of swashbuckling heroes and moustache-twirling villains. I think of flamenco dancers, bullfighters and cowboys. I think of wild horses, of motorbikes, of leather jackets. The temperature soars. I imagine glass shattering and light bulbs exploding overhead. The room vibrates with energy. His veins heave with life. His blood roars and eyes gleam. He is possessed.

Joolz McLay

I, Carry, responded by sharing stories and memories about my own son as a boy and as a man. I wrote about the ones locked in, trapped in the system, the school, the home, even the therapist, me. When we talked about these boys we used words like 'beautiful', 'dangerous' and 'vibrant'. It felt liberating to use these words about men and to talk and think about the energy of the male. We shared stories about different boys who came to therapy, the boys seeking mothers, the boys lashing out and the boys who'd retreated into corners.

We talked about the way we stood between the different worlds, the different characters, the different areas of the boys' lives. We also talked about the different feelings the boys stirred within us. We were talking about the privilege of listening and watching, of the walk down the clinic corridor, closing the therapy room door, leaving it open, the last words whilst pulling on the jacket, half whispered, half heard.

We were women of the twenty-first century giving each other permission to love, fear, and be amazed by the boys with whom we worked. We connected them with our own men, the boys in our hearts.

Carry Gorney, Joolz Mclay

Action research and Socratic dialogue

Through-the-looking-glass group work has similarities with action research, whose dialogic basis is Socratic, non-analytic (Saran and Neisser 2004; McGill and Brockbank 2004; Dinkelman 2000; Crockett 2000). It welcomes discussion of action, thoughts, feelings, without privileging the rational and cognitive, seeking to enquire into social processes without adherence to modernist individualism, in which the individual is the seat of change. It critically recognises and challenges the prevailing discourse and dominant paradigm, denying any 'innocence' of those which structure and force us culturally and politically. Socratic dialogue helps develop clarity, insight and therefore an understanding of an appropriate course of action: an effective reflective practice process. 'Paradigm shift', 'double-loop learning', or 'peak experience' (or 'epiphany': see Joyce 1944) are key. Exposing experiences to critical scrutiny in *action learning sets* can enable individuals to perceive and potentially alter previously taken-for-granted 'paradigms' or 'stories' which culturally frame aspects of their experience. They can then effect change.

In a university-wide cross-disciplinary action learning project at Innsbruck University, lecturers engaged in action learning. 'They articulated their own *practical theories* . . . It was only when faculty members learnt to accept what they regarded as strange and different in their colleagues' attitudes, that processes of collective reflection and mutual understanding could develop' (Schratz 1993, p. 130).

Careful facilitation of reflective practice to enable the development of group work and teamwork can allow windows and fruitful spaces to open.

7

WHY NARRATIVE?

Wherever we walk we put our feet on story.

Cicero

A man is always a teller of tales, he lives surrounded by his stories and the stories of others.

Sartre [1938] 1963, p. 61

I'm not sure I can tell the truth . . . I can only tell what I know.

Cree hunter in Clifford 1986, p. 8

Why story or narrative rather than thinking, talking and discussing, or writing 'critical incidents' or 'events' or case notes? Stories create memorable and comprehensible structures with clarifying devices like causality. Stories are attentively listened to and remembered, such as Clough's powerful story about special educational needs (Clough 1996), and Landgrebe's about care of the dying (Landgrebe and Winter 1994). 'The deceptive power of [story] lies in the fact that single startling cases stick in the mind' (Macnaughton 1998, p. 202). Writing, exploring, and discussing our essential narratives is a route to taking responsibility and control of our lives, professional and personal.

Many hold their failures inside, allowing them to smoulder and decay; others step into self-destructive habits; others tell [and write] stories.

Borkan et al. 1999, p. 11

Our storied nature

Information is retained in the human mind as narrative. We do not go to a particular section within a file within a drawer within a cabinet in our memories, we go to a particular place in a narrative: an association of events, faces, voices, place, foods, and sense of roughness or softness. Since the Enlightenment we have suffered under mechanical metaphors that bodies and minds are machines. We are not. Our feeling, cognitive, physical, spiritual selves are intermixed; they condition and are conditioned by political and cultural contexts. All are experienced, understood and expressed as narrative. Narratives express the values of the narrator; they also develop and create values in the telling.

Narratives are central to human understandings, memory systems and communication, whether we know it or not. Lives are made sense of and ordered by the stories with which they are recounted: told and retold daily through actions, memories, thoughts, dreams, habits, beliefs, speech and behaviour patterns. We spend our lives storying and re-storying ourselves, and contributing to wider social stories around us: it is as natural to being a person as eating and breathing (Bruner 2004; Doyle and Carter 2003; Charon and Montello 2002).

Educators know that understanding occurs when elements are expressed as stories (Clark 2002; Doyle and Carter 2003; Allan et al. 2002). This is a mature acceptance of how we are, rather than an assumption that only children need stories in order to understand (Gheradi and Turner 2002).

Daily constant interaction with other individuals, systems and organisations requires management, generally at a non-conscious level. Everyone shifts between a range of personae as they move in and out of days, and of each other's lives. Among other roles I am mother, wife, lover, sister, aunt, neighbour, colleague, professional, friend. In order to reduce anxiety, and ensure I relate more or less appropriately, I need to be aware of the history of each of these relationships and its meaning in terms of today's behaviour. I also perceive that I exist within a set of geographical places, within a time-frame, as well as a political and cultural structure. My set of stories of myself has a chronological structure reaching back to farming forebears, a space structure locating me in Essex, Singapore, Cambridge, Derbyshire and London, and so on. To an extent all these tell me who I am, and how to relate to others, and to society.

If our lives were not constantly told and retold, storying each new experience, we would have no coherent notion of who we are, where we are going, what we believe, what we want, where we belong, and how to be. Just as my skin holds my organs and body fluids in a form which is recognisably me (to myself as well as others), my psychosocial selfhood relies upon my grasp of my narratives of relationship, chronology, and place.

We are embedded and enmeshed within the stories and story structures we have created, and which have been created around us: some we are aware of, some very much not. Family doctor Mark Purvis was unaware how deeply his life and work was affected by his brother's death when he was 9, until he wrote a reflective practice poem about it (Chapter 2).

These stories form a complex volatile system. Complex, because my apparently coherent life is constituted out of a range of interrelated plotlines, characters, and situations. Volatile, because it constantly changes with every individual action or event: mine and those around me.

My success as a person, or more correctly perhaps my happiness, rests on my ability to juggle this complexity, and my flexibility in response to the volatility and constant change created by my own behaviour, that of others, and of my social, political and professional surroundings. It is what a growing-up child learns, and a beginning professional in training and early years practice. It is also what an effective adult or professional continually undergoes.

Everyone naturally, to a lesser or greater extent, reflects, seeks support and advice, accordingly alters their behaviour, challenges others, and even drastically changes their life situation. Life changes such as a new job or house, marriage, birth, bereavement, illness or disability necessitate reformulations.

Constant repeating and refashioning of life stories is an essential part of living with their complexity and fluidity, but it can be uncritical. The stories told over coffee, or reflected upon in the car, are told in order to create a coherent and live-with-able structure. These reflections might ask: 'How could I have done it better?', or 'Do you think Mrs S thought it was OK?' The answers, whether in solitary reflection or in conversation, are unlikely to be challenging. Perceiving the taken for granted story structure for what it is, and seeking strategies for development, cannot be done in the car or over coffee. The car would certainly crash, and drinking colleagues become bewildered or even angry.

An extreme example is the sexually harassed secretary who complains to her friends, loses sleep and self-confidence, but continues to invite sexual advances unaware. Few colleagues have commitment and ability to support deep development. Similarly a professor and departmental head with a severe alcohol problem creates all sorts of explanations for the situation, none of which touches on the central problem, despite sincere efforts of his staff. No colleague, within the normal everyday departmental structure, knows how to challenge, or help him to see. The secretary or HoD becomes more and more enmeshed, more and more stuck.

These story structures, even while shifting and changing all the time, often seem inevitable, how things are, inviolable even: a set of taken-for-granteds. But each one of us is responsible for the creation of many of them and aspects of others, for connivance at, and even uncritical acceptance of wider social narratives or 'norms'.

People vary a great deal in awareness of their story structure. Some, like Hamlet, struggle with it daily: questioning and reformulating their understanding of their own agency and control. Some, such as Celia in George Eliot's *Middlemarch*, live in blissful unawareness.

Some authorities have taken this further and postulated a non-storying type (Strawson 2004a, b). This might be true of the autistic. But everyone else, at the very least, retells aspects of their day for re-creation, listening and re-storying collaboratively (*re-creation* is used advisedly here). They make further sense of their lives by relating to the social, political and spiritual narratives in which their lives are embedded: news or drama on television or radio, in newspapers, magazines and literature. Booker (2004) maintains that our stories 'emerge from some place in the human mind that functions autonomously, independent of any storytellers conscious control' (p. 24).

Taking responsibility

Education clarifies and develops personal stories, and the way they articulate with, impinge upon, and are impinged upon by societies' stories. Even rote learning is only effective if accommodated: 'I am the kind of person who knows times-tables.' Professional development aims to support in taking responsibility for integrating the learning from these accounts.

Reflective practitioners strive to recognise responsibility for their own life stories, the structures around them, and their actions within those structures. They can then create strategies for responsibly taking charge of as many areas of experience as possible. They also want to learn critically from the stories of others. Frank (1995, 2004) describes dynamic involvement with narrative or story as working *with* stories, rather than *about* them: 'what counts about any story is what those who hear it [and who tell or write it] choose to do with it' (2004, p. 209). Franks calls the *practical wisdom* this develops *phronesis*, from Aristotle: '*Phronesis* is the opposite of acting on the basis of scripts and protocols; those are for beginners, and continuing reliance on them can doom actors to remain beginners' (2004, p. 221).

Some practitioners or students come to professional learning with an assumption that tutors take responsibility. The slowness of reflective learning frustrates them, with its constant reflexive involvement. Surely the authorities should just tell them?

Well no. This is not multiplication tables. When addressing the very stuff of our lives, only the protagonist – the main character – can tackle it from the inside, with the help of the outside perspectives of peers, and the expert support of tutors. In order to take responsibility for professional actions, and some of the actions of others, we need a clearer perception of how we build our world, and how others build it around us: its narrative and metaphoric structures and content. This perception will enable, necessitate even, change and development.

Why narrative-based reflective practice?

We are brought up surrounded by stories: they flow through us and ratify us from birth, telling us who we are and where we belong, what is right and what is wrong. Many are traditional, whether or not they have been given contemporary dress. Tales where wicked stepmothers receive come-uppance explain that mothers can be horrid quite often, but good will ultimately conquer over evil (Bettelheim 1976). Lévi-Strauss (1978) tells us our myths offer us ways of classifying and ordering our society. We do not tell our mythic stories, they tell us. A language created each time they are told, they provide ways of dealing with the complexity of human relationships, and strange and often scary psychological worlds.

Small children are clear about story structure (Rowland 1984). A child requires any story to be told to the end. Their imaginative play is often continuous story, and first writings have a good grasp of structure. Ask a small child about their drawing or painting and they will tell its story, rather than describe the images.

We too live our lives by telling stories about them. These stories are constructs. Life as it is lived is not structured like an *adventure*; adventures only happen in stories (Sartre 1938). And the story has to be communicated: told, or read. It cannot only be thought:

'Is that the end of the story?' asked Christopher Robin.
'That's the end of that one. There are others.'
'About Pooh and Me?'
'And Piglet and Rabbit and all of you. Don't you remember?'
. . .

'I do remember,' he said, 'only Pooh doesn't very well, so that's why he likes having it told to him again. Because then it's a real story and not just a remembering.'

Milne [1928] 1958, p. 31

Stories are the mode in which our culture is transmitted, from history books to *The News*, or bedtime readings. Stories create the way we see our place in society, and the way we perceive it as moulded around us: telling us what to expect of each other and ourselves. They shape and make sense of our world by reiterating the social and political order. Soap opera, Verdi, strip cartoons, and Shakespeare tell us what is good and what bad, what likely to succeed and what fail.

These meanings are usually implicit, as in Aesop's *Fables*. New Testament parables are perhaps the closest to didactic storytelling, with explicit meanings. Had Jesus and Aesop omitted the story, the lessons would not have been remembered for millennia. We remember to sow corn on good fertile ground rather than among stones; that it is more comfortable to assume the unattainable bunch of grapes is probably sour; and that killing your father and marrying your mother is not a good idea (Sophocles' *Oedipus*).

No story has only one meaning. A writer may perceive certain meanings clearly, and formulate specific questions. Different readers perceive other meanings, and pose different questions.

The ambiguities of a fiction may be thought of as representing (in some sense) the ambiguities of the author's and the reader's personal awareness. The questions posed by the text are questions about the writer's and the reader's own experience and values.

Winter et al. 1999, p. 23

Questions and theories arising from a single text may conflict: stories are essentially ambiguous. Discussion following readings can be fruitful because everyone has their own view of the message. Many insights into a story's implicit meanings will be new to the writer and other listeners, and widen their view. 'A story by its very nature resists singular interpretation. Story captures nuance, indeterminacy and interconnectedness in ways that defy formalistic expression and expand the possibilities for interpretation and understanding' (Doyle and Carter 2003, p. 130).

Each reader views a story from their individual viewpoint, often refreshingly different from that of the writer. Perceptions of experience and selfhood are conceived, enmeshed within the frame of social, political and psychological understandings: we cannot know ourselves and our experience independently.

Individual experience has been described in the reflective practice literature as raw and authentic (true); yet it is no more and no less than another story: a story which others will cap with their own, or their own view. The fundamental importance of narrative and story to medicine is well documented (Charon 2000b; Greenhalgh and Hurwitz 1998; Montgomery Hunter 1991; Brody 2003; DasGupta and Charon 2004; DasGupta 2003; Engel et al. 2002) Narrative, particularly auto-biographical, has been explored extensively in initial and in-service teacher training and research (Phillion 2002a, b). Storytelling has been used by Reason (1988) as a research method, dealing with personal rather than professional development. Abbs (1974) and Lewis (1992) both use personal and autobiographical writing with trainee teachers.

An alternative programme in teacher education (Clandinin et al. 1992) examined the potential for collaboration between students, schools and universities by making spaces for the stories of each to be shared. This proved a dynamic ground for understanding, assessing and reassessing experience. 'It is in restorying ourselves that it is possible to remake experience' (Clandinin and Connelly 1990, p. 31). Connolly and Clandinin's three-dimensional space of narrative enquiry looks at a dense weave of multi-perspectival, multi-chronological, and multi-located set of stories (Connolly and Clandinin 2000). Phillion and Connelly (2004) use this 3-d space of narrative enquiry to help educate people to work in complex situations of diversity. Writing stories has been found to be a powerful tool in fostering teachers' professional growth (Huber et al. 2004).

> What matters is that lives do not serve as models; only stories do that. . . We can only retell and live by the stories we have read or heard. We live our lives through texts . . . Whatever their form or medium these stories have formed us all; they are what we must use to make new fictions, new narratives.
>
> Heilbrun 1988

Narrative reflective practice

The narratives and metaphors by which we structure our lives, the taken-for-granteds, are questioned and challenged: making the familiar strange, and the strange familiar. All our life stories can be questioned; many can be altered or struggled against. Life does not present us with inevitable chronological consequences of certain actions or events: we are free to choose how we act and influence others.

We have to take full responsibility, and can try out different characteristics for ourselves and colleagues; alternative ways of perceiving our environment; fresh angles from which to grasp our roles as protagonists of our life plots. This might entail the disappearance of a comfortable characterisation and plot development: the baddy might have previously unperceived good qualities, the good adviser might be lining his own nest, the impossible workplace might have a magically transformable space, the terrible blunder might have good consequences. And, of course, the opposite.

Bringing our everyday stories into question is an adventure. No one adventures securely in their backyard. Professionals need to face the uncertainty of not know-ing what is round the corner, where they are going, how they will travel, when they will meet dragons or angels, and who their comrades are. They even have to trust why they are going. A student commented: 'What a relief it is to know that this uncertainty is essential; knowing that makes me feel less uncertain of being uncertain. Now uncertainty is my mantra.'

Certainty does not generate the flexibly questioning enquiring attitude required by learning. An experienced practitioner learns all the time, and is open to being wrong. 'Certainty goes down as experiential knowledge goes up' (Phillion and Connelly 2004, p. 468). Some senior practitioners, in my experience, find this hard, being the most defended against reflective practice. Their defensive and self-protective reasoning is proof against uncertainty and doubt. Their sense of themselves in their role is too uncertain for them to lay it open to enquiry.

Practitioners engaged in effective reflection explore experience, values and professional identities, and express aspects within certain personal and profes-sional bounds which they expect to be respected. They are appropriately open to have understandings challenged, willing to have beliefs questioned, and coura-geous in discovering aspects underlying and affecting daily behaviour, of which they were hitherto unaware. They are open, willing and courageous *enough*: too much can be a recipe for disaster as can self-protective closedness.

An awareness of the complex interrelatedness of stories within practice facili-tates an awareness of roles in relation to clients, students, colleagues and peers, and an effective working grasp of ethics and values, and can develop responsible empathetic attitudes. The acquisition of skills and experience in relating to, and handling, the everyday narratives of professional life develop this comprehension of complexity.

Writing about professional life can develop awareness of narrative structure (plot, characterisation, chronology, environment), sensitivity to perspective (from whose point of view is the story told?), and the function of metaphor, simile, metonymy, alliteration, assonance, etc. Interpretive abilities can be developed: the narrator's role (omniscient?, reliable?), the value of multiple perspectives (viewing the same situation from the point of view of doctor and patient, teacher and student), and inherent ethical and value structures depicted.

Reflexivity entails examining taken for granted roles and values in relation to individuals, organisations and systems, models and metaphors unwittingly lived and worked by.

Jim Nind: personal narrative and well-being

I discovered reflective writing to try and make sense of my experience and my feeling of alienation, having been ousted from my first headship in

Leicestershire by conservative elements after eighteen months struggling to establish the kind of school I could really believe in.

I started writing a serious reflective journal having got an angry spleen-venting account of events off my chest. It attempted to deal with the deeper issues surrounding the abiding sense of compromise I felt as the national curriculum took hold and I worked to re-establish myself.

My reflective meanderings channelled towards a Masters dissertation using Clandinin and Connelly's (1994) Personal Experience Method. I also began writing poetry with a depth of intent last experienced in mid adolescence. This self-counselling slipped readily towards a doctorate. A rationale to a fluid way of working was offered by Ellis and Bochner's (2000) autoethnography through personal narrative, Richardson's (2000) writing as a method of enquiry and creative analytical practice (CAP), and her expanded notion of 'text' and the concept of 'intertext'.

The research process resembled the artistic process. My photo-essays, manipulated photo-images and allegorical stories offered fictionalised versions of myself facing dramas as a way of returning to past events, rehearsing current dilemmas and testing out possible futures. This writing became an exploration of loss and alienation and the reaffirmation and renewal of my being and self-respect. However, neither introspective 'navel-gazing' nor 'cosy', my journey entailed literal and metaphorical revisiting of places, times, and people: reliving some of the trauma, and revealing buried aspects of myself and practice. This invoking the dead, disinterring memories and undergoing uncomfortable mourning for a lost self, was essential for critical understanding.

I started facilitating a degree module. The keeping of a reflective journal became the foundation stone to a range of writing (or text-generating) activities. Course members reflectively explored personal and/or professional well-being issues: their own, or others' within their institutional setting.

The reflective process necessitates the realisation that the personal and the professional interact and interrelate, and that the management of well-being for self and for others are complementary. The internal process of reflection and external processes of pedagogical agency are implicitly linked.

The starting point for course writing has often been the reflective voice of others, such as Sidney Poitier's (2000) cultural induction into racism, Bauby's (1998) account from within 'locked-in-syndrome', Joe Simpson's (1988) 'touching the void' and Frankl's (1985) 'search for meaning' grounded in the Jewish experience of life in a concentration camp. Each draws upon extreme circumstances most of us never encounter, but raises questions many of us recognise.

A variety of poetic texts also offered kindred voices: echoing doubts and uncertainties, invoking and affirming common experiences, and pushing back the boundaries to perception. Mountain Dreamers (Oriah 2000)

Invitation was used to open dialogue about colleagues' deeply held hopes and desires, Stevie Smith's *Not Waving But Drowning* (2002) to provoke thought, and T.S. Eliot's *Little Gidding* (Eliot 1994) as an invocation to exploration and return.

Encouraged by these texts, participants began to write and share poetic and explorative texts, some discovering depth of purpose and long-withheld and unacknowledged emotion. Some had not previously seen themselves as writers.

Telling the stories of our lives offers a realisation that we have been different people at different times and within different organisations, some discrepant (Goffman 1990). There are multiple possibilities for the people we might become (Mearns 1994; Maclure 2003).

As we tell stories that begin to explore the different people we have been, we are, and might become, we begin to query notions of truth, self, and authenticity. In these stories we can creatively analyse various possibilities, projections of self, and philosophical proposals about ourselves and the places and organisations we inhabit.

Exploring narratives of the self and others enables a genuine listening: collaboratively challenging, questioning, adjusting and affirming of our possible selves and ways of practising. It gives us choice and agency. Therein lies the only approximation of authenticity we are likely to find.

Jim Nind

Rosemary Willett writes of clients from her social-worker experience:

Evelyn

Only her father understood Evelyn. Only he knew that there were times when the noises and voices in her head made her angry and she wanted to lash out. There were times when she could not stand the people and bustle in the day centre. Then he took her to sit at the side of the canal while he fished, or to walk in the woods and look at the birds and animals.

Her mother had died when she was 10. Her four brothers and sisters, envious perhaps of her special place in the family, got on with their lives, and Evelyn stayed with her father.

Then, quite suddenly, he was gone. Admitted to hospital for a routine operation, he had a heart attack and Evelyn was alone.

She had to live with people she did not know; there were too many of them and they did not realise that she needed her routine, her space, her time. And she missed her father's comforting presence desperately.

'Evelyn is violent, dangerous. Evelyn has challenging behaviour,' they said. So they locked her up; she was terrified.

Later, she went to live with a family. Happier at first, the toddler's needs competed with her own and she wisely asked to move.

She moved again after she threw a table; she had been accused of lying by staff. Evelyn knew that she was not lying, only saying things as she saw them.

'Evelyn is a gypsy. Evelyn needs to move,' people said. 'Evelyn needs to learn anger management.'

The new place was smaller, quieter, more tolerant. Now she has been there for four years. She spends her days travelling alone. When she is tense, she walks by the canal.

She looks after her bird. 'Roy is happy,' she says.

Mary

Mary sits in her pretty pink bedroom and listens to the trains going by. She finds that their rhythm is comforting. It is the first room of her own that she has had in her 50 years and she is so proud of it.

Mary weeps for her dead brother. 'I love him and miss him,' she says. She grieves for the birthday card with its five pound note, and for the occasional casual encounters on the bus. She did not see him when he was ill with cancer or go to his funeral.

Mary was put away when she was 3; rejected because she was backward and spastic; since then, only people who are paid have given her attention and love.

Mary is well known because she goes round the district asking for cigarettes and cups of tea. She holds up the traffic by being handicapped. At least she can control that.

Mary gave me a plaque for Mother's Day. 'You're like a mother to me,' she says.

Rosemary's afterword

I came to this job after some years away from much contact with people with Learning Disabilities, and was immediately profoundly affected by their interesting, poignant and sometimes dramatic life stories which are not always reflected in Health or Social Services assessments or academic research.

Working as a social worker in a multi-disciplinary team our major role is the assessment, co-ordination and review of services for our users and their carers. We become involved in people's lives offering them clarification, support and some continuity, and possibly most important we give them our time.

In order to provide the services needed, maximise choices and maintain the quality of life which is everyone's right, it is clearly appropriate to evaluate a range of strengths, needs, skills and behaviours. However, it seems to me that during this process we categorise people in a way which overlooks or denies significant parts of the reality of their life experience, and their feelings about that experience.

Some of the language in these stories is deliberately stigmatising, because that is part of the reality. I hoped to give a different slant on why people are as they are: some explanation which may influence practice. Social workers can become institutionalised in thinking and action. We need to be moved by those we work with: a colleague was in tears on reading *Evelyn*, whom she knows well. It is personally fulfilling for me to *paint these pictures*.

Rosemary Willett

Fiction

Stories are not 'true'

These stories are not reconstructions of chunks of *real life*. They cannot be. The *truth* in stories, as in ethnographic writing (Clifford 1986) can only ever be *partial*. No account, however carefully constructed, can ever be *true*. Told from the narrator's point of view, it contains the details they noticed and remembered, interwoven and shot through reflexively with their memories, dreams, prejudices, personal and cultural values, and so on (Denzin 1992); a different narrator, especially one from a different culture, would tell a different story.

Use of the imagination in such as this is not inventing out of nothing (Rolfe 2002). Writers draw upon memories of experiences which have touched them deeply: art is nearly always a working out of complex unresolved, unsorted-out areas of experience. These memories, by their very nature, do not present as straightforward accounts. They present as a muddle of half-remembered inconsistencies: unsatisfactorily *storied* experiences.

Fiction offers a way of experimenting with storying experiences in different ways – less or more realistically, less or more close to the actual events.

Experiment found that the value of people writing about a fictional trauma is as effective therapeutically as if they had written about a memory (Pennebaker 2000).

Case studies, also, cannot be true, detached or impartial depictions, although they concern real people and events (Clark 2002). Necessarily perspectival, constructed edited texts, they can have only 'indirect or partial correspondence with reality . . . despite their apparent verisimilitude' (Pattison et al. 1999a, p. 43). They include biases of inclusion and exclusion, prejudices and values, and are generally written by professionals, not service users.

'The telling and understanding of a really good story' is the best approach to 'the project of narrative [clinical] ethics' (Ellos 1998, p. 315; see also Montgomery Hunter 1991). If this is the case, and if as Bleakley (2005) says, 'case studies are autistic' in their futile attempt to be true, detached and impartial, then fresh methods are needed, preferably from literature, the home of the story (Montgomery Hunter 1991; Brody 2003; Charon and Montello 2002).

Even a video would only record what came within its field – no smell, taste, sense of touch, or sight and sound material outside its range. 'People talk about true stories. As if there could possibly be such things as true stories; events take place one way and we recount them the opposite way' (Sartre [1938] 1963, p. 62). The belief that any study can be objectively true, with a single 'teleological meaning' (Barthes 1977, p. 146), is itself a fiction. Everyone has selective perception:

Selective hearing syndrome: female

He: You are the most beautiful, fascinating, intelligent, witty, sexy, well-balanced, creative woman I have ever met, even if you are a bit moody sometimes.

She: Me? Moody?

Selective hearing syndrome: male

She: You never take the children to the park, or read them a story; you never even cook an egg, and have never made the bed.

He: Bed? Now?

Reflective practitioners often need to examine a particular incident, exploring motives, feelings and thoughts, their actions and those of others, recording it as accurately and as widely as possible from their own memory, and possibly also consulting others' perceptions. And at times fictional scenarios are appropriate: what might have happened, what others might have thought, and so on. And on occasion genre gives the best exploration (as in fairy story, or romantic fiction: see Chapter 1, pp. 18–20). None can be *true*.

Stories might be what we live by. But life as lived lacks the comforting fictive form recognised from infancy, with a beginning, middle and end, clearly defined characters and sense of place. The function of the endless *stories* we tell and write is to give life a spurious, satisfying, recountable, and memorable sense of shape. 'Narrative seeks to redeem life and pain from chaos by creating sequence . . . In narrative form, one event seems to belong before and after others – not to happen randomly but to make sense exactly there' (Frank 2004, p. 213).

The identity, or *character*, of a person similarly is not static or fixed. 'We all talk about "me". How do we know that there is such a person as "me"?' (Chuang Tsu trans. 1974, p. 136). In life as lived identities change and develop; telling and writing stories celebrates this, and enables dynamic understanding.

Stories are created in the recounting of life events. Sophocles, Aeschylus and Euripides depicted the great bloody events of their tragedies off-stage, recounted by such as a messenger. The murder of Agamemnon (Aeschylus trans. 1999) is foretold graphically, immediately before it happens, by the prophetess Cassandra. Such episodes are told as stories – a story within the story of the play – for dramatic effect.

In life 'we always begin in the middle' (Lyotard 1992, p. 116), and 'we are always in the middle' (fourth-century BC philosopher Chuang Tsu). Here is the hero of *Nausea*, in the process of realising that those essential aspects of adventure – beginnings and endings – are only in stories, in the recounting of a life, rather than in life as lived:

First of all beginnings would have had to be real beginnings. Real begin-nings, appearing like a fanfare of trumpets, like the first notes of a jazz tune, abruptly cutting boredom short . . . Something begins in order to end: an adventure doesn't let itself be extended; it achieves significance only through its death . . .

When you are living nothing happens. The settings change, people come in and go out, that's all. There are never any beginnings. Days are tacked onto days without rhyme or reason, it's an endless monotonous addition.

Sartre [1938] 1963, pp. 59, 61

Trying to *live* our lives as *adventure* or *story* could only lead to depression or mental instability: 'I wanted the moments of my life to follow one another in an orderly fashion like those of a life remembered. You might as well try to catch time by the tail . . . You have to choose: to live or to recount' (Sartre 1938, pp. 63, 61). 'The past is beautiful because one never realises an emotion at the time. It expands later, and thus we don't have complete emotions about the present, only about the past' (Woolf, quoted in Holly 1989, p. 26).

Hélène Cixous asserts that only masculine stories have beginnings and end-ings. 'A feminine textual body is recognised by the fact that it is always endless, without ending . . . at a certain point the volume comes to an end but the writing continues and for the reader this means being thrust into the void.' And 'a femi-nine text starts on all sides at once, starts twenty times, thirty times over' (1995, p. 175).

Realising that accounts of practice do not need to stick to what happened in life as lived can offer confidence in the expression of experience, and widen the range of possible ways of reflection. Fiction can omit slow episodes or effectively combine events which took place at different times and with different people. Writing fictionally from deep professional experience can be more dramatic, leap over the boring bits, tackle issues head on; convey multiple viewpoints; sidestep problems of confidentiality, fear of exposure, and some of the inevitable anxiety which accompanies the exploration of painful events.

Writing about 'she' or 'he' rather than 'I' can be liberating. Fiction can feel safer to write – less personally revealing. Later rereading, sharing and discussing can offer a paced way of exploring areas which might otherwise seem too painful to address.

Fiction can be a vehicle for conveying the ambiguities, complexities and ironic relationships that inevitably exist between multiple viewpoints. It can offer an intelligible research summary of the huge body of data that qualitative research tends to provide. The creation of a fiction, with the awareness that it is a creation, can enable the writer to head straight for the heart of the matter (see also Rowland 1991; Winter 1988, 1989, 1991; Rowland (Bolton) et al. 1990). 'Thinking up a plot and a range of characters in a certain context is analogous to formulating a theory of that context' (Winter 1988, p. 241).

Fictional characters and situations take on a life of their own. If writers try to discipline them to do what they want, the writing will be flat, lifeless and dull. Each character is an aspect of the author, and needs full expression via the creative process. This allows expression to the non-logical, non-rational parts of the writer's mind, allowing contact with previously unperceived internal voices.

Peter Clough's stories about education effectively present the reader with challenging issues to reflect upon (2002). In themselves they form a cogent argument for the method of creating stories or narratives as a form of deep critical reflection. But Clough accompanies them with dense explanatory prose: the stories are not allowed to earn their keep by carrying the argument within themselves. And the narratives are perspectivally limited, all being from point of view of fictional Peter Clough.

Critics have been dissatisfied with forms of research or reflection which make overt use of fiction. Just as few are satisfied with the copy of Michaelangelo's *David* in a Florentine piazza free of charge, with no queues: they need to see the very lump of marble from which Michaelangelo himself 'released' David.

Stories, however, are not *objects* like *David*: they are constructions mediated through writers or narrators. A collection of letters – transcribed exactly – between two or more parties is perhaps the closest to being a written *real thing*.

Charon has reflected upon patients' charts as if they were novels. She says 'Literary critics who write about the novel provide useful frameworks for doctors who reflect on their practice' (2000a, p. 63).

Image and reflection

The reflection in Van Eyck's convex mirror in *The Arnolfini Portrait* (National Gallery, London) allows a view of the couple from both sides. Our night sky would be denuded without the power of reflection: the moon and the planets are only visible because they reflect the sun's light.

'The Lady of Shalott', cursed to live her life indirectly through mirror images, wove them into tapestry. When handsome Sir Lancelot appears in her glass she can stand it no longer:

> She left the web, she left the loom,
> She made three paces thro' the room,
> She saw the water lily bloom,
> She saw the helmet and the plume,
>   She looked down on Camelot.
> Out flew the web and floated wide;
> The mirror cracked from side to side;
> 'The curse is come upon me!' cried
>   The lady of Shalott.

Tennyson [1886] 1932, Part 3, p. 82

She dies, of course, because it was her curse only to perceive life reflected. Reflective practitioners need to look at life fully, and perceive right through the mirror rather then merely musing upon reflections. The route is a critical rendering and rerendering of life's narratives, and critical re-viewing of habitual metaphors and other tropes, via poetic form.

8

METAPHOR AND POETRY

Our ordinary conceptual system, in terms of which we both think and act, is fundamentally metaphorical in nature . . . human *thought processes* are largely metaphorical.

Lakoff and Johnson 1980, p. 6

Maybe all poetry . . . is a revealing of something that the writer doesn't actually want to say, but desperately needs to communicate, to be delivered of.

Hughes 1995

Every poem breaks a silence that had to be overcome.

Rich 1995, p. 84

Metaphor uses images from all the senses to aid understanding. Along with narrative or story making, it is a fundamental way of making sense of the world. Examining the metaphorical structures about ourselves and our professional, social, political, and spiritual world is an essential reflexive process.

Some reflective practitioners use poetry for expression. Poetry's conciseness enables it to reach the parts that prose cannot, leaping straight to the heart of the matter. Poetry is an exploration of our deepest and most intimate experiences, thoughts, feelings, ideas and insights: distilled, pared to succinctness, and made music to the ear by lyricism. In order to make its point in as few words as possible, poetry relies on imaginative and insightful image, particularly metaphor and metonymy. For some, it is the only way to explore and express certain things, directly diving for the heart of the issue, with no messing around with sentence structure or grammatical sense: a way of saying exactly what you want to say, and finding out what you need to say (Abse 1998).

> Maybe all poetry, insofar as it moves us and connects with us, is a revealing of something that the writer doesn't actually want to say, but desperately needs to communicate, to be delivered of. Perhaps it's the need to keep it hidden that makes it poetic – makes it poetry. The writer daren't actually put it into words, so it leaks out obliquely, smuggled through analogies [metaphors]. We think we're writing something to amuse, but we're actually saying something we desperately need to share.

Hughes 1995

Poetry and metaphor can enable the exploration and expression of 'things we don't actually want to say', but 'desperately need to share', because meanings are released slowly and kindly. It can also be a graphic way of describing and explaining something, and gaining clarity for the writer (Perry and Cooper 2001). Leslie Boydell describes the leadership programme she directs for the Institute of Public Health in Ireland as:

> a team of horses pulling a heavily laden wagon. The horses are of different sizes and colours and they are pulling at different speeds. One has the bit between its teeth and is going full tilt, another is taking it easy, a third wants to eat grass, while another is grumpy and nipping the others. But every so often we pull together and we fly. I am sitting on the wagon, inconspicuous, without a whip or loud voice. I constantly keep my eyes on the road ahead to steer around any dangers. Other people come on board for a while and ride with me and use their greater strength to control the horses.
>
> Leslie Boydell (Denyer et al. 2003, p. 19)

Cecilia Forrestal, in describing the programme as an opened jigsaw box, depicts her learning graphically; here's an extract: 'Well look at that! I thought that blue piece was definitely the sky. But no. It is water. And that piece of 'cloud' is part of the 'snow'. Who would have guessed I could be so wrong? Now I can see the value of that sharp edge: you would have to have it to give shape to the whole picture' (ibid., p. 22).

Jane Wilde, Institute Director, saw the programme as jewel-like pictures in the windows of a model building (ibid., p. 27), and:

> The stones in the river are dull and grey
> The sky low and gloomy lies on my shoulders
> And clouds are in my head
> A heron balances on a stone in the river
>
> We watched and waited for each other
> He held my gaze. Balanced
> Silent, still, surveying
> Later, gently with ease, he flew
>
> Jane Wilde (ibid., p. 44)

Metaphor

Metaphor is the frame through which we perceive, understand and feel. A form of cultural interpretation, it is fundamental to communication, values and ethical beliefs and practices. 'There is no liberation from metaphors and their interaction; there is only awareness of the benevolent /malevolent multiplicity of meanings' (Frankenberg 1986, p. 607).

We need to take responsibility for the moral and social consequences of the metaphors we use: 'Metaphors can kill' (Lakoff 1991), and 'Evocative language can take on a pernicious and evil power if the wrong metaphor is chosen – we are liable to be captives of our own phrases and must be careful how we speak' (Osborn 1993, p. 306).

Yet we are unaware of most professional, political and social metaphors and metaphorical systems; used unwittingly, most are taken off-the-peg from peers and the media. We are also unaware that when we struggle to conceptualise, grasp or explain an issue, the struggle we are engaged in is most often the search for the most appropriate metaphor. I asked a group of medical undergraduates if one could give an example of metaphor. They looked blank and rather scared (I could see them thinking 'we're scientists . . .'). One responded: 'I can't think of any, my mind's a blank sheet.'

The dominant metaphors in our culture are static. Elements which are fluid and action based are often expressed as *things*, commonly commodities. Nursing and teaching are relationship based, but relationships are messy and unverifiable. Teaching has become a thing to *plug a knowledge or skills gap, a module*; nursing *delivers packages of care*. We have *human resource management*, rather than *personnel*.

Everyone has a metaphorical way of understanding their lives (Brody 2003). Some people perceive their glass as half empty and others half full: a metaphorical expression of native optimism or pessimism.

A reflexive awareness and conscious use of our own metaphors and metaphorical systems therefore is vital for agency, awareness of the ways we impact upon the lives of others, control of our own values, and in order for us to affect professional or cultural value systems. If as professionals we want to care for, educate or heal people, we need to understand and harness the way we view our professions, and the way they are viewed by society.

The way an issue is understood cannot be changed without changing the metaphors, or metaphorical systems, which express it. By paying attention to the metaphors we use, we can become critically aware of hitherto uncritically accepted and repeated world views. We can *choose* the conceptual frameworks which construct our values, understandings, and feelings and therefore our actions.

Used as a poetic device, metaphor is visible: poets and readers do not believe love is really a red, red rose. But scientists can believe theirs, and persuade the public, for example that the body is a machine (Pickering 1999): the metaphor becomes invisible. Here is a family medicine practitioner (GP) using metaphor to help him to perceive how he might be experienced by a patient he is unable to help:

Nigel Gibbons: portrait by a patient

If he was a dog he'd be an old greyhound,
tense and stiff but droopy round the middle.
If he was a cat he'd be a Siamese
small eyes, and coming over all superior, but lazy.

If he was a wild animal he'd be a weasel
cunning and sly and always wriggling and slipping away from you.
If he was a bird he'd be a heron
tall and staring at you with beady eyes, and then darting at you.
If he was an insect he'd be a busy bee
bumbling about and blundering into things and no use at all.
If he was a fish he'd be a fat trout
just sitting there, and then suddenly shooting off.
If he was a farm animal, he'd be a donkey
awkward and just not quite right.
If he was a bit of furniture, he'd be a tallboy
all big and shiny and domineering, but just a lot of empty space up at the
top and not much use down below. You keep putting things in but you can
never get anything out when you want it.
If he was a car he'd be an Austin Cambridge
years out of date, mediocre, middle of the road, too big, using up too much
fuel, and you can't get the spares.
If only he wasn't the way he is, he'd be a proper doctor.

I was asked as an exercise to write a piece about a patient. I chose this one
because of her familiarity. I found it quite a satisfying experience to share a
distillation of my observations with others as a sort of anecdote. It was a
pleasure to be able to tell a story involving some of my observations, display-
ing anonymously some of what would otherwise have slipped into oblivion.
It was written in a spirit of affectionate resignation about the impossibility of
making any real medical progress in this case. Reflecting about my consultations in this detached and analytical way, and writing a parallel piece about
the imagined observations of me by the patient, taught me that I should be
acutely aware of the signs and signals that I give out when talking to people,
just as much as I am aware of what I observe.

Gibbons 2003

What is metaphor?

Metaphor consists in giving the thing a name that belongs to something else;
the transference being either from genus to species, or from species to
genus, or from species to species, or on grounds of analogy.

Aristotle trans. 1995, p. 105

Metaphor can allow a grasp of the ungraspable, make visible or audible that which
is normally invisible or inaudible. Have you ever touched, heard, or seen a feeling,
emotion, or spiritual experience? Metaphors, however they are created (with
words, paint, or music), give these vital everyday areas of our lives tangible form.

The human mind thinks concretely: what *is* love, anxiety, guilt? Love is the most beautiful, scented flower you can imagine; anxiety is a beast gnawing at your guts, and guilt is the heavy bird you should never have killed, strung inescapably around your neck (Coleridge [1798] 1969). T.S. Eliot described this search for the right image thus: 'And so each venture / Is a new beginning, a raid on the inarticulate' (Eliot [1936] 1974, p. 203).

Images from the five elements are common shorthands in our culture: *my body was leaden, their heads were lumps of rock, our legs turned to water, he talked hot air, she breathed fire*. The body as container is another prevalent image.

Metaphors enable the verbal painting of pictures, the creation of symphonies, banquets, perfumes, silk, the use of all five senses in grasping an issue as fully as possible, and to use 'cognitive, affective and somatic ways of knowing' (Shafer 1995, p. 1331). C.S. Lewis (1961) said that some moments of his grief for his wife could only be described in metaphor. With utter precision and conciseness, a powerful image is created. 'My throat is very sore' hardly compares with 'my throat is on fire'.

> Metaphor is the rhetorical process by which discourse unleashes the power that certain fictions have to redescribe reality . . . The metaphorical *is* at once signifies both *is not* and *is like*. If this is really so we are allowed to speak of metaphorical truth.
>
> Ricoeur 1978, p. 7

Metaphor, with its power of 'metaphorical truth' is an essential aspect of our mental and physical understanding, the 'open sesame' to memories and understanding. 'Metaphor is the "aha!" process itself' (Shafer 1995, p. 1332). And to Arnold Modell, a psychiatrist:

> metaphor [is] the currency of mind, a fundamental and indispensable structure of human understanding. It is by means of metaphor that we generate new perceptions of the world; it is through metaphor that we organise and make sense out of experience . . . The locus of metaphor is now recognised to be in the mind and not in language . . . metaphors have their origin in the body. There is a privileged connection between affects and metaphor. As feelings are to some degree beyond our control, translating such feelings into metaphors provides us with some degree of organisation and control. Through the use of metaphor we are able to organise otherwise inchoate experiences, so it is not surprising that somatic experiences, such as affects, are transformed into metaphors . . .
>
> Modell 1997, pp. 219–20

Plato relied on metaphor to explain his theories. His exposition of the ethical responsibility of philosopher-educators is widely remembered and clearly understood through his graphic *cave* metaphor (trans. 1955).

Susan Sontag wrote a polemic (1991, p. 91) against metaphors, particularly battlefield ones, being used in medicine and healthcare. This metaphor system is commonly used for a disease such as cancer, which 'doesn't knock before it enters . . . a ruthless secret invasion' (1991, p. 5).

'The use of metaphor implies ways of thinking and seeing that pervade how we understand the world' (Elkind 1998, p. 1715). Audrey Shafer argues that anaesthesia is much more complex than the commonly used metaphors seem to suggest (1995, p. 1339). The *under* anaesthetic metaphor 'supports an uncomplicated, unitary theory of anaesthetic action . . . new metaphors may need to be developed to help us completely understand how anaesthetics work'. She also points out that *down* is normally metaphorically construed as bad, perhaps related to the image of devil and hell as underneath, and heaven above (*bottom of the heap*, *under the weather*).

Metaphors can also enable contact with otherwise hidden memories:

Cognitive metaphors form bridges between the past and the present; metaphor allows us to find the familiar in the unfamiliar. This means affective memories are enclosed as potential categories; we remember categories of experience evoked by metaphoric correspondence with current perceptual inputs. We can think of ourselves as owning a library of categorical memories of pleasurable and painful experiences, all of which at certain points in our life will be activated by means of metaphoric correspondence with current inputs.

Modell 1997, p. 221

Traumatic memories lose their connectedness with the rest of material in the memory and prevent the sufferer from effectively living in the present and looking to the future. The sufferer is isolated and inward-looking. Writing can make such memories more safely accessible and communicable, by using image and description; it can communicate strength to the writer. Writing, as a powerful communicating force, can help to overcome that isolation (Harris 2003).

Metaphors are a route to expressing abstractions, memories, ideas, thoughts and feelings, and of exploring and making constructive contact with painful or difficult areas of experience and memory. Effective metaphors can appear to be created by accident in reflective practice, *coming from nowhere*. Facilitators guide writers into allowing images to bubble up, presenting themselves on the page. This is the artistic process. It only seems like accident because we are so used to the Cartesian understanding of the self: 'I think, therefore I am'; these metaphors do not arise through cognitive processes. Such powerful images occur once we have the courage to be 'absent-minded', or to pay attention to absent-mindedness (as Freud suggested about parapraxes). Coleridge called it 'That willing suspension of disbelief for the moment, which constitutes poetic faith' (1817).

If reflective practitioners are encouraged to experiment *playfully* with words – *doodle* with metaphors – they can find they've 'absent-mindedly' found a way into all sorts of areas of experience of life, as well as into those locked categories of memory described by Modell and Harris. Metaphor can reveal because it does not come at these elements head on; it sidles up without coming too close, giving a non-traumatic image for a traumatic event. A writer or artist might not even understand their own metaphor at first (as dreams are frequently not understood); when they do, it is the indrawn breath of 'aha'.

Reflective practice metaphor exercises

There are many ways of encouraging professionals to become aware of some of their habitual metaphors, and to use metaphor's enabling power to perceive hidden things. They also create powerful new metaphors, like Boydell, Wilde and Forrestal above. Megginson and Whitaker ask management development participants to create metaphors for their career, using these in a structured development exercise (2003, pp. 34–6). Julie Hughes's education students, in a metaphor-creating and exploration exercise, gave in-depth explanations why teaching was disco ball, river, road network, and mountaineering.

As a warm-up I often ask people to write a list of binary pairs which spring to mind (see Chapter 10). They then play with these metaphors, like assigning one of the pair to patient or student, and one to themselves. Charles Becker, a therapist, wrote this:

silk & sand	I put the smooth on her rough
light & dark	she's in the light and I'm in the wings
Hansel & Gretel	I'm a boy and she's a girl and we're searching our way
mountains & streams	she flows round me and I stay fixed
horse & cart	she takes the lead and I follow on
grass & green	she's growing while I reflect her colour
sad & happy	I carry her tears as she learns to smile

Charles Becker

Kate Milne, a family doctor wrote about sunshine and showers:

My depressed patient and I. I am the sunshine. He is the showers. I try to brighten his life with pleasantries to help him pull through the storm. Maybe I am too light-hearted and I am minimising his sufferings. When the rain is fine the sun makes a rainbow. As the shower becomes heavy it clouds out the sun. Are my football stories irritating and patronising? He now chooses to see my colleague.

I found it useful putting my feelings down on paper as the situation put me in a dilemma. By sharing it with my group I was able to put the episode into perspective. It was interesting that the patient concerned is now causing my colleague some anxiety also. Maybe it is transference.

Kate Milne

Quite often practitioners use metaphors unwittingly, as when Jo Turner wrote about rowing (Preface), and Jenny Lockyer drumming (Chapter 13). Such metaphors take writers by surprise. Here is a searching self-portrait:

Jug by Sam Kyeremateng

A terracotta jug sits on a stone floor, in a dark space. A dim light illuminates the spot on which it sits. The Jug ponders its existence in the world. It surveys the gloominess of its surroundings. Why am I here? Who am I? What am I? The unspoken questions are unanswered.

The Jug ponders itself. It was crafted with care. Someone had lovingly sculpted its form. Taking great care moulding its short spout and stout handle. Despite this the questions remain unanswered. The labours of its maker could not fully explain its purpose. It understood it was a jug. By its own admission it knew jugs could hold all manner of things. But it could not hold all things at once, and it could not decide what it should hold. It was not enough to be simply a jug, was it? It did not think it wished to be an empty vessel, and it did feel so very empty. It thought of all the things it could hold: water, wine, oil, or even marbles.

If it held water it could be used to sustain people or to hold beautiful things like flowers. If it held wine it could bring life to a party, solace to the lonely and joy to sad. If it held oil it could fuel a fire, or ease the workings of some great machine. If it held marbles it could be an ornament to be admired and adored. As the thoughts danced through its imagination the Jug realised that in the darkness of this room it could see no water or oil or wine or even stones let alone marbles and even if it could, it could not decide how to choose between them all. The Jug sat empty.

The Jug sat in silence. In the distance the sound of footfalls tapping the flagstones pierced the darkness. The Jug pondered a new thought. Perhaps someone would come and make the choice. Someone would find it and fill it up with something that would make it something worth being. Delighted by the prospect it sat thinking soon it would find the answer to all its questions. As the steps drew closer the Jug's excitement changed to anxiety. What if the person chose the wrong thing? Once filled with wine it could no longer hold water for fear of tainting the taste and vice versa. Would oily marbles have the same appeal? Panicked by the new dilemma the Jug remained frozen in the spotlight. The steps stopped. The Jug sensed the gaze of the unseen figure. After a moment the silence that had nurtured its thought became unbearable. The steps clacked back into life then faded.

The terracotta jug sat on a stone floor. In the silence it decided it was better just to be and not ask too many questions. To be an empty jug was enough for now.

Sam's afterword

I wrote this at a time of uncertainty: I'd like to think the sort of uncertainty that everyone experiences from time to time. Primarily it was about career paths. There was also, though, uncertainty about my place in society. As a black Scotsman (or Scotsman of African origin to be pc) I often wonder about my place in the world and what my attitudes should be. Being young, male and black all have their own associated dilemmas. Whilst I am undeniably Scottish, I have a deep love of my African roots. All this is further complicated by the media concept of *blackness* which is very different from that which has been passed to me by my parents. In my experience there are very few role models for the young, black Scotsman even in today's multicultural world. Even now the only one I can think of is the guy who was in *Porridge* with Ronnie Barker and I'm sure he doesn't count.

The story was never meant to be a self-portrait. I think I was just trying to capture certain emotions. It was certainly never meant to be published. Only now reading it again do I realise how embarrassingly personal (and at times sad) it is. Despite the blushes I am happy for it to be published as it surprises me by capturing my thoughts at a certain moment in time. I guess I hope that someone else might gain some comfort knowing that they are not the only ones to have similar thoughts of uncertainty.

Kyeremateng 2003, pp. 101–2

Poetry

Ted Hughes thought poetry should be an uncivilising force (Middlebrook 2003). Poetry strips away cloaking veneers, lays bare thoughts, ideas, feelings, values, dilemmas about identity, etc., through image, metaphor and other poetic devices. These devices allow insight subtly, and graciously: acceptably. Take another look at the poetry by Jo Cannon, Mark Purvis, Maggie Eisner and Nigel Gibbon in this volume. They all employ lightness, humour, gentleness, image, communicating vital messages succinctly, subtly, yet surely.

Sir Philip Sydney was desperate to 'faine in verse my love to show', yet could not find a poem good enough: '"Foole," said my Muse to me, "look in thy heart and write"' (Sydney 1965, p. 165): he had to write it himself. The right words can be used in the right place, and only them; and these right words might be ones no prose writer could possibly put together.

Finding the right words and the right place is not always easy, but once found they offer expressive insight to reader, and clarity of understanding to writer. The poetic mind knows better than the cognitive: 'I like poetry because I can't make it do what I want it to do, it will only do what *it* wants. I didn't want to write the poem I did write; I wanted to write a nice glowing poem about being a mother' (a medical course member).

Poetry often uses image, such as metaphor or simile, to express vital experiences in a few words. Strict form, such as sonnet or villanelle (controlled rhyme, rhythm, syllables or repetition), is often preferred for expression of deepest experiences. Such control seems to contain the otherwise uncontrollable unlimitedness of grief for a friend's death from AIDS (Hamberger 1995), the work of a busy clinician (Campo 1997), or unrequited love (Shakespeare's sonnets). But 'Poetry should be . . . unobtrusive, a thing which enters into one's soul, and does not startle or amaze it with itself, but with its subject', and: 'if poetry comes not as naturally as the leaves of a tree it had better not come at all' (Keats 1818).

Poetry writing, utterly absorbing and rewarding, offering immense surprises, tends to be self-affirming, as well as challenging and demanding. It draws upon deeply held memories, knowledge, values. Initial drafts can be intuitive, intensely absorbing, hypnagogic even, the writer allowing the hand to write with no conscious mental direction: 'That willing suspension of disbelief for the moment, which constitutes poetic faith' (Coleridge 1817). Winnie the Pooh clearly read Keats and Wordsworth: '"It is the best way to write poetry, letting things come," explained Pooh' (Milne [1928] 1958, p. 268). 'Poetry is the spontaneous overflow of powerful feelings; it takes its origin from emotion recollected in tranquility; the emotion is contemplated till by a species of reaction the tranquility gradually disappears' (Wordsworth [1802] 1992, p. 82).

Laurel Richardson (1992) 'breached sociological writing expectations by writing sociology as poetry. This breach has had unexpected consequences for my sense of Self'. She presented a research interview in very carefully crafted poetry, finding it 'one way of decentering the unreflexive 'self' . . . In writing the Other, we can (re)write the Self' (p. 136). Writing about another in poetry, particularly in the first person singular (I) is writing about the self as well as the other. Her research poetry writing was a deeply reflexive experience.

Angela Mohtashemi uses poetry in management consultancy:

I write myself to make sense of organisational life. I have kept journals for ten years and couldn't imagine living without the place where I can hear my voice and practise being me. This poem explores the implied contradiction in Targeted Voluntary Severance: selecting people for redundancy with an apparent 'option' to go.

Targeted voluntary severance

We targeted them. Singled them out
Because they were old or simple
Didn't have the required milk
Dried up cash cows.

We asked them. It was voluntary.
When they wondered what would happen if . . .
We talked of subtle pressures. And no cash.
Best go now we said.

They were severed. We couldn't wait
To get them out. Gave them boxes
To collect their bits. Stains on the carpet
Affect morale.

And now they are gone.
Those who remain
Speak in whispers.

Angela Mohtashemi

Sarah Gull, medical course supervisor, wields expressive haiku:

A Japanese lyric form of 17 syllables in lines of 5, 7 and 5 syllables (Drabble 2000), has a formal structure providing support in framing ideas. Could it be that the structure within a medical course: timetables, deadlines, examinations and so forth, are of neglected value in supporting students to think for themselves?

Educational
Objectives officially
Prescribed
Dull the mind.

Could learning be an
Exploration of the world
Without
Set limits?

Yet ways of learning
Should enable the student
To adapt
To Change

Sarah Gull

Janina Chowaniec explores similar themes in verse:

In research and in teaching
we are now supposed
to anticipate outcomes
that are easily measured.
The culture of audit
has fully espoused
the commodification
of academic endeavour.
These changes in climate
have lead to confusion

fragmented identity
general distress,
for now we are living
the widespread illusion
that only such changes
will lead to progress . . .

My years in full-time research were spent continually extending my knowledge and skills in adaptation to changes in the direction of science funding
and prevailing paradigms . . . But at its worst (and most intensive), it
becomes a form of prostitution – of our subjects and ourselves, and is relentless, exhausting an futile. Now, the whole of HE is expected to commodify
itself, driven by external pressures.

Chowaniec 2005, pp. 267, 269

Reflections in water

Linda, despite being partially sighted, drew my attention to a bridge over
Durham's river, which her husband had described: I saw a powerful metaphor for
reflective practice.

Bridges

Her hand on my arm
so I can be eyes for us both
on the stony path by the river,
she stops, *look at the arch*
of the old bridge and its reflection.
I can't see it, but can you?

The reflection wavers as a duck passes;
stone arch, and reflected arch together
make a perfect circle.

We've written together, shared pools
of deep thought, mirroring our lives
yet different: the one reflecting the other
touching, feeling, tasting, listening,
seeing beyond sight.

Gillie Bolton

Completing the circle

A season ago we shared
A moment that captured our lives
Meeting, crossing and leaving;
The circle so perfect in stone and water
Would soon break
We parted on another bridge
Returning home, to live separate lives.
Even when the reflection is not visible, in shade or dark
The possibility of rejoining the circle is ever present
And vision is more than sight.
As our sharing of thoughts, ideas, experiences and feeling
Continues.

Linda Garbutt

9

ASSESSMENT AND EVALUATION

The life without examination is no life.

Plato trans. 2000, p. 315

'Rabbit's clever,' said Pooh thoughtfully.
'Yes', said Piglet, 'Rabbit's clever.'
'And he has brain.'
'Yes', said Piglet, 'Rabbit has brain.'
There was a long silence.
'I suppose', said Pooh, 'that's why he never understands anything.'

Milne [1928] 1958, p. 274

Assessment is a perennial problem. Can such sensitive material be assessed and how? It is fairly easy to assess knowledge, 'or skill or competence that can be learnt through instrumental reasoning' (Ixer 1999): Rabbit cleverness. But through-the-looking-glass reflective practice develops and nurtures wisdom and understanding. Evaluation is easier, as straightforward communication, even negative, is part of through-the-looking-glass reflective practice. But it can require dynamic new ways of perceiving and understanding: 'You've made things really difficult for me, you have. I shall never be able to teach the way I used to again' (Rowland and Barton 1994, p. 371).

Assessment

Including reflective work, particularly journals, in assessment can inevitably inhibit the process, and thus reduce its value. My students draw and comment upon private reflective journals and writings, and do not submit 'raw reflection'; Brockbank and McGill make a similar distinction (1998).

> If reflection is to be regarded as a core facet of individual professional competence, then we need to know far more about its structure, substance and nature . . . none of the work on reflection thus far has effectively tackled issues of oppression in the teaching and learning environment . . . A particularly loud note of caution must be sounded in relation to the fact that some commentators still inherently endorse reflection as a skill or competence that can be learnt through instrumental reasoning. This leads to the assumption that course planners need only structure assessment in such a way as to

encompass a new outcome called 'reflection' . . . It is clearly the case that the nature of reflection does not fit the competence model . . . The fear is that reflection will become seen as a self-indulgent or 'soft' subject that cannot be afforded, that standards will fall, and that users will receive a poorer service as a result.

Ixer 1999, p. 514

The increasing prevalence of standards, high-stakes testing, and outcomes assessment obscure the value of reflection, and much else, from fields of vision . . . There is a risk that the value of teacher reflection will be diminished and overwhelmed by standards. How will the habits of reflection and questioning survive under . . . the pressures of standards-driven curriculum . . . Will the habits of reflection that we seek to develop in future teachers become devalued simply because they are difficult to evaluate, summarise, and report?

Ward and McCotter 2004, p. 244

David Boud (1998) considers it inappropriate to assess reflection, that assessment will destroy 'raw reflection', i.e. disable students from involving themselves in the process of 'raw reflection'. He also points out that effective reflective practice needs to be unboundaried, which makes an assessed formal learning context, where clear boundaries are necessary, inappropriate. An assessed formal learning context can only too readily lead to instrumental or rule-following strategies, which apart from stultifying the reflection can also unethically seek inappropriate levels of disclosure and confession.

There is no widely accepted means of identifying or assessing reflection. Nor is it clear whether attempts should be made to assess the degree of reflection demonstrated by the developing professional . . . The relationship between the ability and willingness to be reflective about one's professional development, and one's ability and willingness to write reflectively is unclear.

Sumsion and Fleet 1996, p. 122

Sumsion and Fleet conclude that 'reflection appears unsuited to quantitative assessment', though they fear this makes 'reflective practices vulnerable to criticisms about their credibility' (p. 29).

Beveridge maintains: 'there is a real danger that creating assessment criteria will have the effect of killing off the spontaneity and individuality of the exercise' (Beveridge 1997, p. 42; see also Rust 2002). Beveridge feels tutors are in a cleft stick with assessment: without it (mathematics undergraduate) students do not see the process as being sufficiently worthwhile; the effect of it, however, can be to prevent them from expressing themselves freely. He points out how reflective journals provide not only opportunities for students to offer their own assessment, but also useful course evaluations.

Ken Gale has encountered assumed assessment bias; here is a fragment of a conversation:

1st student: '[One of the tutors] marked my first assignment and said in the feedback that I could have made more reference to the work of the critical theorists and later writers in that tradition, such as bell hooks and Paolo Freire. I thought, on reflection that that was fair but do I assume from that that if he is marking the next assignment I need to draw on those sources again?'

Ken: You think that we are going to mark your work on the basis of our own personal preferences, without looking at the critical and reflexive quality of your writing?

2nd student: So how can we really know what is relevant to a particular assignment? I can understand that we have to address the assessment criteria but it seems clear that the tutors might find it hard to avoid preferring one kind of content to another.

Ken: You don't have to reach conclusions that you think a particular tutor might like but if you draw a range of thinkers into the conversation that you set up in your assignment and allow them to engage with each other within the text that you create then you are much more likely to provide a critical and reflexive context within which your work can develop. Don't forget also that your assignments are second marked and externally examined so the likelihood of your work being unfairly marked in this way is greatly reduced.

Winter's solution is *Patchwork Text* assessment (2003). This requires students to present a series of fragments created over time from their learning experience, synthesised into a final submission: 'an essentially creative process of discovering [and presenting] links between matters that may seem to be separate' (Winter 2003, p. 121). Tutors in business, social work, nursing, sociology and Greek tragedy responded that it developed academic rigour, commitment, motivation-driven learning rather than to pass exams, willingness to take risks and tackle complexities and dilemmas, ability to think independently and present critical arguments, integration of personal and professional issues, critical reading, and varied writing abilities. It also allows assessment of the *process* of learning, as well as the *product* (Smith and Winter 2003; Maisch 2003; Akister 2003; Parker 2003), though 'the most difficult aspect has been persuading myself to "let go", release students to really take ownership' (McKenzie 2003, p. 160).

Ken Martin's solution to the assessment problem is triadic assessment – by self, peers and tutors:

Once we have agreed on assessment criteria, triadic assessment becomes possible. Class discussions defining criteria are usually terrific, each group seems to bring out something new, though students find it difficult. The usual criteria are flagged up but debating definitions drives home the problems with interpretation of language and difficulties with objectivity and validity.

The exercise concentrates the mind and provides the real stimulus for tri-adic assessment. This term's exercise produced two new points that could form part of the definition of critical analysis. One was the use of metaphors in critical analysis.

Self-assessment is usually quite acceptable to students, though many find it difficult criticising peers, and being self-critical initially; some find it empowering. However, many students get very thoughtful, honest, accurate and insightful about their own work very quickly. It can help refine ideas and boost esteem. The standard of reflective practice and reflexivity is certainly helped by self-assessment. I think that including 'insightful comments in self assessment' as part of the 'reflective practice' criterion has given it a higher profile. In a small way, perhaps, triadic assessment opens that 'secret garden' of assessment to some scrutiny and collaborative analysis.

Ken Martin

Winter et al. (1999) do not tackle the issue of assessment affecting, or even destroying, the students' confidence in expressing themselves freely and explo-ratively, nor the ethical problem. They point out how it is always difficult to assess work presented in a new format, and that, despite explicit criteria, examiners always have to make, and cross-check, interpretations, and be guided by 'tacit knowledge'. They conclude that:

> in the end these difficulties can be resolved, and they are essentially not very different from the problems of academic assessment in general. As with any assessment decisions other than those involving multiple choice tests there is an inevitable component of subjectivity. But if assessment is explicitly based on the professional criteria [below] (or an equivalent specification), and if examiners devote time initially to sharing and discussing their responses to groups of texts, judgements can be agreed as to whether the work fulfils the given criteria and with what varying degrees of success.
>
> Winter et al. 1999, p. 148

Moon discusses the 'need to decide whether the student is being assessed on content or on the writing, the process of the writing, or the product of the learn-ing' (1999b, p. 34), which again should be clarified in assessment criteria, and in teaching. Moon offers a set of assessment criteria (1999a). The assessment criteria for Richard Winter's reflective writing course were designed to synthesise profes-sional and academic educational objectives as follows:

- careful detailed observation of events and situations;

- empathising with the standpoint of other people;

- noticing the various emotional dimensions of events and situations;

- addressing the complexities of issues, events and situations;

- making connections between different events and situations, and between specific details and general principles derived from a range of professional knowledge;

- demonstrating learning, in response to both professional experience and the process of reflecting upon/writing about it.

Winter et al. 1999, p. 108

Carlos Sapochnik uses a dynamic form of reflection with university design students; material for assessment is developed organically from reflective course work:

Writing is a learning and assessment strategy in the interpersonal/study skills component of a graphic design first-year undergraduate skills module (50 students). Reflectivity is modelled in all workshop activities (e.g., discussing issues in pairs – foursomes – whole group; career planning undertaken by students working in pairs interviewing each other on their strengths, weaknesses, goals and strategies), and prompt sheets at the end of every activity invite students to reflect on outcomes, surprises, satisfactions, dissatisfactions, and possible future strategies. These reflections are collated, annotated and transcribed at the end of the module by students as an essay submission. Writing thus becomes artefact-making. The objective is not the artefact itself (writing), but learning by reflections on the process of producing it.

Most submissions praise the learning thus made, but this enthusiasm might be partly due to possibly unconscious needs to satisfy tutor/readers. Nevertheless, many students engage with and explore issues of uncertainty, not necessarily suggesting improvements to learning practice, but often recognising dilemmas. Such accounts are usually very honest, preoccupied with how to manage reflections (e.g., feeling insecure to speak up in group activities; a wish to lead in teamwork) and also quite moving.

My assessing criteria is subjective: grading is difficult. I pass (I do not grade) those sufficiently comprehensive papers where engagement with the writing – even if not with the activity – has taken place, and to feedback in writing by posing further questions ('You state x was the case. Why might that be?'; 'How could you have done y differently?'; 'Would you consider a pattern in your performance through all the activities?', etc.). This process is lengthy (i.e., uneconomical within current time resources) but, I believe, essential. Having found a reflective voice, the student must be responded to in an equally reflective manner.

I trust that ongoing reflection based on written submissions, my own teaching diary, the photographs I take during and after some events (e.g., teams building towers with newspapers) and the module feedback forms, will assist me to refine, develop or discard this approach.

Carlos Sapochnik

David McLaggan's art therapy students

use artwork as well as writing for their reflective practice in their own time, sharing experiences fortnightly with peers at the university. Though many find the reflective work very useful ('when you have clients in your thoughts you need a private space'), initially many found the sharing burdensome. They felt they had to be careful about doubts, confusions etc. because of the difficulty of the transition from the safe private space of placement to the university, and because of assessment. Also many clinical institutions are beginning to claim students' material, even private process notes, as their property. Once they became more confident the peer-mentoring reflective practice was private and confidential, they were able to use the process fully. [see also Chapter 6]

David McLaggan

McDonell et al. (2004) have effectively used and assessed video stories for reflective practice. And Claire Whewell reports: 'The best student final assignments often use vignettes from learning journals, unpacked using critical incident analysis. This allows a richness and depth to their self-assessment against the Standard for Chartered Teacher (2002), and provides a useful and clear platform from which to take their next steps.'

Evaluation

Evaluation is feedback from participants on the experience of a course: helping facilitators improve practice. Summative evaluations give participants' experience of the whole course; formative evaluations are undertaken at the end of each session, and help form the remainder of the course.

Students gain more if they are supported in tackling negative thoughts and feelings at the time, rather than brood and complain too late. Peer-mentoring (see Chapter 6) can help as participants can share doubts with a peer before expressing them to facilitator and group.

My short-course participants write anonymously what was good on one paper, and on another what could have been better. When we have more time they spread the positive sheets on one table, negative on another, and go round reading all, marking each one negatively, positively, or with a comment. At a course beginning this process can share hopes, expectations, fears, or personal objectives. Comments can be transferred to flipchart or typed up and fed back as part of final evaluation. Or they write brief (ten-minute) evaluative stories, using the same approach for evaluation as for the course. We read back with no comments, an affirming and warm way to end: the stories tend to refer to the life of the group as a whole. An anonymous form is needed to elicit negative points.

Drawing formative evaluations, pioneered in Sydney universities for a range of disciplines and courses (McKenzie et al. 1998), gave different information, inventively and informatively, from participants' written evaluations. One drew a juggler juggling a variety of commitments, another falling at the last of a succession of high hurdles. Anonymity can be obtained by, for example, a postbox to collect evaluations. I think the evaluation process needs to be useful to participants, rather than just a chore.

Students' reflective writing can offer effective course evaluation in my experience. Beveridge developed course structures in the light of students' reflective journal material. A student science teacher 'Barbara' was supported by her tutors in reflecting on how her practice 'did not mesh with her beliefs about how she wanted to teach' (Abell et al. 1998, p. 133), and what to do about it.

> What we have learned about our students led us to take action on the elementary science methods course . . . Interestingly our finding that methods students lack an understanding of first graders' abilities mirrors our lack of understanding of the preservice teachers. While our students were observing, writing about, and discussing the actions of first graders and their teacher, we were learning about them.
>
> Abell et al. 1998, p. 506

Joelle Fanghanel describes reflective practice in the professional education of university lecturers:

> Reflective practice is an underpinning approach I use to dispel any idea that teaching could be 'taught' through the acquisition of tricks and techniques. Providing a framework in which professional activities are continually evaluated and refined, its ultimate aim is to encourage conceptual change, understood as improvement.
>
> My approach to reflective practice has moved from conceiving it as a purely cognitive kind of activity (i.e. uncovering cognitive processes that might help me make sense of what is going on in any teaching situation through recall or critical incident analysis) to a much broader sociological perception. I have found that reflection should bear on structures and environments that frame professional practice, as much as – or perhaps more than – on intellectual processes. This has brought me closer to a more critical stance, similar to Zeichner (1994) or Brookfield (1995), as understanding of external constraints are very important in creating the conditions for change.
>
> Each programme lecturer has his/her own ways of promoting reflective practice. Many of the seminar activities are reflective in nature: relating theory to practice, solving case study problems, reflecting on strengths and weaknesses of systems (including the funding councils, the quality assurance

agency, university procedures etc.). All our assessment tasks also demand that students reflect on their practice in a variety of ways.

Students are also invited to analyse their own behaviours in critical incidents, following Johns (1995) (below). And the discursive specificity of reflection is illustrated through a writing and debriefing exercise in which students outline the main benefits obtained from taking into account the broader context (below).

Students keep a record of their teaching with particular groups, with specific reference to what they do in class, what happens, including their observation of individual behaviours, and their reflection as to how to work more effectively with that particular group.

My research has shown, however, that reflective practice is an elusive and metamorphic concept, subject to wide-ranging interpretations and applications. An essential recipe for success is that it should not come across as a bolted-on activity, but rather pervade the curricular approach.

Critical incident analysis

Consider a teaching event through the stages below:

1 *Phenomenon*: Describe the experience/incident/matter to investigate
2 *Causal*: What essential features contributed to this experience/incident/ matter?
3 *Context*: What are the significant background factors to this experience/ incident/matter?
4 *Reflection*: What was I trying to achieve? Why did I intervene as I did? What were the consequences of my actions for myself/others? How did I feel about this experience when it was happening? How did others feel about it? How do I know how others feel about it? What factors/knowledge influenced my decisions and actions?
5 *Alternative actions*: What other choices did I have? What would be the consequences of these other choices?
6 *Learning*: How do I feel about this experience/incident/matter? Could I have dealt better with the situation? What have I learned from this experience? What will I do/not do next time?

From Johns 1995

Reflective writing

Part 1

- Write for *five minutes without stopping* an account of something that did not go quite according to plans/ a conflict / an incident you have experienced in your teaching or rapport with colleagues.
- Narrate/ summarise this incident to your partner.

Part 2

- Now write a reflective statement on the same incident using the following prompts: What happened? What action did you take? What did the other party/the class do? What external factors impacted on this event? What alternatives did I have? What might have happened if I had acted differently? What lessons might be learnt concerning the external environment?
- Now discuss with your partner the difference between the two narratives, not the actual content of your second narrative which is private.

Joelle Fanghanel

10

HOW TO BEGIN WRITING

The captain unlocked his word hoard.

Beowulf trans. 1973, p. 12

I learned the science of letters . . . and this opened before me a wide field for wonder and delight.

Shelley [1820] 1994, p. 119

But Eeyore was saying to himself, 'This writing business. Pencils and whatnot. Over-rated if you ask me. Silly stuff. Nothing in it.'

Milne [1928] 1958, p. 153

Words, our everyday communicating tool, can be taken for granted so easily. After all, *in the beginning was the Word*. But writing is an art form, like painting and music. There are many more different ways to write than there are writers, because each develops their own voice. It can have as complex a form, process and set of variations as any other cultural form, say music or algebra. Each piece of writing belongs to the writer while it is being crafted – an adventure into their own thinking. When shared it becomes a joint journey: reader and writer together. Eeyore did not have the confidence to try it, perhaps because he had been put off at school by being told he couldn't do it. But it can be a thoroughly, satisfyingly straightforward process.

This chapter is a practical guide to writing: for practitioners, or facilitators. It helps unpick assumptions, and support a rediscovery of the *wonder and delight* of Frankenstein's monster. It covers what reflective writing is, for whom, and why, how, where and when it might be written. Reflective writers own their writing, and only share it with a reader when they are ready. Above all it is not only a learning tool, but something to be wielded and enjoyed for its own sake.

Introduction to writing
Trust the authority of the writing hand

Reflective practice writing is creative, a way of gaining access to each practitioner's deep well of experience not always accessible to everyday channels. It is akin to that used by novelists, poets or playwrights (Goldberg 1986), diarists

(Rainer 1978), or for personal exploration (Schneider and Killick 1998). The writer allows the pen to write whatever needs to be written, with no forethought, reference to grammar, spelling, punctuation or literary form. Grammar and so on do not matter at all at this stage: they can so easily be sorted out later if necessary. After all, the ancient Greek's *trivium* was grammar, logic, rhetoric.

A valuable mode of expressing, sharing, assessing and developing professional experience, writing is excellent solo and with colleagues (Rowland 1993), and as an effective research tool (Winter 1991). Students, moreover, write in order to express themselves, store an aide-mémoire, present an argument, demonstrate knowledge, explicate experience, or create a piece of literature. Educators write alongside their students; if not, something is wrong. Students and colleagues are most ably supported by tutors with first-hand knowledge and experience of the processes themselves (Murray 1982).

Artistic writing is used because: 'art takes one over a threshold, out of the rut, it questions custom, the "taken-for-granted"', and 'writing taps tacit knowledge – brings into awareness that which we sensed but could not explain' (Holly 1989, p. 75). 'The function of art in the full extent of its expressions includes the deliberate and subversive challenge to everyday understandings and interpretations of events' (Smyth 1996, p. 937).

Writing is essentially different from talking. It can enable

- contact with unexamined thoughts and ideas;

- contact with completely forgotten memories, and leaps of understanding and connections;

- expression and exploration of issues of which the writer is aware but unable or unwilling otherwise to articulate, communicate and develop.

Speech or thought can be forgotten, or shift and change like Chinese whispers, and vanish on the air. Conversations which both parties remember completely differently, and each party is certain their recollection is correct, are only too common. Writing leaves clear footprints on the page.

- These footprints aid progressive thought. Writing stays in the same form to be worked on whenever the writer is ready.

- Rewriting and redrafting, to get closer and closer to what needs to be expressed, is a self-educative process.

- Writing is private, a writer is their sole own interlocutor until ready to share with another: safer than talking. Since something said and heard cannot be unsaid, spoken utterances are habitually severely edited, usually unconsciously. Writing can, to a degree, evade this police officer-editor; it can be creative and rewarding, tending to increase self-confidence and be a pleasure in practice.

- Writing can be torn up or burnt unshared with anyone, even the writer themselves, if necessary.

- Writing is longer, slower and more laborious than thinking; writers are therefore less likely to *rabbit* than talkers. Greater depth and breadth, and more immediate access is engendered.

- Images or tropes such as metaphor are appropriate and readily used, giving indirect access to feelings, thoughts, knowledge, ideas, memories not accessible to non-image contact (Pennebaker 2000; Modell 1997).

- Fiction is an appropriate written form. It can protect confidentiality, be less exposing, more dynamic, and can convey ambiguities, complexities and the ironic relationships which exist between multiple viewpoints. Furthermore the re-creation of a situation exactly as it happened is unlikely; it will be recounted as experienced through the writer's own senses, as felt and thought about by them. This can allow the exploration of the experience without worrying about getting the *facts* just right. Research shows a fictional approach offers the same health benefits as writing directly about a traumatic event (Pennebaker 2000).

- Creative processes tend to increase self-confidence and self-esteem.

Why writing?

Suspend your disbelief

This writing is essentially playful. Creativity *is* playful: one of the aspects of its appeal to audiences and artists (musicians 'play'). Art is not thus denigrated; rather it grows up the role of playing from the purely childish arena to which our modernist culture has relegated it. Writing can be enjoyable, but it also requires courage to plunge into it wholeheartedly. The serious (but safe) and too heavily enforced rules for writing we learned at school have to be unlearned, as Jenny wrote: 'it's not easy is it to unlearn bad learning?'

> Might we not say that every child at play behaves like a creative writer, in that he creates a world of his own, or, rather rearranges the things of his world in a new way which pleases him?
>
> Freud 1995, p. 54

Freud reckoned the grown-up version of playing is fantasising. Creative writers surface fantasies and rid us of some of our tensions around fantasies – about which we are ashamed and secretive. We vicariously enjoy writers' fantasies. How much more powerful to write our own, however big or small, in a playful way.

The sound of pencils on paper
An occasional sigh, or sniff, a page
Torn roughly from a notebook, or
Scrunched and discarded
I twist a lock of hair around my finger and glance up.
Someone is frowning,
Another, smiling . . .
Everyone concentrating.
Time's up. (But this isn't an exam and doesn't feel like one)
There's a growing excitement – like that moment when someone is about to
open the present you've given them . . .
My gift to them, theirs to me – words on paper.
We're sharing very private thoughts . . .
Thoughtful silence and lots of laughter too.
It's a kind of communion.

Becky

Becky is referring to the explorative stage of writing too often left out, to the detriment of skill and confidence. To be literate and make full use of that literacy requires confidence. Writing does not come easily to many because of our early didactic training. We have all spent many years learning *proper* ways to write: the essay with its sequenced argument; the sonnet form; the short story's beckoning beginning, slick middle, and sting-in-the-tail end; the punchiness of the journalistic voice. Writing, for most professionals, is for reports: a burdensome and long-winded, hated but essential means of justifying work to authorities. All too often we strive to imitate successful writers, to please our teachers, editors, line managers: we have lost ownership of writing, forgotten we have our own voices.

Reflective writers can trust themselves in the very first vital stages of writing. These stages can transform that hitherto frustrating time of seeming to have an empty head with no writing in it at all, to writing a telling account. Never again (well, not quite so much) that 'Oh no!' fear of a clean sheet or empty screen.

Many find it easier to begin writing in a group, being given the process stage by stage. There is no opportunity for delaying tactics, like anxiety about subject, and the *Internal Critic* doesn't have much opportunity to whisper how useless they are. Some find writing alone less inhibiting. Writing a second piece can feel more difficult. Two students once wrote great pieces during the session, received interesting suggestions for development, but merely typed out their original pieces with a few amendments to bring to the next session. They came from a culture, I think, where imaginative flair was not expected of students, and couldn't maintain it without group encouragement.

The first two stages of writing will be discussed in detail, partly because they are the vital self-explorative, self-expressive stages required for reflective writing. And partly because they are the stages all too often skipped over. The later stages of writing ensure the writing communicates to a published audience. These are beyond the scope of this text (but see, for example, Albert 1997, Wade 1994, Doubtfire 1996). Suggestions are made as to how a reflective piece of writing can be developed.

> Our discussion may focus on the thoughts, feelings and experiences which led to the piece, on the way it was crafted, or both. The trust we have developed means we may quickly move from empathising deeply with a writer's grief at the death of a loved one to suggesting their piece would be more powerful without the last sentence.
>
> Maggie, Sheena, Clare, Mark, Becky

First stage
Your writing is a gift to yourself

- Choose a comfortable uninterrupted place and time, and writing materials you like.
- Make sure you have everything else you need to hand – like coffee and chocolate biscuits.
- Be able to time yourself to write without stopping for about six minutes.
- Allow another 30–40 minutes or so after the six, in order to do the next bit.

Without stopping to think too hard about it, jot down right now:

- your feelings about undertaking a piece of writing;
- your thoughts on the advantages and disadvantages of writing reflectively.

Adam's reflection upon writing

Take time to calm down, sit back, change gear. Nice and comfortable in here. Quite a few things I've thought about writing today. Nice to just let things just come out and sit on paper for a while. Not quite sure what track I'm on at the moment but don't worry something will come along in a bit. Good technique this. Doesn't matter. No one's going to read this later on – so don't worry about it – so can write anything.

Adam, undergraduate writing group

How to start
You can't write the wrong thing. Whatever you write will be right – for you

The initial stage of writing can be explorative communication with the self, and need not be shared: invaluable for reflective writing, and the same for stories, poetry, reports or essays. Some create everything clear in their heads before writing; most feel there is initially nothing, or a jumble. I find all sorts of things to do before I begin (looking up one more reference, watering the plants): delaying tactics. This method can help prevent the dither – 'What am I going to write?' – by dumping mind-clutter onto the paper. Some of these will be useful, some only a shopping list (or scurrilous moan about a colleague). Stow all that safely on paper and the mind is freed to continue. Invaluable elements of which the writer was unaware can also surface. Writing rules (grammar, logical sequencing, etc.) are NOT used.

> I write without thinking much, trying to overcome all kinds of self-criticism, without stopping, without giving any consideration to the style or structure . . . only putting down on paper everything that can be used as raw material.
>
> Llosa 1991, p. 45

Begin, like Llosa, by allowing the pen to write:

1. **Write whatever is in your head**, uncensored.

2. Time yourself to **write without stopping** for about six minutes.

3. **Don't stop to think or be critical** about your writing, it will probably seem disconnected, rubbish even.

4. Allow it to flow with **no reference to spelling, grammar, proper form**.

5. Give yourself permission to **write anything**. You don't even *have* to reread it.

6. Whatever you write it will be right: it's yours, and anyway no-one else will read it.

Lots might be written, or only a little seeming rubbish. Six minutes' writing sometimes turns up gold, sometimes dross. It is always useful, however, for beginning to scratch the surface.

Six minutes

I'm clearing out the rubbish
I'm emptying my mind,
The trouble with this task is that
I don't know what I'll find.

I came because I want to write,
I wanted to move on,
And if I keep on writing,
Maybe I can move the stone.

Perhaps what lies beneath is ore,
Of course it may be dross,
But let the chance go just once more,
And all there'll be is loss.

Janet Tipper

Six minutes
Here I am
Now.
It's hard – Something
I don't know what,
Yet I know
I feel and yet I cannot
Say – or write
the words too slow the thoughts
Who – am I and why I think
that I can come and give.

It's clear – I think – I don't
know, I'm not sure
Will it be OK, can I do
This – I am there – or – here?

So hard, too easy to fill all
the spaces – a thought in
a word it can go to all places!
A life, that is mine, I want
To be known – my heart it is
beating through gates that
are open.

John McAuley

I always do my 6 minutes, but then I screw it up and throw it away without reading it. I realised when you said you should read it through that while I am doing my 6 minutes, which is complete and utter garbage and can even include a shopping list, weird exclamations and verbal tics, I also have another current slowly going along in my mind which is deciding what to write about in the next bit of writing and then I sit at the end of the 6 minutes and think, oh THAT is what I am supposed to do. Sometimes I don't want to do it and I try to do something different but it is the thing that has appeared in the 6 minutes that is very insistent and demands to be written.

Helen Drucquer 2004, pp. 203–4

Writing a reflective splurge

Forget about grammar, syntax, spelling – for now. They block the inspirational flow. Correct them later

Now write straight away about *a time when I learned something vital*. Focusing on a particular occasion is particularly facilitative. Alternatively a theme may have arisen in the six minutes. This is still first draft: no one else need read it. What matters is capturing what is there to be written.

- Write in the same way as the six minutes, allowing the words to arrive on the page without planning or questioning. Don't look over your own shoulder, questioning what you write.

But this time:

- **Write with a focus** – the story of a vital occasion. Try not to ask questions – yet. The most common blocking query is: *why have I chosen this to write about; it's not nearly important enough?!* Well, everything is important: try to ignore this police officer.

- **Choose the first event which comes to mind**. Try not to reject it, for whatever reason. The more anxiously the *right* account is sought, the more the really right one – the one thought of first – will slide away.

- **Only allow about twenty to forty minutes in which to write**. The more time wasted thinking, the less time there will be for writing. I have known students set an alarm clock, and stop when the bell rings. On the other hand, if you find you want to go on, and on, then do.

- **Recreate the situation as memory gives it**, with as many details, as far as possible, rather than an idealised *what you would rather have happened*.

- **Consider it fiction**. Even if the situation is recreated as closely as possible to the memory, thinking of it as fiction can relieve embarrassment or fear of confidentiality loss: these things happened to a character. It can also allow experimentation with elements at the hazy edge of memory. Or if it seems less important to explore the actual event, considering it fiction can offer freedom of expression, rather than *what really happened*.

- **Spelling, grammar, syntax, usually flow** naturally in this kind of vitally charged writing. If infelicities or repetitions do occur, they can be corrected later.

- **This writing does not need *good form***. Stories have proper beginnings, middles and ends: life doesn't. The same sort of glorious muddle format as it originally had is appropriate now. Musings on the event (what you should/should not have said, for example) may arise: let them. Writing is endlessly plastic, and can be altered and tidied up later, before anyone else has to make sense of it, or embarrassingly read innermost feelings.

- **The pen can effectively notice details**: tone of voice, clothing, spoken words, seeming incidentals, and feelings. As the experience is replayed, vital details begin to emerge. Write them ALL down.

- **Allow reactions, emotional responses, feelings**.

- **Refrain from judgements at this stage**.

Another thing I've learned about reflective writing is that writing about a difficult event when I am a novice leaves me much more vulnerable than when I write about difficulties in something I am expert at. I have been keeping a reflective journal on these experiences.

Maureen Rappaport

Write for about twenty minutes according to the above *reflective splurge* way of writing. Remember this writing is for you. You need not share it with anyone.
    Write about:

A time when I learned something vital

Be as creative in your understanding of what constituted *vital* in your choice of *time when* . . . and in your understanding of *learned* – there are many ways to learn.

Bev's midwife's story

It was 1971 and I was working on the labour suite in Xmouth. Sister was a bossomly, matronly figure called Miss Lane, with iron grey hair and a face carved in granite. She exuded no warmth but appeared competent and in control. She certainly liked to control her flock of sheep – her nurses – and also her flock of rams – her doctors.

We were all in fear and awe of her; she had favourites and could be extremely sarcastic and make life difficult for those she did not like and her voice lashed out at people. Unfortunately this extended to the patients and she could be very prejudiced.

The girl was young and unmarried, scared to death and in labour for the first time. An enema was ordered for her – 'high, hot and a hell of a lot' – by Sister Lane. She was subdued and in misery, kept in isolation because she was socially unacceptable.

Her pain was intense and the medication seemed to be slow in appearing and the support she was offered was peripheral and minimal. Sister was in total control and had decided to make this young girl her mission.

I felt excluded and unable to offer support – we all did, we all stood on the periphery – watched and observed what this youngster was subjected to. Sister did the delivery and everything was clinically correct and cold, cold, cold as ice – she allowed no family support into the delivery room.

I don't know what trauma was taken away by this young girl and what processes were set up for her in her future. I do know that the scenario had a profound impact on myself about what to do and how to be with women in labour. About power, dominance, control, exclusion and the withholding of warmth and love to anyone in distress.

From another source years later I learnt that Sister had had a breakdown of some description. Part of me thinks this was divine retribution and another part reflects on what we do to ourselves as human beings when we become so rigid, fixed and inflexible. And part of me reflects that had I made different choices at certain times of my life that that could have been me.

Bev Hargreaves

Further writing: read, extend, vivify

Trust the process; have faith in yourself

When the first *dash* is finished, reread everything (including six minutes scribble), taking notes:

- with an **attentive yet open, non-judgemental** mind, looking at content rather than form;

- with an **openness to divergent connections** previously perceived as separate, or inappropriate together; specifically links between six minute mind-clearing and the later writing;

- and with an **openness to underlying links and to fresh understandings** and awarenesses;

- **additions, alterations or deletions** can be made;

- fill out the narrative with as much detail as possible, remembering we have **five senses** – smells and sounds as well as what things looked like can give vital clues, as can time of year; discomforts; intuitions; what people said, and the tone of voice they said it in.

Everything is significant.

Ask some of these questions:

- **Is the nub of the situation pinpointed?** The most vital issue might be located or clarified by looking down the wrong end of the telescope at a seemingly mundane trivial matter. As with fractals, the tiny recapitulates the great; and it is a great deal easier to concentrate metonymically on the small than the unwieldy.

- Notice **contrasts** within the story.

- Note the way **officialese/jargon** can be used to conceal.

- **Try not to come to an answer**, or even a definitive question – yet.

Fiji and reflective practice

It's at 4 o'clock in the morning, when I can't sleep, that's when I get the pen and paper out.

Working as a counsellor at the University of the South Pacific is an idyllic experience in lots of ways. The Rogers and Hammerstein set every time I look out of my office window, tropical colours and scents. But the sheer cultural complexity of the university community here at the main campus in Fiji is enough; add to that race, gender, sexuality, status and other aspects of diversity I'm meeting every day in the job and the lack of professional consultation and the isolation from any group of counsellors with a Code of Ethics and Practice is enough to keep me awake. So, I write it all down. The feelings of inadequacy, of excitement, the confusion and doubts, contradictions and discoveries.

Some of the writing I've kept, some was torn up into very small pieces, too awful to reread, the thoughts too negative to carry around any more. Scribbling it all down, in complete privacy acted as a safety valve. I could be my own 'supervisor' and avoid the worst of the isolation. I also started to suggest writing to some of the staff and students who came for counselling. Some were using their third language, English, to speak to me and were thousands of miles away from their village in another remote part of the Pacific. The writing gave us the possibility of a bridge.

Mustn't grumble, that so very English maxim is turned on its head. You must grumble, I would say, but do it on paper and in your own language.

Jeannie Wright

Types of writing, and topics

Autobiographical narratives, fictional stories with plots, poetry or songs, dramas or descriptive passages are all appropriate. Detailed accounts of experience may be followed by a piece of reflective interpretative thoughts; or these may remain unwritten until discussion with group or mentor. Subjects for writing may be suggested by a group. Each piece of writing will also generate ideas for fresh writings. Here are some from my groups:

> changes
> a conflict
> in control
> taking care
> a dilemma
> a celebration
> a moment of joy
> a sensitive subject
> a clash of interests

> a conflict of loyalty
> a misunderstanding
> a frustrated episode
> a missed opportunity
> a parting or beginning
> a case for compassion
> an evocative occasion
> an extremity of emotion
> the most dangerous time
> a breach of confidentiality
> a time when I was incapacitated
> the blowing of the pressure valve

Bev reread and thought about the midwifery sister and the young unmarried mother, wondering about the Sister's mental breakdown. The group discussed it, sympathized with her pain at the memory. Feeling guilty she had not attempted to make things better for the patient, Bev was comforted that there was nothing she, a young student, could have done. But she wanted to try to get to the bottom of what was driving this Sister in her cruelty. She decided to attempt to see the story through her eyes:

Bev Hargreaves's story from Sister's perspective

I trained in the days when nurses were real nurses – the nurses today don't know what hard work is and are frequently cheeky so need to be kept firmly in their place.

The medical staff need organising, but I usually manage to keep them doing what I want them to do.

I'm responsible for the Labour Suite and feel proud of the lying-in ward and our suite of delivery rooms. I run the department like clockwork and I like the routine of the place. I live in here so am always able to keep an eye on the place.

Some of the nurses are good and I get on well with them, but others need to be kept firmly in their place at all times.

I love my work, I'm really dedicated to it, I've given my life to it and have no family of my own.

Midwifery has changed a lot since I came into it and the mothers now have better analgesics during labour – mind you, some of them still scream and shout and need firm handling.

I don't like messes in my delivery area, the clutter of husbands or other family members, and if I had my way I'd ban them all; but there is this growing tendency to ask the husband to be present at the birth.

I like things to be orderly, to have well-behaved mothers doing what they should do, and I don't agree with children out of wedlock.

I remember this young girl came in – she must have been 17 years, arrogant and demanding – I thought I'd soon knock the stuffing out of her, lick her into shape. Anyway it was not right that she should be with the other married mothers so I decided that I would look after her.

She wanted pain relief far too early and started yelling and screaming, so I had to be really firm with her, she was not going to get the better of me. She had medication when I deemed it was the right time, anyway she soon didn't have the energy for arrogance – and such a noise she made at the birth I couldn't let her hold the baby until she had calmed down.

Anyway that's my role, to keep control – control of everything, I'm not here to be liked, I'm here to do a job.

Bev Hargreaves

Share your writing with a peer

Your writing has the power to influence another, and them you

A peer's responses can open up fresh avenues. They can support towards deeper levels of reflection, as well as see accounts in wider institutional contexts, or on the national social and political stage. Seeking just the right person or people can be a worthwhile endeavour. E-contact can be a good substitute (see Chapter 4). A colleague at work might be right, but they or a partner at home *might* be *wrong*: emotionally charged relationships may not offer different enough perspectives.

Reflecting on a critical incident is still within the confines of one's own perspective. Reflecting with another person, with the written incident before you, can bring added insights.

Jane

- Be positive and supportive; negative opinions are more readily received when preceded by positive.

- Comment on *writing*, not on *writer*. If writings are considered as fiction, if characters and their actions are fictional, then the reader has as much right to suggest ways of thinking and of developing them as the writer. The likelihood of hurt or loss of confidentiality is reduced.

- Safety for participants to say what they feel and think is offered by written or oral discussion being confidential to the parties involved, unless they specifically decide otherwise.

- Writers can usefully make it clear to mentors if they have any particular parameters for the discussion.

- Beginner writers feel everyone's writing is wonderful except their own: apologetic competitions are unfruitful.

- Choose a colleague or fellow student with whom to share writing.

- Use the above guidelines to support the development of other appropriate ones.

- Enjoy deepening the reflective process, whether verbally or in writing.

Sometimes reading my work feels exciting; sometimes gratifying; sometimes heartbreaking; sometimes even faintly dangerous.

Becky

Reading a piece aloud is like writing a song and singing it – it's not just your creation, it's your interpretation, it's putting your own voice out there.

Sheena

Reading in the group can give the writer the courage to examine painful events in a truthful way. The group holds the writer's hand through a raw and painful life event.

Mark

Developing writing

Thinking inhibits creativity, believe it or not. Let it flow

Writing additional pieces (like Bev's), can deepen and widen understanding. The writer explores *what would it be like if* . . . , being the *other*, different endings, or altering other essential aspects. This is fiction: written to surface and reflect upon the deep well of experiential knowledge and understanding in all professionals. Psychological benefits of fiction writing are the same as when writers try to stick to what actually happened (Pennebaker 2000). Writing as the *other* is an exploration of the other's experience, not what I would think, feel and do if I were them:

Her: You always think of yourself!
Him: I've always been good at empathy!
Her: You!
Him: Yes, putting myself in their place, imagining I'm them.
Her: Yes. If you were them what would YOU be thinking; what would YOU do! You always think of yourself!

Here are some developmental ideas. A group or a mentoring pair will develop their own, appropriate to their own writing:

- Give the story a title.

- Have protagonists other than the main character aired their opinions and standpoints? How might they have told the original story? Try writing from a different or opposing point of view.

- Write a similar story from the point of view of one of the other characters (like the client, or an observer to the main events).

- Rewrite the story with the gender of the main character(s) switched.

- Write the next chapter.

- Write a commentary on your own or another's text, either as yourself or as one of the characters.

- Retell the story with a different ending or focus, e.g. happy for sad.

- Write what a particular character is thinking at any one moment.

- Write about a (some) missing character(s). Like a photograph, a story is always an unreal and slim slice of reality – think of the area beyond the frame.

- Rewrite the story in a different style/genre: newspaper article/fable/narrative poem/children's story/romance/detective/sci-fi/fantasy (see Chapter 12).

- Write *thought bubbles* for vital (or puzzling) characters at significant points in the narrative.

- Rewrite the story with the focus of control/power altered.

- You are a reporter: interview a character from the story.

- Take a character who's just left the action; what might they be doing/ thinking?

- Write a letter from yourself to one of the characters, expressing your puzzle-ment/anger/sympathy. Write their reply.

- Write a letter/transcribe a telephone conversation between two characters.

- List the objects/colours in the story. Are they significant?

- Write a film/dust-jacket blurb for the story.

- Continue the story six months/a year later.

- Consider asking someone who was involved in the *real* situation to write their own version; or interview them.

- Explore the area which puzzles you.

- **Ask what if? *Invent your own!***

> Write the next piece. The best things in life *are* free.

Still not satisfied she'd understood Sister's deep embitterment, Bev's group encouraged Bev to get inside her mind better. She concentrated on Sister's past:

Bev's final story about Sister

I had to write the first chapter: I don't want people to get beyond the shell that I now am. And as I reflect on the hardness, rigidity and controlled automaton that I have become I am upset and scared, scared to remember what used to be – I was in another life and country then and I don't know if I can bear to remember . . . to feel again.

Once upon a time there was a bubbly, friendly 5-year-old called Mary Ellen Rose. I was brought up in the country and loved animals, ponies, rabbits, badgers and foxes and knew where to find all of them.

I was one of two children, Robert was younger than me by two years and I idolised him. He was a blond, blue-eyed cherub, into mischief and dragging me with him.

My father was a clothier and worked long and hard hours. My mother was one of those delightful, warm, cuddly people who give a lot to others – we were a small family in a close-knit community – a happy and exuberant family, not at all remote as happens in some families.

I had many friends and we were a large and boisterous group who loved to go dancing, hiking and cycling together. I also had a special friend called Joe, who became my sweetheart and life-time partner. He was tall, dark haired, rather serious and intense and we had long involved conversations about the meaning of life – the sort that you have at that age. He was my best friend and eventually my lover.

I don't know when I decided that nursing was for me. It was hard work in those years, but I always wanted to care for anyone who was sick, so I went and started at the local cottage hospital – so young and naive and green, but so proud of my uniform.

And then the war came and so many of my childhood friends went marching off, including Joe and Robert.

I haven't let myself dwell on the last time I saw them both, especially the last time I was with Joe – too bitter-sweet and it hurts, I hurt even after all these years. I hurt more and more after the news came that they had both died together in the same battle – I felt old and cold and grey, a bone-deep coldness that I couldn't shake off – the same coldness I felt when I had the miscarriage which was hushed up and never spoken of . . . I had almost forgotten . . .

Life had to go on; I buried myself in my work; everyone around me was suffering losses; there was no time for grief – self-indulgent nonsense. No nurse could be selfish: too much to do, so many broken bodies and souls – no, don't think, just concentrate on this job in hand, survive.

And so I lost my ability to be, to fully live my life, to allow myself to feel – too painful to feel.

I never again met anyone I fell in love with, or anyone I have been close to. I have just buried myself in my work.

Bev Hargreaves

A reflective writing course evaluation

It was a new experience for me to be able to share experiences in the written form in a trusting and stimulating place. I was surprised how easy it was to write about previous experiences, and, once the setting was right, how the ideas flowed. Over the months we laughed, cried and discussed our work together and I found I gained confidence both in my ability to write but also the value of it. Somehow writing it down enabled me to get to the essence of past experiences and events in a way that discussion alone cannot. From the beginning Gillie encouraged us to write whatever came into our heads; this felt very different from the prescriptive writing I had been doing as part of my Masters.

I discovered I wrote about the more profound and painful experiences and sometimes wondered if I wanted to share them; however, whenever I did it was very valuable.

Shirley

Brief warm-up writing exercises for reflective practice work

These can take very different lengths of time. Some are challenging, some very affirming and group forming. The *how to start writing* preliminaries above are vital, such as: this is unconsidered, off-the-top-of-the-head writing; it is private, belongs to the writer, and need go no further than this group. Each writer reading silently back to themselves before reading to group or partner is vital. They also need to be told at the start that they will be invited to read out to the whole group or their small group, but that they can choose not to read out if it feels inappropriate. Many of the following exercises will occasion quite a bit of laughter. Some might bring tears, especially if given longer. Both are fine.

These exercises are best done with the facilitator giving instructions in order as participants finish each section. I suggest participants complete each section before being given the next. It is most useful if they do not know or want to question why they are doing each element. People are usually keen to 'play the game' if they trust the facilitator.

Names

1 Write anything about your name: memories, impressions, likes, hates, what people have said, your nicknames over the years – anything.

2 Write a selection of names you might have preferred to your own.

3 Write a letter to yourself from one of these chosen names (optional).

4 Read back to yourself with care. Read to whole group.

Truths, lies and fantasies

1 Write one truth about yourself, one wish, and one outright lie.

2 Read back to yourself; read to whole group.

3 Choose and write down something from someone else's list you might like to borrow for your own wish or lie list. This does not have to be shared with the rest of the group (optional).

Clothes

1 Describe a favourite set of work clothes in detail, including any features such as mends.

2 Describe the buying of these clothes briefly.

3 Describe one occasion when you have worn them.

4 How do these clothes make you feel?

5 Describe your least favourite work clothing. When do you wear them and why? Why do you dislike them?

6 Read back to yourself with care. Read to your small group. Comment on each other's helpfully.

Observation 1

1 Write about entering your office or place of work first thing.

2 Focus your mind on what you observe as you arrive. Note everything, remembering you have five senses.

3 Reread to yourself.

4 Mark five things which strike you most: do not ask why these.

5 Redraft this into a short, tight piece focusing upon the five chosen images (optional).

6 Describe what is yours in this environment, and what is institutional or belonging to someone else (e.g. previous occupier) (optional).

7 What would you like to change about (a) things in this space, (b) the way you use or respond to this space?

8 Discuss with the group. What has this exercise led you to think about your place of work, or your way of arriving there? Has hearing their writing affected your thinking about your work environment or you in it?

Observation 2

1 Write about entering the workroom or place of a colleague you admire.

2 Note what you observe as you arrive: remember you have five senses.

3 Reread to yourself.

4 Mark the five things which strike you most: do not ask why these.

5 Redraft this into a short, tight piece focusing upon the five chosen images.

6 Compare this with your observations of your own work space. What does this make you think and feel?

Observation 3

1 Describe a patient/client/colleague that you know well. They will never see this, so you can write anything: 10 minutes writing. (If you are working with a group of colleagues choose someone they do not know.)

2 Write phrases in response to this list, describing these characteristics:
   - gesture or movement
   - way of walking or sitting
   - turn of phrase, or saying
   - habitual mode of greeting
   - the quality of their speaking voice
   - something about their clothes
   - a colour (might not be one they wear)
   - a sense of touch – quality of handshake, for example
   - any smell associated with this person
   - any sounds other than voice (e.g. keys jangling)
   - any taste (perhaps you always have coffee with them)
   - anything or anyone they remind you of
   - what do they make you feel
   - and so on . . .
   - if they were an animal what animal would they be? (phrase)
   - if they were a piece of furniture what would they be?
   - If they were a season or weather what would they be?
   - a food?
   - a drink?

- a flower?
- a form of transport?
- and so on . . .

3 Write as if by this person: a poem, story, letter to someone other than you (e.g. to their child, mother, or the local newspaper), shopping list, things-to-do list . . . (optional).

4 Read back to yourself with care. Read to your small group. Comment on each other's helpfully.

Metaphors

1 Respond to each of these, creating a list of phrases:
   - if my work were an animal what animal would it be?
   - if my work were a piece of furniture what would it be?
   - if it were a season or weather what would it be?
   - a food?
   - a drink?
   - a flower?
   - a form of transport?
   - and so on . . .

2 Use the items of the list to create a description of a place, or a very short story or account. If a cat and a cup of cocoa figured as the first and fourth items in your list, your account or description might have a cat lapping from your cup of cocoa while your back is turned (optional).

3 Read back to yourself with care. Read to your small group. Comment on each other's helpfully.

From another point of view

1 Write a five-minute piece from the point of view of one of:
   - your work coffee mug
   - your work chair
   - your work mirror
   - or similar . . .

2 Read back to yourself with care. Read to your small group. Comment on each other's quickly and helpfully.

Milestones

1 List the milestones of your life and/or career – VERY QUICKLY.

2 Read back: delete or add, clarify or expand as you wish.

3 Delete all the obvious things; try to add some not very obvious things (e.g. the occasion you first really squared up to your HoD).

4 Read back to yourself with care. Read to your small group. Comment on each other's helpfully.

Key relationships and spiders

1 Put a relationship word relating to one particular person in the middle of the page in a box: e.g. boss, colleague, client, secretary.

2 Write words or phrases which arise in relation to this person anywhere on the page; allow them to cluster

3 Read back your spider to yourself, adding, deleting or filling out as you wish; list the words/phrases, or join them up into a piece of prose (it doesn't have to make perfect sense).

4 Note down any thoughts arising about this person or any other as a result of this.

5 Read back to yourself with care. Read to your small group. Comment on each other's helpfully.

Lists

1 List twenty (fifty or a hundred, depending on time) things (phrases) which make you (facilitator to choose from list):
  ● focused and productive
  ● furious
  ● happy
  ● serene
  ● lazy and unproductive
  ● unco-operative
  ● etc.

2 Reread and order this list with most important at the top

3 Read back to yourself with care. Read to your small group. Comment on each other's helpfully.

Memories

1 Write a line for each of these:
  ● something you saw which struck you yesterday
  ● a memory of a smell from a very long time ago
  ● a sound from yesterday, last week or month or year
  ● a taste for tomorrow
  ● a touch in the future, or a feeling about the future

2 Read them out to the whole group with no comment. If the group is very large, each person to read only one of their phrases. This can feel like a group poem.

Proverbs or clichés

1 Write a list of proverbs which occur to you, e.g. 'a stitch in time saves nine', 'locking the stable door after the horse has bolted', 'moving the goalposts'.

2 Take each in turn and write what you feel about this – whether it is useful or negative, helpful or infuriating when said to you.

3 If possible write by each one whom you associate it with (e.g. my mother always said that!).

4 Can you invent a useful one (optional)?

5 Read back to yourself and share with the group.

Binary pairs

1 List as many binary pairs as you can (e.g. needle and thread, horse and cart, Adam and Eve, knife and fork).

2 Picture yourself and one other work person: client, colleague, whoever.

3 Write who is which from your pairs (e.g. I am the needle and my client the thread); note which ones seem not obvious to assign.

4 Choose five of these. Write them a bit more elaborately (e.g. I am a big fat shiny darning needle; she is a long length of dark grey wool darning a huge hole in the heel of this old sock).

5 Read back to yourself with care. Read to your small group. Comment on each other's helpfully.

11

THE LEARNING JOURNAL

The periods when I undertake this [writing] activity can be unsettling just as much as they can be therapeutic. They are vehicles for me to test out the very basis of my assumptions and re-evaluate significant portions of both personal and professional life.

Sonya

Try to love the *questions themselves* like locked rooms and like books that are written in a very foreign tongue. Do not now seek the answers, which cannot be given to you. *Live* the questions now.

Rilke [1934] 1993, p. 35

A learning journal is a particularly personal and unstructured form of reflective writing. An organic exploration to support reflection rather than a product, all the writing suggestions in this book are appropriate, depending on writers' needs, wants, and situation. The secrets of effectiveness are: write for yourself; use the methods in Chapter 10; and write about episodes of experience, including:

- what **you and others did** on any particular occasion;

- what **you thought**; what **others might have thought**;

- what **you felt**; what **others might have felt**;

and take into consideration the power of the simple pronoun 'I'. Reflective authors are not like Victorian children: best seen (in the credits), but not heard (in the text) (Charmaz and Mitchell 1997). 'Writing a journal calls on students – and [educators] – to relearn a lost language. We are trained to favour academic over expressive language, which includes the use and valuing of the first person singular. Ironically, it seems that the very requirement to write in the first person singular may be an important reason why journals contribute to improved learning' (Moon 1999b, p. 34). Oddly, Moon herself does not write as 'I' (2004).

I like this idea of writing. I wrote poems in my youth, like we all. Then, writing for what? But now it feels comfortable, like a silent friend, there unquestioning, uncritical.

Rita

This chapter covers what and how, exemplified from practitioners and lecturers; discussions of assessment are in Chapter 4, more examples in Chapter 5.

Logs, diaries, journals

These words seem to be used interchangeably in professional development. It is useful to distinguish between them, as each one has its uses (see Holly 1989).

Logs straightforwardly record events, calculations or readings, like ship's logs. Their usefulness is as an aide-mémoire. Anorexics have been required to keep logs of their food intake and symptoms.

Diaries, at the other extreme, can contain anything, be confidantes like Anne Frank's (1947) or Virginia Woolf's (1977, 1978, 1980). One of the oldest forms of literature in the West (Simons 1990; Blodgett 1991), diaries were traditionally kept by women who, being more confined, needed confidential interlocutors. Early novels were in diary form (e.g. Burney 1898), I think because of the illusion of illicit reading since a diary is generally written for the self alone.

Diaries can be confessor, confidante or special friend (Anne Frank called hers Kitty) for a writer trapped in a tiny social circle, or a place of creation such as a writer's (e.g. Virginia Woolf's). These diaries contain stories of happenings, hopes and fears, memories, thoughts, ideas, and all attendant feelings. They also contain creative material: drafts of poems, stories, plays or dialogues, doodles and sketches. Thorough information on how to keep an effective diary is covered in Bolton (1999a) and Rainer (1978).

Journals are records of events, thoughts and feelings about a particular aspect of life, or with a particular structure. A journal can record anything, and in any way, relative to the issue to which it pertains. So a reflective practice journal is like a diary of practice but in addition includes: 'deliberative thought and analysis related to practice' (Holly 1988, p. 78).

A form of personal development journal uses structured series of sections, such as: *relationships, work, dreams, here and now, the more distant past* (Progoff 1987). Like professional journals, Progoff's contains deliberate thought and analysis, intimate explorations of events and feelings, and attendant feelings. Many find it useful, some too structured. A left-hand column journal (Megginson and Whitaker 2003; Argyris 1991) records events in two columns, the right focuses on the event, the left on what did not happen: suppressed thoughts, feelings or impulses to action.

Qualitative research journals record researchers' findings, and thoughts and feelings about those findings, quotes of exactly what people have said, quantitative data such as tables and figures, and descriptions of focus groups or interviews. The writing might be publicly shareable data, or personal and private (Etherington 2004). Politicians' journals record their years in office. Travel journals were particularly popular in Victorian times; travel writing still uses this intimate personal form.

These documents (some virtual, others painted), might be intended to be read by a wider audience, unlike a diary, but more like a log. Politicians, and some artists intend publication, but many are written for a very small audience: research journals and teachers' or nurses' reflective journals. Practitioners keep reflective journals primarily for their own learning, but also to share parts with their supervisor, or portfolio group, reflective practice group, staff development group, or Masters cohort.

I now feel quite sad about this journal and the ending of the group. This journal represents for me the space which this course has given me for my 'whole' life so far. It has given me intellectual space and opportunity – physical space from work and social group – spiritual space . . . also psychological space to rethink my responses, reactions, motivations, expectations and hopes (this passage cut from journal, for personal reasons). I'm more able to take risks and I have thought of things I'd like to do which I've previously not thought as possibilities in the past . . .

Elaine, Masters student

The writing has been a real eye-opener for me. I was sceptical at first, partly because the *reflective journal* has almost become a cliché in nursing education, but also because I was anxious about others reading my gibberish . . .

I will continue to write a log because Gillie was right. Things come out differently when written down. Feelings and thoughts can creep up and surprise you in writing. I will always be grateful to this course for giving me the space to discover this. And when you discover something for yourself you use it!

Ann, Masters student

A letter to my patients

I am listening, really I am.

I have to be honest, though – sometimes it's hard to pay attention. If my focus seems to shift away from you to the clock, or the door, or the computer, please don't think it's because I don't care.

Let me tell you something, my friend. I've got problems, too. Sometimes my problems are bigger than yours and I'm hanging on by my fingernails. But I'm the one with the desk and the prescription pad.

And what am I doing while you struggle to explain yourself to me? I'm holding myself together, is what I'm doing. I might distractedly put my hand up to my face while your words hover between us. Just checking I'm in one piece.

I'm not painting my toenails, that's for sure.

I'm not snuggled up under my duvet, drifting off to sleep.

I'm not licking a rapidly melting chocolate ice cream cone.

I'm sitting here, listening to you.

So make the most of me.

Becky Ship

Becky (family doctor, GP) explained that when 'I distractedly put my hand up to my face' it was to ensure her *work mask* was uncracked and in place, to protect her vulnerable private face.

The learning journal: an introduction

Writing things down in itself sharpens perspectives, breaks things down into clearer 'elements' and brings up further questions which facilitate learning.

Liz

Learning journals are cornerstones of reflective practice, collections of expressions of thinking and explorations, charting personal reflective critical backgrounds to experiences and understandings, like a map. Types of writing can be experimented with: dialogues, metaphor exploration (Etherington 2004), visualisation, fiction, etc. Private and confidential, elements can be extracted and discussed with peers, mentors, supervisors, or included in portfolios. Privacy can enable free expression, the telling of secrets. As one practitioner said: 'writing things down without worrying what other people think is the most powerful thing about this kind of writing'. And, 'I must say I like this idea of keeping track of your thoughts.' A dynamically rewarding process (Benner 1984; Beveridge 1997; Bolton 1991, 1994, 1995, 1999a; Boud et al. 1985; Morrison 1996; Schon 1983) reflective journal writing is an interactive process requiring commitment and energy:

By keeping a personal-professional journal you are both the learner and the one who teaches. You can chronicle events as they happen, have a dialogue with facts and interpretations, and learn from experience. A journal can be used for analysis and introspection. Reviewed over time it becomes a dialogue with yourself. Patterns and relationships emerge. Distance makes new perspective possible: deeper levels of insight can form.

Holly 1989, p. 14

Reflective learning journal writers:

- take responsibility for discovering personal learning needs, and attempt to ensure they are met;

- learn by examining vulnerable areas, the cutting edge;

- question, explore, analyse personal experience: actions, thoughts, feelings, and what peers feel, think and do.

Shepherd (2004) developed an effective intensive learning journalling process for his Ph.D. research as a management adviser, commenting that it had to be enjoyable to work well. Glaze (2002) reports how a reflective Ph.D. journal deepened, enriched and enhanced research, making it more relevant and applicable. Directors of clinical psychology training courses in Britain's south-west report their use of journals (Stedmon et al. 2003): in one the content remains private but is used as a basis of a third-year reflective essay; another uses it in the appraisal process; the third involved it in reflective tutorials. Bonnie Meath Lang tells of her deaf students' journals, shared with peers and teacher, helping them know each other better and communicate more effectively (Meath Lang 1996).

> It was only through reading *Writing Cures* (Bolton et al. 2004) that I discovered that what I had been doing for years as a personal resource was called 'Reflective Practice'. I simply have a large loose-leaf notebook, and take five minutes – or an hour – to write down what's on my mind: anxieties, dreams, experiences, bits from books, puzzling psychotherapy sessions, relationships, ideas . . . you name it.
>
> The main benefit is that I stop obsessing or ruminating about them, because I begin to disidentify with what's bugging me – get it out of my head and down onto the page; and then I can begin to understand. The second is that I find I may have written one really interesting phrase. The third is that I glimpse I may have an idea for a paper . . .
>
> If I'm too upset, it doesn't work, or I just can't bring myself to write.
>
> Nathan Field

Types of writing

Writers normally constrain themselves to types of writing appropriate to specific tasks: letters (business or personal), short story, journalism, shopping list, academic or professional article, report. A journal can contain anything, in any order, for no reason other than that the writing comes out that way. A journal, for example, might contain free-flow *six minute* writing, stories, poems, musings or reflections on what, why, how, when, who, why, dialogues with the self, fictional dialogues or monologues with others such as patients, clients or students, analysis of motives and actions, philosophising on such as ethics, evaluation, assessment of practice, description, fantasy used to aid insight, cathartic writing, letters, extended metaphors, ethnography, sketches, cartoons, descriptions of dance, diagrams. Experiment!

The thing

A journal is an object, a possession. I recommend appropriate and pleasurable investment. A loose-leaf folder, mine can hold all shape's and sizes: A4 sheets of my handwritten or typed writing, letters, newspaper cuttings, journal papers, pictures, and all sorts. And I like to write with a 2B pencil with a rubber on the end: I never rub it out, but I might; a soft pencil whispers to the page. Some people prefer to buy a nice book. One nursing group had between them: a suede covered book, one decorated with bright children's pictures, one plain but a glorious red, another a shocking pink folder and pen.

Typing is likely to produce a different kind of reflection from handwriting, looking more organised and deliberate, inviting analytic revision. A pen feels more permanent than a pencil; a fountain pen feels more professional and sophisticated than a biro. Coloured pens and paper for particular emotions and feelings can take writing in interesting directions, as can different sizes of paper: A1 for anger, the back of an envelope for when confidence is low.

Experiment!

Subjects

- The relative status and roles of
  - tutor and student
  - physician and patient
  - nurse and doctor
  - social worker/therapist and client.

- The effect of this sense of hierarchy on work/self.

- The balance of responsibility between peers.

- The influence of informal contacts between
  - peers
  - non-peers.

- Personal/professional gains from supervision/courses/groups.

- Personal objectives and how these have been achieved.

- Taking responsibility; the role of shame and guilt.

- The match between
  - expectations/hopes and reality
  - clients/patients and you
  - students/staff and you.

- The effect of the forces of anger, compassion, denial, etc.

- Discussion/conflict – has it been useful/destructive?

- The difference between a goal-directed project and a process-focused one.

- The value of uncertainty in a world where science knows the answers; are there even a few right questions?

- Changes and developments in professional practice.

These reflections might make us more accountable to

- ourselves;

- students/patients/clients;

- society and superiors;

by developing greater:

- self evaluation/knowledge;
- flexibility (more able to perceive the other point of view);
- critical awareness of dilemmas rather than being overwhelmed;
- willingness to collaborate and learn from colleagues.

Why a learning journal?

New experiences happen all the time (events, memories, inspiration, learning, practice, research . . .), affecting us in myriad ways. Muddly periods of accommodation, particularly starting a new, big thing, are a positive developing process. A flexible tool in the process of learning, a learning journal helps in the grasping or filling out of vital issues which might otherwise become lost, and charts the development of personal learning. Parts of it may be shared with tutor or colleagues, but it must primarily be *for the writer*. It:

- helps clarify thinking;
- allows you to express feelings about yourself/peers/tutors/course content/your writing/others' writing;
- helps identify misunderstandings/non-understandings;
- can help you identify needs;
- can inform dialogues between you and your tutor/peers;
- allows you to perceive links between knowledge/experience – past/present.

How?

A learning journal could include reflective running notes on:

- experiences with colleagues, clients or students;
- personal experiences which impinge on work or course;
- group sessions;
- interactions with peers/tutors;
- any other learning/teaching situations past or current;
- things you did/would not *say*, but did *think* – for whatever reason;
- feelings about your writings;

- comments on readings;
- any increase in your knowledge;
- increase in your ability to articulate and identify issues;
- the expansion of your depth of vision and understanding;
- changes in beliefs, theories, attitudes, relationships or practices;
- anything else you want to get off your chest.

These notes might include:

- fears, hopes, anxiety, expectations, values, beliefs;
- useful ideas or methods to try out or consider irrelevant or impractical;
- development of arguments or opinions not fully developed or expressed;
- explorations of changes of opinion;
- details of what you found difficult to understand or do.

Useful tips

- This is for *you*: not to be shared at first.
- Discover what you think by writing free flow (see pp. 145–7) for part of the time.
- Experiment with writing: exploratory, descriptive, judgemental, story, poetry, anecdote, reflective musing, vignettes or portraits, lists, interview yourself.
- Date entries: you won't remember.
- Make entries soon after significant events: you'll forget.
- Fill out notes taken during teaching/learning sessions.
- Explore by playing devil's advocate: arguing the opposite of what you think.

When?

Any or every time; when you want. The most creative times might be when your cognitive powers are at lowest ebb: midnight or 4 a.m.

'Aren't you going to bed *yet* Mum? Are you *still* working?'
'No, I'm not working. I'm just writing.'

Write about an event at the right time for you. Left too late, events lose impact and interest: attempted too soon they may be too raw:

If the experience is very close, I feel inhibited . . . If the closeness of the real reality, of the living reality, is to have a persuasive effect on my imagination, I need a distance, a distance in time and space.

Llosa 1991, p. 44

For whom?

For you, primarily; for your colleagues; some of it possibly for tutors or supervisor, or for assessment.

With whom?

Co-mentoring, paired support with a colleague each reading the other's material and supportively commenting, can be extremely useful, as can belonging to a group. Or your journal may inform work with supervisor or mentor.

Where?

Anywhere: in a café, in bed – perhaps difficult on a bike.

This, from an academic counselling department head, was written in a café:

A student tells me she is experiencing severe insomnia, and I feel helpless, feeling only inner compassion. A colleague, in the canteen, looking ashen, laments his own bureaucratic burden and his impotence about finding any end to it. Again, I can only feel for him, sit in silent solidarity. Sometimes, with a client, while listening to a complex narrative of inescapable suffering, I will become aware of some stillness, in me, between us, a sensed original sanity.

Is this what is meant by a wounded healer? Wounded, yes. Healer, I'm not so sure. We seem to have created and live in such a wounding, adversity-generating culture, that healing – wholemaking – often seems a forlorn hope, empty slogan, uphill struggle, aspiration rather than reality. Perhaps healing, counselling at its best, is only found in timeless moments. The sacred fifty-minute hour, oasis in today's wilderness, symbolises – and occasionally is – such a moment.

If counselling isn't the place for lachrymal freedom, where is? If counsellors become tame, professionalised, 'audit-minded' rule-keepers, how can they free? If I can't overturn my adversity, de-oppress myself, practise what I teach, and practise what I feel, who can?

Colin Feltham 2004

Learning about journals with students

Stephen Trotter uses learning journals with prospective and veteran teachers, and to examine his own professional actions. His use of journals developed considerably as he understood reflective processes better, and perceived journalling's potential:

Engaging in reflective practice requires individuals to assume the perspective of an external observer in order to identify the assumptions and feelings underlying their behaviour and then to speculate about how these assumptions and feelings affect practice . . . However, I have found this process may be hampered by 'Fundamental Attribution Error' whereby the student places too much responsibility for causality on external factors rather than personal volition . . .

Examining 'personal volition', however, and the attendant feelings and experiences, seemed to me as a behavioural psychologist initially not only foreign, but fraught with miscues. However, I now consider the miscues an essential process in the construction of a *Teaching Schema*. I initially chose to have my students report in a *Dragnet* style of *Just the Facts* [but] I came to realise this emphasis on objectivity and emotional distance was counter-productive to my instructional goals.

I slowly found myself more interested in the Journals of students who had violated the rules and strayed into the subjective meadow. The entries were both enlightening and in many instances poignant. I began to see the Journal entries as a mirror of a student's ever-increasing awareness of the act of teaching . . .

The examination of one's teaching behaviour may [however] be so painful as to serve as a disincentive and foster a defence mechanism of denial. Therefore in the teaching of the reflective process I find it helpful to try and increase the focus on positive behaviours and the identification of replacement behaviours . . .

I have [also] found that without prior training, entry content is likely to be observational and reactionary rather than reflective.

Trotter 1999

Claire Whewell's students are post-experience Masters and undergraduates in teacher education:

We are committed to developing collaborative learning communities that feel, look and sound safe. We team-teach where possible, and work with small cohorts (up to 20), split into 'home groups'. These meet for single days, interspersed with guided self-study of reading, writing and gathering evidence from their classrooms to develop personal explorations. Space and time is allocated in small groups to the development of ideas through essential professional dialogue and storytelling. Processes of professional dialogue, discussions and exploration, often leading to a meeting of differences, provide a broader grounding for personal exploration.

Initially group time is taken to build a quality learning community, in which concerns and beliefs and issues such as confidentiality are shared. A final 'home group' collaborative task is to present to the whole group.

We provide students with a 'learning journal' (Moon 1999a) from the start: essentially a non-assessed private space. Many students do not initially warm to this form of free writing, so we provide appropriate focused questions, often connecting reading with explorations of their professional practice. Sometimes students are requested to share their writing with their 'home group'. If writing is not comfortable, other forms of expression such as images, poetry, mind maps are used. The secret of success is to ensure a revisiting of entries over time. Some students use a double-entry system, others prefer to use different colour pens – the possibilities are endless.

Students, in pairs or triads, use Tripp's critical incident analysis for unpacking shared narrative extracts from learning journals, using structured questioning (Tripp 1995a, p. 27). Developing the skills of critical analysis allows issue explorations, such as relationships and power, with staff and pupils. This can lead to a consideration of implicit, messy and often unexpected attitudes and values.

The best student final assignments often use vignettes from learning journals, unpacked using critical incident analysis. This allows a richness and depth to their self-assessment against the Standard for Chartered Teacher (2002), and provides a useful and clear platform from which to take their next steps.

Claire Whewell

Journal use, in glorious variety

Journals are used in many different ways in professional and higher education. Rita Charon's medical students are each given a new blank book, and fruitfully share extracts with her and each other in seminars (2000b). Kember et al. (1996) undertook a qualitative and quantitative examination of how effective reflective journal keeping enables more fruitful tutorials and seminars for education students. Moon offers a thorough analysis of journalling with education students (Moon 1999a). A deeply enquiring, theoretically and methodologically thorough study indicates how to set up reflective diaries (including critical incidents) in nurse training (Paterson 1995). Glen et al.'s (1995) analysis in nursing is equally useful. Love (1996) describes a fruitful study of student nurses and patients keeping and comparing parallel diaries. GPs (family practitioners) kept diaries of their emotional response to situations in order to reflect upon them, in a study by John Howard (1997).

An in-depth study of pre-service (student) teachers' journals concludes that they 'provide occasions for students to find their own voices to explain, describe, challenge, or question their experiences in the field' (McMahon 1997, p. 211). Taleb Durgahee reports wonderful work using journals and reflective groups to foster awareness and understanding of ethical issues with palliative nursing students (1997): 'because I had to write my diary, I was much more aware of the issues before making decisions', 'being aware of my beliefs, actions and my practice are crucial in ethical decision-making, I have learned to reason and think clearly'. Taleb comments: 'the students are helped to realise that there is no magic formula for ethical decision-making. Instead, the process of writing in the diary followed by group discourse enables the analysis of relevant and important factors to be considered in morally challenging decisions' (Durgahee 1997, pp. 140–1).

Best stresses the value of a journal 'as a process of integration' for *containment*, and *therapeutic space*: a safe place to put experiences and emotions, however bad. These can then be reviewed more safely at a later date: the material will have remained the same on the page in the interval, but the writer will have moved on and be able to reassess the situation, their feelings and thoughts. She also calls it a *play space*: 'space to explore and confirm' (Best 1996, p. 298).

Mathematics undergraduates' use of reflective journals has been reported by Beveridge. 'Students are expected to write 1–2 sides per week on selected topics of interest', and develop 'their ability to think deeply about their own needs' (1997, p. 35). Students hand in a version of their journal for assessment. Interestingly about half the entries concerned 'controlling their learning environment' (p. 38). Beveridge reports: 'The need to work at their own pace on individual skills was presented so forcefully through the journals that I reworked the second year module to include a significant amount of individually learned material.' Lecturers learn and change, as well as students. He concludes: 'those students who are better able to notice and feel their successes learn more' (p. 42).

In a reflective journal project in business management, a company's employees kept journals called *thinkbooks*: 'participants were asked to record significant events, make observations on their performance, analyse their actions, draw conclusions, note learning points, and make suggestions for further action' (Rigano and Edwards,1998, p. 436). Realising the journal's impact after three months, Vincent's daily entries changed from 'organising daily routine . . . to a process of reflection leading to growth' (journal entry, p. 440). Vincent carefully structured this process himself, using readings and other texts on effective behaviour such as de Bono. The researchers concluded Vincent's success stemmed from *owning* the process. Realising he needed to share his reflections to develop further, Vincent's company offered facilitated reflective writing in work time.

Angela Mohtashemi, a management consultancy coach:

I have recently been coaching a new consultant, a recent and very bright graduate, who was working on a complex and difficult business change project. He was often overwhelmed with the challenges of becoming a consultant, the change between work and studying and staying away from home at the client site as well as understanding the company he was working for and the complexity of organisational politics. The journal I encouraged him to keep became a survival mechanism for him and a rich source of learning. The following extract, which is a free word association, gives a strong sense of how his perception of the culture of the company merges with his own state of mind. Here is an extract from his journal:

NewCo pointless old tired stale dark cold unfriendly confusion anxious bleak stagnant slow protracted conflict going round in circles repeat same old parochial trivial dread going through the motions denial escape fight withdraw individual shell distance myself scared bitten stress pedantic process machine automation indecisive conflict avoidance stupid panic macho picking holes unhelpful barrier don't care apathy ridiculous small-minded prejudiced siloed blinkered unappreciative arrogant waste of space obstruction denial deaf clueless machine hierarchical fragment disintegrate plural infighting political playing games Machiavellian agenda effort failure antagonism conflict embarrassment hide away secretive behind closed doors inefficient paper-pushing overly complex dispersed resentful bitter stuck repeat

Angela Mohtashemi

Reflective journals read by tutors can have a particular use in cross-cultural student nursing communication, in increasing facility with the language, and in fostering critical thinking (Hancock 1998). They are also useful for maintaining 'a student-driven view of coherence to taught modular higher degrees', given the fragmentation, loss of continuity, and problematic choice of modules occasioned by modularisation (Morrison 1996, p. 322).

Morrison introduced education higher degree students to in-depth reflective journal writing throughout their period of registration. They undertook an assignment drawing upon journal data and reflections, and discussed contents with their tutor. Evaluation proved 'increased skill in articulating and crystallising issues and arguments'; 'increased confidence and ability to interrogate and critique issues'; and 'growing self-awareness'. They appreciated the opportunity for 'self-analysis as a basis for planning for self-development'; 'enhanced enjoyment and satisfaction in the course'; and the 'openness to self . . . as an opportunity to recharge themselves'. They even reported 'they were initially prisoners of their own expectations and perceptions and how the process of reflection has been an enabling and liberating experience – freedom *for* self-realisation' (Morrison 1996, pp. 323–4).

Fins et al. (2003) introduced palliative medicine students to a reflective practice process of immersion in the context of care as 'participant observers', with no clinical responsibilities. Observing and reflecting on psychosocial and ethical issues and patient-centred advocacy in 'highly empathic and emotional' (p. 308) journals, students share these unique perspectives with peers. This course counteracts the informal medical curriculum of detachment, and Shem (2002) would say – inhumanity.

Masters in Higher Education students

> were encouraged to keep a research diary of observations and interpretations they have made of an aspect of their teaching; accounts of their thinking in response to the discussions of the group; critical responses to

any of the literature encountered; evaluative comments about the course itself; and so on. They were private documents to which no one else, including the tutors, had any rights of access. The material from them might be used in informal seminars on the course; it might be used as a basis for later publications; or to identify issues which require further exploration with other participants or the course tutors. The research diaries would also be a major source of material for compiling a portfolio of work relating to each module . . .

We were concerned that these portfolios should be seen as working documents, as tools for thinking through ideas about practice, rather than as final products . . . What seemed to be of immediate importance was that participants should see their own regular writing to be a fundamental part of the enquiry process.

Writing in such a way as to explore the professional values which underlie practice is not easy. Such values are always difficult to express. Their articulation needs to be retraced as they become questioned and new experience is brought to bear on them. Thus we would expect the participants to refine those ideas in one portfolio which may initially have been raised in an earlier one. They would pursue themes of enquiry across consecutive portfolios.

Rowland and Barton 1994, p. 371

Facilitation of journals

Journals need to be carefully introduced and facilitated: 'The act of writing alone does not move pre-service (student) teachers beyond a preoccupation with themselves toward a broader conceptualisation of critical enquiry into the practice of teaching and their roles as educators' (Hoover 1994, p. 92). Hoover's teachers wrote about day-to-day frustrations and problems but the journals did not seem to 'encourage reflectivity, particularly thinking about teaching and learning in light of theory, contextual factors, and ethical issues' (p. 92). Kruse (1997) has also found that teachers make variable use of journals. A few can maintain deep focused reflection within their writing: 'They look for innovations and new pedagogical forms of practice with a specific purpose in mind.'

However: 'Teachers who are less focused in their reflective activity concentrate on the enduring dilemmas of classroom practice. Their reflection is cyclical in nature, never resolving the issues that plague them; thus they remain "stuck and searching for new ideas" as they struggle to maintain their professional self-esteem' (Kruse 1997, p. 56). Hoover (1994) suggests dialogue journal writing, teachers reading and commenting on each other's journals, or teacher and supervisor might overcome this problem, as trialled by Staton (1988) and Bean and Julich (1989). I would suggest carefully facilitated group work is needed as well.

Deeply reflective writing and understanding does not come readily to graduates of our schools and universities. The barriers are high (Newton 1996). There is evidence in the literature of trainers and facilitators having difficulty in facilitating journal and story writing, and therefore finding it ineffectual. Bellman gives three-quarters of a page to exposing her own inadequacy in introducing and supporting this valuable mode of reflection. She quotes her co-researchers' reasons for not writing their journals, e.g. 'embarrassing', we 'reflect anyway . . . over a drink with the girls', 'couldn't see the relevance', 'too depressing', 'you forgot to give me one', 'I find it a threat because someone could read it', 'no one else was doing it', 'I don't see the point really' (Bellman 1996, p. 136). Wellard and Bethune (1996) report similar lack of success, blaming the students, and unwittingly giving an example of how *not* to facilitate reflective journal writing.

Journals can be in danger of being used in inappropriate ways, if they are read or assessed by superiors. A practitioner can feel under pressure to *confess* or disclose professional or personal material. Julie Hughes, teaching mentor of post-compulsory education trainee teachers describes an effective provision:

Julie Hughes: 'I didn't have a voice until I joined this group'

I engaged in journal dialogue with all new teachers individually through from induction. This creation of individual and personal dialogues allowed me to monitor that the reflective journey was not simply an examination or description of personal and professional experiences. Instead my inter-text dialogue challenged assumptions and choice of content.

Dialogue offers a way for 'us' as teacher educators and researchers to view and represent ourselves as 'them', making visible to our mentees that we are 'experiencing' rather than 'experienced' practitioners. It works against the power relations that function to locate the 'other' in a dialogue as a unified speaking agent (Butler 1990).

Verbal honesty within the group was mixed in the first semester, and written journals often expanded upon issues mentioned briefly during sessions. The group were organically creating the conditions for dialogue that could be extended into a written format. It was still very early in this professional programme for some of the group to be comfortable with more in-depth self-disclosure and self-analysis, particularly in writing.

In the first semester my written dialogue: my comments, questions, thoughts, supportive statements and disclosures with individual students contained writing in the margin, in-text comments, and extended comments at the end of the journal. All dialogue was handwritten, personal and dated, sometimes with different coloured gel pens, stickers and sometimes illustrative drawings.

A sense of expectancy emerged and trust engendered, allowing an attitude or disposition to dialogue and reflection. In the second semester two students per week shared their journals with the group. They were writing for self and each other from this point: 'I do like the idea of sharing our journals with peers.'

Dialogue reflection and refraction represented multiple perspectives and perceptions, suggesting resistance to the reproduction of self as mirror image. Dialogue then allowed the participants entry to material with multiple reflective layers; for some an unsettling process as the dialogue roles were no longer formed through choice. In-text comments, as I had modelled, were very common, particularly supporting, understanding and agreeing. It was clear that all this enhanced the journal writing. Dynamic conflict and contestations were growing, as was self-awareness and the valuing of invention and interpretation.

Journal writers found they could be somebody else, reinvent self as teacher and dialoguer (having a dramatic effect upon classroom practices for some). In adopting different narrative voices and genres they were able to challenge and talk back to themselves reflectively, though some writers felt it was their role to 'entertain' their readers with comedic narrative style.

Some writers struggled with the journal's content and writing style: dialogue can be intrusive, enforcing censorship. Sensitivity is vital to encourage honest reflection and risk-taking on the part of all dialogue turn-takers. The embodied set of writers and listeners in turn re-story the narrative by offering multiple perspectives. Probing and adding information in dialogue allowed other voices to come into play, and create awareness that meanings were being made in conscious and unconscious ways. Language choices and assumptions were probed, and individual and social identities challenged.

Unpredictable horizontal reflective dialogues are potentially a subversive discourse with their exploratory and elliptical nature, and possibility for multiple contradictory and conflicting realities. Reflective practice can destabilise former certainties if travel leaves well-trodden pathways and literacy practices (Harrison 2004, p. 177). MacLure (2003) suggests we need new metaphors representing the layering of realities: of fabrication and assembly, of borders and interweaving, of deferral and becoming within the journey analogy. Dialogue journals offer a tapestry always in the process of becoming. As experimental representation (Richardson 1990) they are a transgressive and open writing genre always partial and situational, always temporal and contingent. There is no prescribed 'getting it right': in the telling and retelling they are 'getting it differently'.

Dialogue journal writing demands the blurring of boundaries and literacies. Textually and conversationally incomplete, it potentially offers a model for reflection that challenges excessive outcome-based approaches. Dialogues of participation 'as a gradual "coming to know"' (Winter 2003, p. 120) are dependent in part upon social assembly and an understanding for writing as a social and politicised practice (Clark and Ivanič 1997). Dialogue journals offer recognition of the plural and multiple text and challenge institutional norms of reflective writing.

Julie Hughes

Journal writing enables an ongoing self-dialogue with some of the otherwise quiet or silent voices within (see Rowan 1990, Bolton 1999a): knowledge, intuition, analysis, inspiration and feelings. It enables standing back, taking a long reflective look, and allowing fresh views to form: a route to *loving and living the questions themselves* (Rilke 1934):

> Writing taps tacit knowledge; it brings into awareness that which we sensed but could not explain.
>
> Holly 1989, p. 78

> This writing process is really helpful. It enabled me to find a synthesis of all those things going round and round in my head.
>
> A group member

12

WRITING IN GENRE

Life never does more than imitate the book, and the book itself is only a tissue of signs, an imitation that is lost, infinitely deferred.

Barthes 1977, p. 147

Man is an animal suspended in webs of significance he himself has spun.

Geertz [1973] 1993, p. 5

We have many selves and many potential voices, one clamouring for expression as fantasy, another wanting nurturing towards haiku. Fairy story, romantic fiction, detective, fantasy, fable, and so on are particularly valuable as they offer clear formulaic rules, and archetypal characters, place and situation. The writer is set free from the trap of attempting to depict realistic characters, chronology, events, and environments, AND from the creative bother of inventing people, plot, place. 'Writing "works" because it enables us to come to know ourselves through the multiple voices our experience takes, to describe our contexts and histories as they shape the many minds and selves who define us and others' (Holly 1989, p. 15). Mercedes Kemp asked students to write in genre, to '*create* self through textuality and language's inherent undecidabilities, as in the writings of Hélène Cixous' (2001, p. 353). This chapter looks at different prose genres and their use, and examples of practitioners' poetry (both formal and free verse).

Story

Things come out because the story lets them out.

A reflective practice writer

Everything has a ripple effect in a book; in the years of introspection, I grow. For me, it's like meditation or prayer.

Allende 2000, p. 6

Unlike poetry, in which from the first word to the last you are placed in a world of extraordinary sensibility and delicacy or dynamism, a novel or a short story is a text in which it is impossible to be intense and creative all the time and to sustain vitality and dynamism in the language. When you tell a story, the moments of intensity must be supported by episodes that are purely informative, that give the reader essential information for understanding what is going on . . . [It] is not possible in a novel, as in a poem, to use only intense, rich language.

Llosa 1991, p. 95

There are stories and stories: whodunnit, social realism, sci-fi, thriller, comedy, aga-saga . . . I can only represent a few in this book. A writer's chosen genre gives a specific slant: adding an extra dimension to reflective writing work. Everyone views the world and their life in genre: comic, epic, soap, satire . . . Think of a colleague: when they tell stories of their life, are they the hero(ine) of a romance, moral tale or tragedy? Few people realise such habitual genre can be played with; but it can, with startling effects.

People unwittingly live in genre, just as they think through metaphor. As soon as I suggest different genre to a group, several will set off instantly and unthinkingly towards *romance* or *detective* or *fairy story*: a particular genre will grab them (see the teacher's use of romantic story, Chapter 2). A nurse tried to write *doctor-nurse romance*, swapping the roles to male nurse and woman doctor. She could not make it work: the genre relies on a power structure of habitual male dominance. We all laughed, but learned a great deal about medical-nursing relations, and the way they are seen by 'the public'.

Amanda Howe: Strange Love

A good-looking patient – that's a change. And smart – so why is he living round here? New patient card – always a frisson of expectation, so easy to impress on first acquaintance by a charming manner and efficient style.

He tells me he's in a hurry – 'got to get to London on business, just needs some antimalarials' as he's off to the Far East tonight. Exotic lifestyle then – and wonderful scent, Opium for Men? His shirt is white, bit creased, touchingly ruffled. Does he smoke? No. Keep fit? Yes. Drink? A smile – eye contact – 'now and again, how about you?'

He's flirting! But I don't mind. Married? No. Lives alone? Mostly. Will he be in Sheffield long? No, 'fraid not, just passing through.

I take a chance and suggest he might like a blood pressure check 'since he's obviously a busy man and probably doesn't get much chance to look after himself'. An excuse really. I see a masculine forearm, and some rather stylish leather braces, but not much flesh. Oh well – this is feeling rather unethical anyway.

He leaves, thanking me, shaking my hand – the firm dry grip of all romantic heroes. After he's gone, I notice the name on the computer. It reads Bond, J: patient I.D. number 11 – 007.

Amanda Howe

Fantasy, folk tale, fable, myth

Now that we have no eternal truth we realise that our life is entirely made up of stories . . . truth is made of stories. So we can rehabilitate myth . . . myths are the stories people live by, the stories that shape people's perception of life.

Don Cupitt 1991

Fantasy is currently appropriate. Cultural, professional, political and familial forms all seem to be in flux, with constant imperative innovation: we constantly have to change how we do things, our colleagues, and to whom we are answerable. Increasingly work is on a movable stage. No longer can one be a GP to the same families, a village school teacher teaching children whose parents they also taught, or a midwife remembering the birth of the mother. Fantasy deals with people not knowing in what dimension they live, what kind of being they will meet, what kind of communication is appropriate. The only thing which remains constant is the values of the main characters, which, as in *Star Trek*, are usually strong and moral. Events either turn out very right or very wrong: part of our relentless attempt to create moral order in a chaotic world. Confronting elements in our everyday world by exploring fantastic ones has been called 'structured fabulation' (Gough 1998). Huxley's *Brave New World* (1932), Orwell's *1984* (1949), Shelley's *Frankenstein* (1820), and Pullman's *His Dark Materials* (1995) are examples of fantasy which both create and critique our own world.

Fairy or folk tales and fables traditionally have a similar function. Using character archetypes (like ancient Greek stories and plays), they help us to make sense of perplexing lives and fate. Just as people tend to tell their lives according to a particular genre, so they relate to particular archetypal characters. Are you, or a colleague, wily beautiful Scheherazade, Baba Yaga the witch, Anansi the tricksy spiderman, the boy who knew the king was wearing no clothes and was not afraid to say so, or perhaps 'Mudjekeewis,/ruler of the winds of heaven' (Longfellow 1960, p. 37)?

John Goodwin, higher education tutor for adult learners, uses fiction writing for reflection. His teaching team also undertakes reflective writing sessions to share professional issues. This was written in a half-hour *automatic* writing session, using folk tale to distance the writing, creating an objective voice: especially useful when staffing had become a tense matter.

John Goodwin: Pathway

She sat in a small dark room. Scared. Bored. Miserable. Alone. The woodman had left for his day's work in the forest bolting the door firmly behind him. Clunk went the bolt. Clack went the lock.

She waited for the hours to pass. Heavy long hours. Darkness began to fall in the forest. Birds made wing in the thickness. Clack went the lock. Clunk went the bolt. The door of the room was flung open wide. She peered out. No woodman.

'Hello,' she called. No voice answered.

'Anybody there?' she called again.

Still nobody answered. She got to her feet and went timidly to the door. Nothing but blackness. Her foot hesitated by the open door. Dare she step out? He had forbidden her to do so yet forward went her foot and touched pine needles on the cold earth. An owl shrieked.

Earth shrank. Pine needles vanished. There was no forest now only a clear path onward which she began to step slowly along. Cautiously. Nervously. Then there were others walking along the path each like herself stepping nervously and holding themselves back a little. At both sides of the path plans sprang up. Each was in gold writing on rolls of parchment. Each had a big red wax seal on it stamped with a crest of arms.

Then the plans began to speak. Excitedly. Enthusiastically. Happily. They sounded like her. Yet it was a strange and mysterious language. A language she'd never known in all her life. How she wanted the language to go on and on. Never stop. All the others along the path were speaking in the strange new language and now her lips moved too just like the rest.

The pathway was pulling her on. So on she moved. Quicker. Easier. All the others were moving too with the same ease and comfort. The pathway climbed skywards. It twisted and turned and the going was harder. Some fell off and were not seen again.

She had climbed long and hard and when now she looked back at the way she had come all she could see was a mirror. On the mirror was a bold and clear image of herself. Oh how she had changed. There was no way back now to the forest. The lock and bolt were broken beyond repair.

John Goodwin

Parody

Parody helps us understand (or deride) an everyday matter. Students often write such as: 'Shall I compare thee to a heap of shit . . .', parodying Shakespeare's *Shall I compare thee to a summer's day* (Sonnet 18). Like fantasy, parody often uses archetypes to which we all relate.

Susanna Gladwin: problem-solving

I did once and once only use a form of writing to help me resolve a problem: and it was amazingly effective – so rather surprising perhaps I've never used it since. It used the simple device of taking the A.A. Milne, *Winnie the Pooh* (1928) format and style, and using his characters – Tigger and Eyeore and so on – as a sort of allegory to represent the various people and their relationships as I saw them in my own psychodrama. The extraordinary thing was, I started writing it in the vein of spleen and hurt and anger, a means of venting my spite against those who had hurt me. But as I went on, I found the very act of writing (and I suppose using that particular model) induced a feeling of generosity in me which spilled over not only in the little story (now lost!) but into the real-life relationships as well.

This actually did have a permanent effect on my working life, because it awoke me to an effect of creative writing I'd only intellectualised about before. I determined to introduce this form of writing into my English Literature students' experience, and from that small beginning a whole undergraduate degree course in writing has now sprung.

Susanna Gladwin

Gillie Bolton: Take care

You are about to enter a danger zone
Wear protective clothing around your heart
Take off your shoes

Writing can seriously damage your sadness
Writing can seriously damage your nightmares
You are in danger of achieving your dreams

Writing is addictive
Remember the dangers of secondary contamination
Others might catch it from you too

You are in serious danger of learning you're alive
You are in serious danger of laughing out loud
You are in serious danger of loving yourself

If it gets in your eyes, consult your loved ones
If it gets in your mind, cancel your therapist
If it gets in your heart, hold on tight

Gillie Bolton

Writing for children

I cannot stress too strongly the power of writing for children, and writing as a child. It opens up straightforward, lucid understandings and insight 'a child's wise incomprehension for defensiveness and disdain' (Rilke [1934] 1993, p. 46). Jonathan, a physician, speaks to his *writing self*, a child:

My head is full. Full of stories and poems. Some of them I've written and some of them I've listened to. And we've talked about writing stories and poems. I told my friends about the stories and poems that you've written. I wonder – would you write me some more? And will you read them to me?

And can I read my stories to you? Can we learn together about writing stories and poems? Can we? Can we?

Jonathan Knight

Mairi Wilson: Dear Sarah and Jenny,

I know you have been puzzled about my job as a doctor for many years, especially because I always tell you, you say, when you tell me about your illnesses, that it will get better on its own. But that's the truth; people come to me all the time with things they perceive as illnesses which are not illnesses at all, or, if they are, will get better on their own. There is very little use of the skills and scientific knowledge I struggled so hard to get into my brain and regurgitate at the right moment for the examiners. A lot of my work involves creating a pleasant space and place for people to come to when they feel they need help. What we do in there barely matters very often, but making the place welcoming and relaxing goes a long way to helping people feel better, and helping people feel better is the main part of my work.

People bring all sorts of problems, but mostly they don't need medicine, just another person to talk to, and perhaps some reassurance that everything is going to be okay. But it's difficult being a constant parent to so many needy children, especially when nobody looks after you as well.

As I get older, I am coming to the conclusion that the National Health Service has missed the point for the majority of people. There are many who need things like a hip operation to relieve their pain, but that is not what doctoring was all about before hip operations became possible. Doctoring before industrialisation, for want of a better term, must have been about being available for people: the priest, the professional confidante – the one who hears the unspeakable. Nowadays we put everything in terms of illness and disease, and pills or operations to 'cure' people, but they don't cure people really. For the main part, people and problems are much more complex and we really only ever scratch the surface.

I would like not to be embroiled in the machine that is the N.H.S. today. I would like the opportunity to be genuine and honest with people, without having to sell them something which, for the main part, I don't believe in – sometimes I feel like a dodgy car dealer, which is a bit of a funny thought, isn't it?!

Mairi Wilson

Autobiographical reflective stories

A large proportion of reflective stories are based on direct experience. The term autobiography was invented at the start of the nineteenth century (Cox 1996). Such stories represent writers' viewpoints: a way of exploring and making sense of impressions, understandings and feelings. DasGupta and Charon describe a 'personal illness narrative exercise': 'Affording students and residents an opportunity to describe and share their illness experiences may counteract the traditional distancing of physicians' minds from their bodies and lead to more empathic and self-aware practice . . . one means toward recognizing, acknowledging, and incorporating the physician's self-story into their clinical practice' (DasGupta and Charon 2004, pp. 351, 355), and 'offer unique subject positions from which to view and critique medicine' (DasGupta 2003, p. 242). Medical training tends to disembody doctors, separating them from patients: a Cartesian split of patients as bodies, doctors as minds (and women are bodies, men minds). Writing personal illness stories helps heal all these splits, enabling medical students to enter patient worlds, and men women's worlds.

Julie Hughes's students undertake a *learning autobiography* exercise:

This exercise is launched on day 1 of our post-graduate teacher education course. The responses have been wonderful in general: a fantastic scene-setting to a reflective programme. Students review and update at the course end:

Welcome to your first reflective writing task for your teaching portfolio. You may handwrite or word process, and include illustrative images/references/drawings. References and citations are not required.

Writing task outline

Consider your learning journey so far:

- Describe/illustrate the journey, choosing your own starting point.

- Thinking about yourself as both actor in this autobiography and audience for the writing, attempt to pull yourself back from your description and think critically. It may help to visualise your journey as a film narrative and position yourself as the viewer.

- It is vital this is not simply descriptive; critically reflect upon how/why/what/where and when.

- Please consider:
  - How have you arrived at this destination?
  - What have been the challenges, trials and successes so far?
  - Why do you think you were challenged or succeeded?
  - Who/what helped and/or hindered you?
  - What do you know about how you like/dislike to learn?
  - Why do you think this is?
  - What positive and negative connotations/associations does learning and teaching hold for you?
  - Why teaching?
  - Why now at this point in your life?

- What beliefs and values underpin your desire to be a qualified teacher?
- Why do you think you hold these beliefs/values?
- What can you do to make a difference?
- What are your personal and professional goals for the next 9 months?
- What are you excited/worried about now?

Mavis Kirkham: the wisdom of nausea

In recent years, I have cared for several women who have had long labours at home with successful outcomes. During these labours, I have inevitably become tired. In each case I have had a similar experience. After a long period with no apparent problems, I had to leave the room because of nausea. On some occasions I actually vomited. After a wash and a walk round the block to clear my head, I returned to the labouring woman. On each occasion she then started to push.

My first reaction to this was the traditional female response of blaming myself. I concluded that I am getting old, tired and possibly past coping well with long labours. I arranged better back-up against my own exhaustion and need to leave women at a crucial time.

Then I heard Susie Orbach give a lecture in which she described physical experiences of counter-transference in her practice as a therapist. This, and subsequent discussion with her, led me to realise that my nausea occurred at the same point in each labour.

My next labour was a 41-year-old primigravida, at home, and the pattern recurred.

My stomach somehow picked up that the woman was approaching second stage well before I could see or hear any signs. Because I learned this through my stomach, rather than my intellect, I had to leave the room, later returning with fresh energy that was picked up by the tired woman and her tired supporters.

This experience led me to ponder a midwife's ways of gaining knowledge, which are discounted because they do not appear in textbooks and are not congruent with measurable medical knowledge. I discussed this with colleagues and became aware how different midwives pick up knowledge from women in different ways. A colleague with an astute sense of smell told me how she is aware of changes in the smell of women as they progress in labour.

The rhetoric of reflective practice takes place within the accepted sphere of authoritative knowledge. Therefore it does not seem to have had much impact upon what we accept as knowledge or our recognition of patterns in our own experience. As women caring for others, we tend not to see our own feelings as important enough to reflect upon.

Reflecting on bodily knowledge has made me aware of the wisdom of my own perceptions and of the ways in which I can learn that are not intellectual. It has also made me aware that I am trained in ways of knowing that prevent me from acknowledging my own wisdom, which made me initially think I was old and inadequate rather than growing in awareness.

Mavis Kirkham

(adapted from *Midwifery Today* 1999, p. 15)

Lane Gerber: we must hear each other's cry

For me the whole 'business' of my writing and the vignettes I use [as a psychotherapist with Southeast Asian refugees] is an attempt to find out what I am thinking/experiencing – which I don't know except as I begin to reflect and to 'talk' in written form about what is moving around inside me. It doesn't take full shape and meaning until I begin the writing process, which creates the meanings out of what has been inside me, unbirthed in thought or language.

I felt very strongly that I didn't want to separate my professional life from my personal life. So my writings about therapy have been about the interaction and wondering about who I am as I am in relationship with the other at the same time I am trying to understand their world.

I began writing letters to friends trying to find my way out of the career morass – really trying to find who I was. And 'writing', such as it was, enabled me to make a bit of sense out of what was inside me that I hadn't been able to do in any other way. Certainly not by talking. And it was the letters and then papers I wrote for grad school in which I found subject matter that counted for the course, but more importantly helped me express my despairs and longings and hopes. For me the writing was discovering something that felt real and true about me at a time when I felt on the verge of losing myself.

Gerber, 1996

Poetry

The inexplicable importance of poetry.

Cocteau [1930] 1968, p. 128

Chapter 8 carries a detailed explanation of poetry's power and value.

Maggie Eisner's villanelle

On a muggy Saturday afternoon after a busy week at the Health Centre, I sat down with two hours to do my homework for the next day's meeting of the Reflective Writing Group for GPs [family medicine]. It's one of my very favourite things – I wonder why I always leave the writing till the last minute. I felt exhausted, uncreative and devoid of ideas. Six minutes *free writing*, recommended by our facilitator as a kind of warm-up, produced a long moan about how tired I was. Then I remembered reading how to write a *villanelle*, and wrote this:

I'm spending too much time on work, I know,
The pressure's putting lines upon my face.
I'd like to sit and watch the flowers grow.

Sometimes I feel the tears begin to flow:
I'm leaden tired, I'm desperate for some space,
I'm spending too much time on work. I know!

Do they want blood? Why don't they bloody go?
I'll crack if I continue at this pace.
I need to sit and watch the flowers grow.

Those piles of paperwork oppress me so,
They never seem to shrink, it's a disgrace.
I'm spending too much time on work, I know.

If I could take my time and take it slow,
If life could be a pleasure, not a race,
Perhaps I'd sit and watch the flowers grow.

If I got bored, there's places I could go,
I'd stretch my limbs, write poetry, find grace.
Must get to spend less time on work – although
I might do more than just watch flowers grow.

When I'd finished it, I felt rejuvenated and alive. It's always good to express my feelings in writing, but I was surprised to feel so dramatically better. Possibly the villanelle, or the challenge of writing in a tight poetic form, had a specific chemical effect on my brain (maybe serotonin reuptake inhibition like Prozac, or dopamine release like cocaine).

Eisner 2000, p. 56

Robert Hamberger: At the Centre (for Kettering MIND)

I've been a social worker for twenty years, and have viewed myself as a poet for about seventeen of those years. I've usually perceived these two aspects of my life as quite separate. The American poet Mark Doty said 'I write . . . to try to figure out my experience by shaping it' (1995, p. 24). It may simply be that figuring out most of my social work experiences doesn't require the shape of poetry. It may be that I find the ways of shaping reflective practice available in the workplace sufficient for most of the time. I've also attempted to shield my writing as something precious for myself, not for my work. I retain a fear of using the experience of others in a voyeuristic way; but the social work poems I have written are usually tributes to people, respecting their courage or their individuality in the way they deal with adversity.

When we all went on holiday they put a photo in the paper. My husband was embarrassed. He said you with all those mental people. I said I'm not ashamed. I've had a breakdown and that's me. Like it or lump it. People think you should hide coming here.

celebrate the woman
scabbing her skin with a matchbox edge
to make her husband listen
celebrate the man
who cracks jokes at the kettle
on bad days

Anyone can get depressed. I can, you can. They want me to have injections. I'm all right without it. If you go in the sun you've got to cover your arms. Who needs that?

they build their papier-mâché time
carefully
shred by shred
so it won't unglue again

This isn't me. I had a job. I had a laugh. Look at my hands now. Mornings are worse. I take another tablet, go back to bed. I want to wake up and be like I was.

at the centre
you can tell your life
to whoever sits beside you
you can touch the shaking woman
say I've been there
and I know you will be well.

At the Centre was written towards the end of my first placement, when I was qualifying. I think writing it helped me to achieve two things simultaneously: to attempt to make sense of meeting a large, varied group of so-called 'mentally ill' people for the first time, and to – as some lines say – *celebrate the woman . . . celebrate the man*. The dedication to Kettering MIND was also important, because I was bowled over by the positive, supportive work they do. I hope that reading the poem feels like meeting a group of new people collaring you, the reader. If it does, that mimics the experience that led to writing it.

A recognition I channelled into writing the poem was that the people I met felt a compelling need to tell their stories: this is my life, my perspective, my experience of the mental illness I'm currently going through. The busy

Day Centre was full of voices – sometimes competing against each other and arguing, but usually sharing a joke, a laugh, and literally supporting each other by their presence. I suppose the poem attempts to give both voice and shape to those voices. The prose sections are simply transcriptions of statements made to me.

The last stanza concerns a creative writing workshop I held at the centre. Two seriously ill women attended regularly. We would all read out the work we'd produced at the end of each session. After Christine read hers, she was shaking and saying that she felt she would never get better. Gillian, who sat beside her, and whose mental illness was as serious and long-standing, calmly said what became the last lines of the poem.

This generous and supportive statement was not only moving, it seemed to sum up the ethos of MIND – of mentally ill people helping each other to attempt to become well again – so forcefully that it stayed with me. It reverberated and I couldn't let go of it. During the placement all these statements dropped into my ear and fizzed inside my head, showing me glimpses of other lives and perspectives, trying to tell me something I didn't know before. Writing them down towards the end of the placement got them out of my head and gave them shape. By setting them on paper, I could let them go.

Robert Hamberger

John Graham-Pole: through the looking-glass

Sitting down to my journal at 6.30 of a Friday morning I jog myself to remember that the first words spilling onto the page are the real ones. I've had that habit for so long of screening out first thoughts and feelings, settling for safe but second-hand ones. Today I get it though: the thought on the top is the ripest.

I'm as much writer as doctor [professor of paediatrics] nowadays. I don't separate them much. If William Carlos Williams could write the first fragments of his poems on patients' charts during house calls, then I can transpose my scribbled stick-it notes into my journal and onto my word processor and call them poetry. When I get up the next day, lo and behold, there they are – my little buddies grinning right back at me. And hey ho, off to work we go together, like Snow White and her dwarfs.

A lot of my work time I spend sitting around on beds. In the bone marrow unit my charges don't say much: their tongues and throats and palates are too sore from their chemo. 'First do no harm' went out of the twelfth-floor window of our modern medical skyscrapers before I'd even made it to houseman. We devastate our patients' body, mind and soul in the name of curing them of the utterly dreadful diseases besetting them. The children at least bounce back, forgetful and forgiving. Meanwhile I talk to their mums and dads. When I take the time to listen well, poems come. The words I hear are not ones heard in the shopping mart.

I have to remember though to value every relationship enough to stop and sit and see (not easy in an environment that often values only what it can bill for). When things are going a bit easier for everyone, I listen to myself making small talk. Not much about the illness or its treatment; they've heard that enough. I try to stay light. No data I know proves solemnity ever cured anyone. I share a bit of my home life and hear about the homes I've never seen of all these people whose children's illnesses I know so intimately. This is when funny poems come, and sometimes I share them.

Mostly though I don't write poems for my patients to hear, although I do write for their benefit – perhaps as much as my own. Poetry seems the very art of service, when it helps me attend, listen, intuit, love. If I take my average clinic experience – yesterday for instance – the twenty children and their families got only a few minutes each of my really seeing them. Too much noise, too many pulls to the phone or to mini-crises, the ever-present time crunch, and sometimes anxiety intruding about what to do with a new symptom or a low blood count. Only a couple of jots made it to my stick-it notes yesterday. But at those moments I had the unveiled sight of a baby; and those children and their mums really got my attention.

I write poems for other people too, especially care givers. Their conciseness helps me make a point in a talk to medical students or nurses or hospice workers. I hope some of my poems are teachers, especially about things hard to put into more words, like this one:

Slant

I'd read them the poem about the nine-year-old
I'd told was going to die. His parents' wish, so
There'd be no conspiracy of silence between them.
How he'd howled for three minutes, then stopped
on an in-breath, played the stand-up comic, offered
jokes. The point about truth-telling opening the
sluice gate to emotion, trust-building, those things.
Afterwards two surgeons addressed me separately,
confidentially. One as much as to say: How dare you?
The other tenderly: Sorry, I couldn't do that:
'Tell the truth but tell it slant.' That's me, my
failure perhaps. Surgeons are really softies.
Acknowledging poems compress: Perhaps you'd
worked up to it a bit. Yes: I'd beat about the bush
a bit, but came at last to it: 'Joey, you're going to die,
go to heaven.' Candour I'd called the piece. Was I
too candid? They'd thought so. For me, I knew
he knew. He knew I knew it: Straight, no slant in that.

Writing this apology for the other poem I'd read and which had upset those surgeons was a good way to think and talk about the issue of candour with children. It's a hard idea to discuss, almost like religious belief. It helped me sort out on paper what I believe about this aspect of doctoring. Perhaps it can help another facing such a dilemma – or at least provoke some lively dialogue.

John Graham-Pole

13

GROUP PROCESSES AND FACILITATION

Socrates: It isn't that knowing the answers myself, I perplex other people.
The truth is rather that I infect them also with the perplexity I feel
myself.

Plato trans. 1958, p. 128

No man can reveal to you aught but that which already lies half asleep in the
dawning of your knowledge . . . If he is indeed wise he does not bid you
enter the house of his wisdom, but rather leads you to the threshold of your
own mind.

Kahlil Gibran [1926] 1994, p. 67

A group has to be formed with care, looked after knowledgeably, and terminated
thoughtfully. This chapter offers detailed *how to* with examples of practice.

A good facilitator joins in a search for demanding questions, but does not know
the answers. The role involves constant awareness of both verbal and non-verbal
contributions, and fine judgements as to the timing and wording of reactions and
suggestions. Low key and unobtrusive, possibly not noticed by some participants,
but the role is certainly vital:

Reflection is a real key to change, but facilitating good reflective learning
experiences is probably more difficult than many anticipate.

Ann

Facilitators and members will find this chapter useful. Participants can support
group processes productively, and get more out of it, by being aware. Such a participant may stop speaking when they know they have said enough, and draw out
a silent member of the group instead; set out the chairs beforehand rather than
waiting for the tutor to do it; be brave enough to break an awkward silence, or
conversely to hold a productive silence instead of nervously and ineffectually
breaking it. They may challenge the facilitator if they feel appropriate actions have
not been taken, reminding him or her 'do we have ten minutes for this activity as
well?'; 'Might it be useful if we introduced ourselves first?' This is not being
'teacher's pet'.

An effective group is run *for*, and largely *by*, its members. Participants are
encouraged to consider and express what they want and need from the start, to
meet their own learning needs. The facilitator is there to facilitate not lead: to

orchestrate and support the group to get what they want, or collaboratively create appropriate objectives. Occasionally a member leaves, wanting something materially different from the others, or they stay and collaboratively modify group aims. Years ago, a participant was not willing to write, only to talk about how writing can help: he had not realised that is what *interactive workshop* meant. He disrupted the whole day. I should have been firmer about aims and objectives, and elicited group support.

Groups always have *hidden curricula*. Everyone brings expectations, hopes and fears, unspoken elements which might either be productive or harmful. Awareness of this and participants' sensitivities is invaluable. And groups often learn something completely different from what the tutor intends. 'School children rarely ask me about my poetry,' a poet told me, 'they ask me about things like my shoes.'

Groups initially test boundaries, deciding how they wish to function, and what they wish to do. Trust, respect and confidence will increase in each meeting, if facilitators support, listen and – facilitate.

We learn from our tutors, teachers and lecturers; we can learn far more from our peers. Participants feel confident enough to create discussions in an effective group. Facilitators keep them from straying from the task, time-keep, support a reasonable balance of contribution from everyone, and so on. Insights into writings heard can be contributed from participants' experience. They can help writers understand what their writing is trying to tell them.

Writing in this way, and sharing it, can be deeply personal; feelings and emotions can be raw and exposed. Confidences normally only drawn forth by supervision, therapy, or deeply trusted friendships can be shared. Careful facilitation and confidentiality make all the difference.

During the course's monthly meetings, [professionals] contribute by reading aloud pieces they have written in the intervening weeks. This can be a subject of the member's own choosing or one that has been suggested by the group. These are kept intentionally vague, such as a *time of uncertainty*. Each piece is discussed by the group. An observer seeing the group in action – with members enthralled and, at times, moved by both sadness and mirth – would appreciate that the age-old art of storytelling is alive and well. In these meetings people's prevalent emotions are laid bare, whether of humour, pain, cynicism or sadness.

This course has encouraged me to be more aware of each day, and is making me more observant. Emotionally charged events no longer make me gulp and bottle things up. I now tend to write about what has happened and how I feel about it. I now keep a jottings pad on my desk and even a notebook in my car. I can be seen scribbling away in a lay-by.

Brimacombe 1996

It is easy for [practitioners] to work in almost total professional isolation, even in a friendly partnership, and it can be hard to admit to mistakes, vulnerability, sadness and even occasionally, joy. If you can commit some of these thoughts to paper, then not only can it be personally therapeutic, but by sharing them with others you may bring insights that can strike a chord and be of benefit to others.

Purdy 1996

Principles

I felt like I'd been given something – real parts of other people.

Elaine

Respect, shared responsibility, confidence and confidentiality are vital cornerstones. Groups contain different abilities, interests and confidence, as well as possibly nationality, ages, types of social background, and both sexes. Respecting these, and respecting the contributions of everyone, ensures the group will gain from diversity. Some talk readily, others are naturally quiet; a balance of contribution is also important.

A group can be powerfully facilitative if it can create its own rules: a relatively safe warm island in life's choppy sea. Issues can be raised tentatively or hesitatingly, aired supportively, and then appropriately taken into the big world. Participants share a specific part of themselves and their lives with each other. Miranda (Shakespeare's *The Tempest*) first met other people just when she was ready for a greater width of contact and experiences; she responded: 'O brave new world, that has such people in it' (V. i. lines 183–4).

Many ingredients create appropriate boundaries to engender confidence and relative safety. Two are:

- members taking each other as they experience them within the closed social system of the group;

- members relating to and supporting each other through discussions of the writing without seeking to question beyond the boundaries of that writing, and the group.

Both help participants write about and share important issues. Participants do not relate to each other as *doctor*, or *senior lecturer*, but Sue or Phil. They do not expose *themselves*, but their writing. They will have had time to write, reread and think about sharing their writing beforehand. It can be helpful if participants treat each writing as *fiction*. Discussions will then focus on what the writer intended to share with the group: on the writing rather than the hinterland of the account. Questions like 'did you *really* . . .?', 'And what happened next . . .?', 'Why did you perceive the senior colleague like that . . .?' can lead to unintentional disclosure.

If writings are considered as fiction, there is no '*really*', or '*what happened next*': characters do not walk beyond the page and do anything. A question will sometimes stray, but often accompanied by such as: 'I'm going to ask you this; please don't answer if you don't want to, but I think it might help.' A group respects a 'no', just as a decision not to read a piece because it feels too personal is respected.

Listening

The group has enabled me to share my writing over the last six years in a supportive and creative environment. This has helped me to both explore and make sense of some of the experiences and challenges of my life. I have improved my confidence and ability to write creatively and have been enriched by the range and depth of poetry and prose which each member has brought to the group.

Shirley

There have been times when I've brought a piece of writing and decided not to read it – the circumstances have simply not been 'right'. And this feels acceptable – comfortable – because the group is sensitive to the mood engendered by each person's writing. I think we have learned to 'hear' better and this has informed our writing. The whole process is evolving all the time.

Becky

I find the process of listening to someone read intensely moving, knowing something of the life from which the writing comes. It helps me know the person more fully. It really is a unique way of sharing.

Sheena

The space created by the group is: supportive, constructive, safe, facilitative, confidential, free from jargon and (almost) free from bollocks.

Mark

Ground rules

Trust, and a sense of safety, is fostered by **confidentiality**. Belonging to such a group, hearing important reflective material, is a privilege. The writings belong to the writers, and the discussions to the group; neither should be shared outside the group without express permission. I remember one group even requesting nothing be shared with life partners.

- A sense of group **boundaries** helps create confidence. Many professional groups choose to focus solely upon work issues.

- **Respect and mutual trust** are facilitative. An attitude of 'unconditional positive regard' (Rogers 1969) can be modelled by the facilitator. A disagreement can be undertaken in a spirit of mutual respect. Discussions will be constructive and friendly if comments are either generally positive, or if negative elements are expressed gently, along with definite appropriate constructive suggestions.

Silence

Silence is powerful in any group, particularly in an interactive confidential group, discussing deeply held principles and problematic practices (for a useful exploration, see Rowland 1993, pp. 87–107). 'The leader must learn to allow for different sorts of silence – the reflective, the anxious, the embarrassed or puzzled' (Abercrombie 1993, p. 118), the angry, the portentous, and so on.

Silence can be experienced as confronting and aggressive, especially if participants feel they do not have responsibility to break it. Silence can be used fruitfully for deep reflection when members feel responsible for their group. If no one in the group has anything particular they need to say, then no one needs to speak. The silence is broken when someone has something to say, however tentative.

A silence might be used, for example, to allow previous words to sink in, and an appropriate ensuing response sought. Understandings and clarities do not necessarily emerge through argument or discourse. The silence following participants' readings are fruitful, allowing listeners to marshal their thoughts and feelings before speaking. Readers need to see this brief silence as positive rather than an indication that the group hates their writing, and listeners learn to use it to think what they want to say. A new anxious group needs the facilitator to support listeners to say something positive quickly, as new writers feel exposed on reading their work. A participant rather than facilitator breaking this silence tends to increase group responsibility for the discussion.

> Sharing our writing weaves connections between us. The special attentiveness as we listen to someone reading their work, and especially in the silence afterwards. There is special pleasure in witnessing each other's writing develop, each in their own way. There is excitement in discovering unfamiliar aspects of people: sensual, lyrical writing by one known for their cynicism, well-crafted, poignant pieces by another who joined the group believing they couldn't write.
>
> Maggie

> Silence is but a feeling silence. Someone has just finished reading their contribution – perhaps a difficult encounter with a patient or a partner or even memories of training and hospital days which still have the power to hurt. The group has lived through that moment with the speaker, shared the emotions, and for a few minutes there is nothing to say. We are amazed at the power of each other's writing. Certainly when we come down to discuss,

with Gillie's help, there are ways that the writing could be made more telling, but the inspiration comes from the group. It is not afraid to face the feelings aroused daily in medical practice and is learning in the safety of the group to translate them into words.

Naomi

More can be said by silence than words: 'a long heavy silence promises danger, just as much as a lot of empty outcries' (Sophocles trans. 1982, line 1382), and Aeschylus pointed out that safety and discretion can reside in silence: 'Long ago we learned to keep our mouths shut/Where silence is good health, speech can be fatal' (trans. 1999, p. 29).

Group function

A great deal of hassle, disappointment, and possibly pain is avoided by initially discussing more or less what participants are there for, how they are going to do it, why, where and when. The group is likely to be organic, with working aims, objectives, duration, patterns and relationships developing over time, but some initial agreement helps.

How many sessions needs to be decided. Six sessions can be agreed, to be reviewed at sessions four and five. Less than three is not so useful, this being the minimum for people to grasp the process and begin to tackle it fruitfully. Reflective practice writing groups generally offer support in professional and personal explorations and expressions to:

- understand more clearly the import and implications of specific experiences;

- discover learning needs;

- enable the sharing of sensitive issues with involved, supportive disinterested (i.e. not such as line managers) others with similar enough experiences;

- reinforce the self-confidence and self-esteem which writing tends to bring;

- support with occasional loss of confidence, writer's block, and lost way.

The group is *not*:

- *a writers' workshop* in which the form rather than the content of the writings are constructively criticised in order to help the writer improve the text (e.g. story, poem or play) with publication in mind – the content of the writing is not considered in such a forum;

- *a therapeutic writing group*, where the content of the writing is focused upon, but in order to support the writer in psychotherapeutic explorations;

- *a chat group* where the writings are read out, and the response might be: 'how nice, now that reminds me how my Auntie Gwen used to . . .'

A group's plot

A closed group with the same members at each meeting (allowing for occasional absences) can enable trust and confidence, as well as listening, understanding and responding skills. The experience of being in a group is different at different stages – a courtly dance, then jive, quickstep, country dance, or tarantella.

A group can be seen to have a 'plot' of *Meeting, Falling in love, Lovers' tiff* (or *Conflict*), *Kiss and make up*, (or *Conflict resolution*), *Mission* 'lovers win over their parents (or don't)', *End* 'lovers sail off into the sunset (or die)', and *Mourning*. What makes a story a story is the way the characters and situation, and the readers' view of them, change and develop. A group does not just get better and better; the duration and shape of the 'plot' will vary for different groups (*Romeo and Juliet*, or a cheap romance):

- At **meeting** members begin to see themselves as a group rather than a collection of individuals. They find out about each other; the lovers tentatively become a couple rather than just individuals. Relationships are characterised by reserve, avoidance of conflict and politeness; few personal risks are taken, and views and feelings are withheld.

- **Falling in love** is the initial stage of excitement and beginning of commitment.

- **Conflict** is the traditional 'middle day' phenomenon when the group has constituted itself and perhaps felt rather congratulatory. Members provisionally sort out their roles, flex role muscles and jockey for leadership perhaps, or push preferred objectives. People can become quite badly hurt in this process if not handled carefully. Argument is a route to finding out more about boundaries and each other; an important stage, engendering creative thinking, such as: Precisely what are we doing here? Who am I in this group? What do I want to get out of it? People are often defensive, assertive, distrustful, suspicious, and do not listen to each other.

- **Conflict resolution** is creating group identity and rules, developing commitment, as well as wanting to nurture and care for both group and each other. Participants are supportive, receptive, and attempt to avoid conflict.

- In **mission** the group has tackled each other, uncovered quite a few prejudices to sidestep, and strengths and skills to harness. They have a reasonable group feel for who they are, what it is they are doing, why and how, when and where they are doing it. They work well together, have mutual understanding and are doing whatever it was they set out to do; or something else which has become more important. They are open, trusting, forbearing, supportive, listening well, and willing to take risks.

- **End** is when the group has done its work and moves on gracefully: with regret and optimism about the next stage for each. Members leave – once more individuals. A 'rite of passage', such as a shared lunch, can ease the parting.

- Facilitators might not be aware of **mourning**. An effective supportive group is bound to leave a sense of regret at its passing.

These stages are simplistic, as for any model. A group is a story authored by all group members. The stages will probably get mixed up, and earlier stages, even if undergone thoroughly, may recur. Conflict may arise at any time and need to be dealt with (lovers continue to tiff, kiss and make up). New rules and guidelines may be discussed. The group may even go back to elements of the first stage and need to get to know each other again in areas which seemed unimportant at *meeting*. *Mission* is reached after at least some elements of the previous stages. All the relationships depicted are within the boundaries of the group: individuals meeting outside the group's boundaries may knife each other or jump into bed.

Characters

A story also relies on character: the talkative and exuberant, the shy and quiet, the silent but anguished, the dominant and bossy, the analytic reasoner, the facilitative, the divergently creative thinker, the moaner, the kindly and motherly, the frustrated rescuer, the frightened pupil, the babbler, the lurker, the catalyst, the logical structurer, the teacher's pet. Troubles sometimes arise when a group contains two or more habitually dominant people; different problems arise when too many are shy and quiet (or even worse, anguished and quiet). Facilitators can gently and subtly encourage members to try new roles.

Different roles may be played in different groups, as in life: mum one minute, teacher or lover the next. A Masters student, described as 'facilitative' in a reflexive group discussion, was astonished, a bit fearful, and kept referring to it. We supported her in thinking it was all right for her to be facilitative. Until then she had clearly assumed a whacky role, with creative ideas but had to have the more serious elements of the course explained carefully. The 'game', leading to this enlightenment, was participants likening each other to animals. We then gently and cautiously teased out what we thought our metaphorical animals 'meant'.

The facilitator also assumes roles as appropriate and with discretion, being a 'good-enough facilitator', taking on each character just 'enough' of the time. He or she may be:

- **Teacher**: giving a keynote talk on an essential issue. Participants usually like this, but too much of it makes for a passive group who do not take responsibility for their learning at other times (as in the *chalk and talk model* in Chapter 5).

- **Instructor**: for a set task. The group undertaking to do what they are told is useful when needed for demanding tasks, such as writing to a certain theme for a certain length of time. Responsibility for everything else is removed, freeing them to be creatively explorative and expressive in their writing. This should be in an environment of enough trust and support, otherwise the writing will not be worth the paper it is written upon.

- **Interpreter**: the facilitator reflecting back a contribution, repeating it in his or her own words in order to clarify and ensure it has been heard. This can increase member confidence, but must be used with care as it can irritate, or reduce members' autonomy. The facilitator might also interpret behaviours, or make connections or linkages between concepts or ideas. This pattern-making or pattern-perceiving can be creative and constructive.

- **Devil's advocate/confronter**: appropriate in certain circumstances. Groups need to be challenged – enough. The facilitator must be reasonably confident in the way the individual may respond. Tears and anger can be very fruitful, but not when engendered by mistake.

- **Compatriot/discloser**. A group in which members reveal themselves, but the facilitator never does, will not work. Nor should he or she cross boundaries by revealing all the skeletons in her cupboard, taking up the group's emotional space and time.

- **Consultant**. The facilitator may respond to a particular wish or need of the group for some information or advice from his or her knowledge and experience.

- **Neutral chairperson**: makes sure the group keeps to the point, to time, that everyone has a say, the subject is appropriately and thoroughly aired, sexism, racism, big white chiefism do not happen, the ground rules are respected, the discussion is appropriately recorded, and so on. Chairpeople are not primarily involved in discussions or activities.

- **Participant**: opposite to chairperson, a useful role on occasion. It creates a warm, coherent sense; the skill is not to lose sight of essential facilitator roles. Members new to group processes think facilitators are participants much of the time, without noticing the chairing, interpretive, confronting, and some directive functions.

- **Manager**: undertakes essential but unexciting organisational and management tasks, ensuring participants arrive at the right time and place and with the right papers and expectations.

These roles are delineated simplistically; in practice boundaries are blurred. Groups rarely perceive experienced facilitators moving between them. Shifting appropriately and smoothly is not straightforward; even a skilful tutor can confuse, anger, alienate or devalue at times.

Authority and power

The facilitator is always in an authoritative role, powerful even. A group trusts him or her to retain awareness of this, and wield it responsibly. Forgetting and playing *participant* too much is as dangerous as becoming *dictator*.

> Trainers need to give considerable thought to what backing they need to enable them to face the full extent of their managerial authority and of the potential impact of this on the functioning of participants. The more they know about their own authority, the less are they likely either to deny it and collude with participants in avoiding powerful learning experiences, or wield it unthinkingly and impose rigid, unresponsive courses. Our argument has been that the more open trainers are about the extent and limits of their own authority, the more open they can be to the professional and personal authority of course participants.
>
> Hughes and Pengelly 1995, pp. 169–70

Facilitators can make errors, which need careful handling. At a day course for university therapists, one wrote about a vital childhood bereavement. The small group sat stunned at the privilege of hearing such limpid, clear writing full of meaning; and clearly of such value to the writer. The writer said he could never have intended to write it, and would not have done so if I had not forgotten to mention they would be asked if they would like to read their writing to their group of six. On this occasion I was lucky: he forgave me, and they all benefited from him reading it. I was on poor form, my daughter seriously injured in hospital and my mother having just died. He had felt secure in the privacy of paper and pen.

Transference, counter-transference, projection, introjection

These terms from psychoanalysis refer to interpersonal dynamics. We *transfer* onto others elements of other relationships. Facilitators can receive bewilderingly inappropriate emotions if participants transfer feelings which, for example, belong to their parents. In *counter-transference* facilitators react similarly inappropriately, treating a disruptive member like a naughty son, for example. *Projection* is when emotions are projected inappropriately: 'I'm sure you are getting at me', might mean 'I really wish I could get at you'. In *introjection*, feelings, such as anger, are swallowed and not expressed, possibly leading to the bottled feelings erupting inappropriately and painfully or awkwardly later. All these happen in everyday life. A facilitator has responsibility to take them into account. Awareness can explain why anger or tears erupt out of nowhere.

Group management

Groups do not happen, they are created and nurtured. Groups which meet for more than three sessions begin to take responsibility for their own functions; participants gain more confidence in sharing tentative – border – ideas, feelings, and memories. A series of at least three sessions is best for people to begin to understand, trust and take responsibility for through-the-looking-glass reflection. An understanding of the following elements is useful:

- *Participants need to know each other's names*. Beginning the first session with a warm-up exercise game (see Chapter 10) helps people feel integrated and involved. Begin the second session with those who don't know a name asking the person across the circle. It's quick and leads to laughter and companionship, as several people speak at once.

- A *formative evaluation* to conclude each session, to check on group satisfaction and personal involvement.

- *Timing*: beginning and ending when expected; participants each need their share of time. Confidence in *time sharing* and *time boundaries* fosters respect, responsibility and security.

- *Reflexive periods* enable groups to examine their own processes critically. Careful facilitation is required to help people to stand outside themselves and their group for a space, in order to be more aware of the rules, values, unspoken assumptions and so on they bring to the sessions.

- *Variety of group size and organisation* aids dynamics. Periods of paired and small-group work during sessions can enable a situation of closer trust: quiet or well-defended participants contribute more, and dominant ones less.

- A supportive yet stretching relationship to participant *roles* (see above).

- *Verbal contributions from as many group members as possible* and as appropriate. Reflexive periods, a variation of paired work with plenary, as well as appropriate subtle facilitation can help participant awareness of the value of their contribution.

- *Problematic participants* can usually be coped with by the group with careful facilitation, leading to greater group cohesion.

- *Open questions*: 'How did you feel about that?', not closed, 'Did that make you angry?'

- *Use of personal pronouns*. People say 'you', meaning 'I' ('You get tired of saying it over and over again', meaning 'I get tired . . .'), 'we' instead of 'I' (an assumption the group agrees with the speaker). The use of 'I' by each speaker can help the group own and be responsible for what each of them say.

- Using individuals' *names* appropriately increases inclusion and value.

- An awareness of the power of *sub-groups*.

- *Non-verbal communications* (facial expression, posture, gesture, blushing, sweating, laughter, crying, and so on) are very informative.

- *Who comments first, and when* after a reading? It is never me: as leader I can readily dominate and inhibit participant contributions. I speak after everyone else, having asked for a quick response for the sake of a new writer. A deeply thoughtful pause as the group reflect on what they have heard and want to say, can prelude a fruitful discussion in an established, confident group.

- *The door-knob*. Just as the session is ending participants may blurt out disturbing or vital information, invariably needing time. Firm time boundaries, aiming to finish well in time, and a reflexive period at session end can help.

- *Listening to, commenting on, and eliciting comments* reflectively on the written experiences of others is a skill to be fostered and enabled by facilitation.

- *Learning how to take the comments and discussions of others*, about writings, needs practice and confidence building. Facilitative, stretching or surprising points come from participants not just the facilitator. I have been asked: 'Now are you going to psychoanalyse me?' Group and facilitator have the responsibility to support writers in extending and clarifying their *own* ideas, not impose views.

Maria Garner: reflective practice in the workplace

As part of addressing poor performance, motivation and staff retention in the local unitary council for whom I worked, I undertook a post-graduate certificate course in business management. I found the reflective journal a safe place to question my actions and answer my own questions. I felt more in control and less stressed. I set out to evaluate workplace reflective practice for the course project.

I delivered three reflective writing sessions after work with twelve strangers of diverse professions. Discussion opened up added dimensions to the benefits of reflection. Participants felt safe to discuss their issues, and could share alternative views and possible future options. Even though participants worked in different areas they described common themes and situations. I tried to give group members experience of as many reflective practices as possible. Much of session one was taken up by clarifying our purpose, ground rules, and allaying fears. Each session started with participants giving a single word to describe how they were feeling, followed by five minutes free-fall writing. Both moved people to an internal focus, and brought them together.

Writing exercises connected past, present and future experiences. The helpfulness of turning reflective writing into poetry or story, and examples, were discussed to encourage people to express thoughts (W.H. Auden's *Funeral Blues*, Jo Cannon's *Performance* [Chapter 2]). No one had written poetry before but were pleased and amazed with the haiku they wrote and shared.

Evaluation confirmed the feel-good factor, lowering of stress levels, and the spreading of reflective writing to colleagues or family: 'It did more for me personally than anything I have tried before, uplifting'; 'Triggered much discussion back at work'; 'It felt like unloading'; 'It provided some answers'; 'I know why it happens now.'

This group was self-selected. The work could not be developed, however, as the council could perceive no organisational benefit. Staff performance and retention continues to fall and sickness levels rise.

Maria Garner

Housekeeping

I keep six honest serving men
  (They taught me all I knew);
Their names are What and Why and When
  And How and Where and Who.

Kipling 1902, p. 83

These 'honest serving men' have served me well for years, too. I call them *can-opener questions*. Used as a checklist in planning and writing, they help ensure I have covered everything. Here are some practical considerations they have suggested:

- King Arthur thought *sitting in a circle* helps everyone to feel equal. A centre table can be a barrier. A circle of comfortable chairs can create more confident intimacy. When only schoolroom chairs are available, packing people in close round a table is good. They all lean forward, creating a gathered circle.

- *The right number of chairs* for everyone makes the group feel complete; it is worth removing the unneeded chairs. Leaving the chair of an absent but expected member can retain a sense of their presence. A group referred to Jenny's empty chair as if she was there, then, when she came in apologetically but expectedly late, slipping into her waiting chair felt warm and wanted.

- *Necessary equipment*, such as an overhead projector, being in place beforehand saves wastage of valuable time.

- *Punctuality and regular attendance* can offer a sense of respect to the group and its work, as well as saving time and frustration.

- *Size* affects group dynamics considerably. Eight is a lovely number; twelve an ideal maximum; four is too few when some cannot come (but may be perfect for a short introductory one-off session).

- *Funds*: who pays what, when, how, how much, to whom (if appropriate).

- *Venue*: is it right?

- *Coffee time*: important because people get to know each other. But when, where, how, how long?

- *Timing*: people like to know at the beginning when they will get their breaks (coffee, tea, lunch) and when they will finish. One parcels out one's energy and commitment unconsciously for the allotted time – surprises in this area are not useful. An unexpected hour on the end of a session, when the energy has been used up, is as unfacilitative as people coming to the finish time before they are ready – they could have invested more energy and commitment earlier, had they known.

Juggling

A course facilitator juggles with co-ordinating these three areas:

Needs of the group

Needs of the individual   *Needs of the task/organisation*

Maureen Rappaport, medical lecturer, reflects on her teaching:

How can I arrange a series of teaching sessions, or one session, where others feel safe to expose parts of themselves and explore their own experiences, their cutting edges of learning, a place where the learning is raw, but a place we learn from? The edge is where our professional experiences, grounded and guided by mentors, cut into our own beliefs, and values, and boy, do they hurt.

I have been experimenting with different groups and various methods. It is hard to keep the group focused on the writing and meanings and not on making their peers 'feel better'. I, too, have to fight against my natural tendencies to 'save' my students when they express difficult feelings and emotions, although I am perfectly comfortable sharing my uncomfortable feelings with them.

Finding my own voice in writing has been so powerful: I'm afraid of smothering others'. It's time to listen to students and residents voices, through poetry and literature and writing among other things. The residents teach me so much. I hope I give as much back to them. It's like the magic between my patients and I. I look up at their sharp minds and clever reason. What do I want to learn?

It never ceases to amaze me that the residents are more self-aware and more self-reflective than I give them credit for. I ask them to write about a meaningful event in their training (20 minutes of keeping the hand moving). Here is Al, 1st year family medicine resident's writing:

> I met an amazing patient recently. I was called down to emergency on my surgery rotation. I was to see a 24-year-old woman with cerebral palsy. When I first saw this African-American with short black hair I thought she was a he, so I got confused.
>
> I approached the patient, introduced myself and began my history. It was obvious that the patient was bound to a bed all her life. She couldn't speak clearly and mumbled her words. It was obvious she depended on others for her care. I began asking her father questions. After awhile she mumbled something and her father started laughing. When I asked what she said, he said, 'she says why don't you just ask me the questions?'
>
> I was shocked and ashamed. I apologised to her and began our conversation. Although difficult to understand I made out her words and realised how direct and concise she was. She was also witty and kept cracking up her dad. At one point I had to stop my 'history' and said, 'I'm sorry, but I just have to say you are one of the most inspiring and amazing people I have ever met.' Despite all the crap in medicine, just the fact that I got to meet her makes it all worth it.   Al
>
> Maureen Rappaport

Drumming

A skilled facilitator, just like any expert practitioner, is not generally conscious of the kinds of issues covered in this chapter: they work intuitively (or with phronesis, see Frank 2004). But even an expert facilitator makes mistakes, has to learn a new method or technique. It can feel dangerous: emotions, feelings and opinions can be expressed and felt with vigour when groups focus on vital issues as in through-the-looking-glass reflection. A participant said: 'The responsibility for encouraging reflection is awesome.' If effective learning is to take place, that responsibility needs to be taken:

> Effective learning is therefore dependent, at least in part, on access to that world of feeling and phantasy, which allows structures of meaning to be recognised, and to be open to change, in a way which facilitates a different (and perhaps more constructive) professional response. Great emphasis is placed . . . on the learning environment, particularly on the need for space and for containment . . . High value is given to creating a space which is somewhat apart from the everyday world, where a reflective mode and a slower pace is promoted, and where it is permissible to allow vulnerability to surface (a view somewhat at odds with the dominant ideas of competence and 'mastery').
>
> Yelloly and Henkel 1995, p. 9

Facilitating an effective group offers immense satisfaction: experiencing people developing, growing, reaching fresh understandings, and learning how to support each other. Effective group work is like learning to drum collaboratively in rhythm:

Rhythm, seamless, breathless, captivating. Ah ha! We do have rhythm. We can do it! Circle of faces, my friends.

Rhythm of the heart, of the step, of the circulation of the blood. Change of the seasons. Night and day. Springtime and harvest. Marching, dancing, walking, skipping, running, jumping, talking, poetry.

Jenny Lockyer

14

REFLECTION ON REFLECTION

'Would you tell me, please, which way I ought to go from here?'
'That depends a good deal on where you want to get to,' said the Cheshire Cat.
'I don't much care where –' said Alice.
'Then it doesn't matter which way you go,' said the Cat.
'So long as I get *somewhere*,' Alice added as an explanation.
'Oh, you're sure to do that,' said the Cat, 'if you only walk long enough.'

Carroll [1865] 1954, p. 54

'I think – ' began Piglet nervously.
'Don't,' said Eeyore.

Milne [1928] 1958, pp. 240–1

This book began with the oxymoron of *certain uncertainty* which is at the heart of reflective practice. The only way to get anywhere in reflective practice is to do it, trusting the journey will be interesting and useful, having faith in and respect for yourself and your abilities to reflect as well as to practise. You do not know where you are going. You never will get to a definitive *somewhere* anyway, just as Alice got to the Mad Hatters' Tea Party – an illuminating experience – but she had to move on again. She later met the Mock Turtle who helped her realise that the most productive journeys are undertaken without set purpose ('porpoise': [Carroll 1865] 1954, p. 88) (see also Aristotle trans. 1953).

Setting out into reflective practice with an open questioning mind, rather than set purpose, can lead to fresh dynamic territory. But that is 'to arrive where we started/And to know the place for the first time' (Eliot [1936] 1974, p. 222). Reflective practice does not travel distances: it makes a great deal more sense of where we are.

This enquiry needs a *thoughtfully unthinking* approach, like footballers are taught not to think, or Eeyore begged Piglet not to. Reflective practice can be hindered by too much self-consciousness and self-awareness.

Letting go of hard and fast notions of myself allows responsibility for a greater range of actions thoughts and feelings, even ones I was previously unaware of. We live in a culture where it is always considered to be somebody's fault: somebody has to pay; someone has the duty to sort me out – doctor, police officer, priest, therapist, counsellor, lawyer. I am not responsible for myself, and who is my self anyway? I am no longer surrounded by a consistent nexus of family, neighbours, priest, the same boss and employees: these figures unreliably shift and change. I can change my body with plastic surgery or drugs, and invent different persona with bell-bottoms or mini-skirt, cheongsam or sari.

An outward consistent sense of self cannot be relied upon. Instead I invent myself anew all the time by telling and writing stories about myself: to make some kind of sense. And I locate and shift this growing self alongside others: through discussion and hearing their stories, and in the wider world through reading and discussing as many relevant texts as I can. ' "I" doesn't exist, one constructs oneself' (Simone de Beauvoir, quoted in Guppy 2000). And: 'The unfinishedness of the human person [in] a permanent process of searching' (Freire 1998, p. 21). Perhaps *me* is not a noun, but a verb, a process: *to me*.

This can only be undertaken by the whole practitioner in a holistic aesthetic creative process, not flinching from the range of human experience:

> The states of mind or feelings that art can excite have been helpfully distinguished in Sanscrit aesthetics, where they are called *rasas*, from a word meaning 'juice' or 'essence'. A fully achieved work of art should flow with all nine of them: their names might be transposed in English as wonder, joy, sexual pleasure, pity, anguish, anger, terror, disgust and laughter.
>
> Warner 1998, p. 7

Reflective practice will never offer solutions or final answers. If such are sought, and seemingly found, they will prove hollow, just as the *meaning of life* being 42 is meaningless (Adams, 1984).

The Ekoi people of Nigeria (Gersie 1992), have a tradition of *story children* from long ago. Each story has to be told and heard for both *child* and hearers to be nourished and run free. Once heard and known, however, the wisdom in each story can never be unheard or unknown: therein lies its power. Listening to and telling such stories changes the teller and listener irreversibly:

> They were not the same eyes with which he had last looked out at this particular scene, and the brain which interpreted the images the eyes resolved was not the same brain. There had been no surgery involved, just the continual wrenching of experience.
>
> Adams [1984] 1995, p. 493

BIBLIOGRAPHY

Abbs, P. (1974) *Autobiography in Education*. London: Heinemann Educational.

Abell, S.K., Bryan, L.A. and Anderson, M. (1998) Investigating preservice elementary science teacher reflective thinking using integrated media case-based instruction in elementary science teacher preparation. *Science Teacher Education*, **82**(4), 491–510.

Abercrombie, M.L.J. (1993) *The Human Nature of Learning: Selections From the Work of M.L.J. Abercrombie* (ed. J. Nias). Buckingham: Open University Press.

Abse, D. (1998) More than a green placebo. *The Lancet*, **351**, 362–4.

Adams, D. ([1984] 1995) So long and thanks for all the fish. In *A Hitch Hiker's Guide to the Galaxy: a Trilogy in Five Parts*. London: Heinemann.

Aeschylus (trans. 1999) *The Oresteia* (trans. T. Hughes). London: Faber & Faber.

Akister, J. (2003) Designing and using a patchwork text to assess social work students undertaking a module in family therapy. *Innovations in Education and Teaching International*, **40**(2), 202–8.

Albert, T. (1997) *Winning the Publications Game*. Abingdon: Radcliffe Medical Press.

Allan, J., Fairtlough, G. and Heinzen, B. (2002) *The Power of the Tale: Using Narratives for Organisational Success*. Chichester, W Sussex: Wiley & Sons.

Allende, Isabel (2000) The Guardian Profile, interview by M. Jaggi. *The Guardian*, 5 February, 6–7.

Anderson, C.M. and MacCurdy, M.M. (2000) *Writing and Healing: Toward an Informed Practice*. Urbana, Ill. The National Council of Teachers of English.

Argyris, C. (1991) Teaching smart people how to learn. *Harvard Business Review*, **63**(3), 99–109.

Aristotle (trans. 1953) *The Nichomachean Ethics* (trans. J.A.K. Thomson). Harmondsworth: Penguin.

Aristotle (trans. 1995) (S. Halliwell, ed.) *Poetics*. 1457 b 6–9 p. 105, Cambridge Mass.: Harvard University Press.

Atkins, K. and Murphy, K. (1994) Reflective practice. *Nursing Standard*, **8**(39), 49–56.

Baernstein, A. and Fryer-Edwards, K. (2003) Promoting reflection on professionalism: a comparison trial of educational interventions for medical students. *Academic Medicine*, **78**(7), 742–7.

Barker, P. (1991) *Regeneration*. London: Penguin.

Barry, C.A., Britten, N., Barber, N., Bradley, C. and Stevenson, F. (1999) Using reflexivity to optimise teamwork in qualitative research. *Qualitative Health Research*, **9**(1), 26–44.

Barthes, R. (1977) *Image, Music, Text*. London: Fontana/Collins.

Bauby, J.D. (1998) *The Diving Bell and The Butterfly*. London: Fourth Estate.

Bauer, L., Duffy, J., Fountain, E., Halling, S., Holzer, M., Jones, E., Leifer, M. and Rowe, J. (1992) Exploring self-forgiveness. *Journal of Religion and Health*, **31**(2), 149–59.

Belenky, M.F., Clinchy McVicar, B., Goldberg, N.R. and Tarule, J.M. (1997). *Women's Ways of Knowing: the Development of Self, Voice and Mind*. New York: Basic Books.

Bell, J. (1992) Cross Cultural Studies. Paper presented to Teachers' Stories of Life and Work Conference, Chester.

Belli, A. and Coulehan, J. (1998) *Blood and Bone: Poems by Physicians*. University of Iowa Press.

Bellman, L.M. (1996) Changing nursing practice through reflection on the Roper, Logan and Tierney model: the enhancement approach to action research. *Journal of Advanced Nursing*, **24**, 129–38.

Benner, P. (1984) *From Novice to Expert: Excellence and Power in Clinical Nursing Practice*. Menlo Park: Addison Wesley.

Bennett-Levy, J., Turner, F., Beaty, T., Smith, M., Paterson, B. and Farmer, S. (2001). The value of self-practice of cognitive therapy techniques and self-reflection in the training of cognitive therapists. *Behavioural and Cognitive Psychotherapy*, **29**, 203–20.

Bennett-Levy, J., Lee, N., Travers, K., Pohlman, S. and Hamernik, E. (2003) Cognitive therapy from the inside: enhancing therapist skills through practising what we preach. *Behavioural and Cognitive Psychotherapy*, **31**, 143–58.

Beowulf and Grendel (trans. 1973, M. Alexander) London: Penguin.

Best, D. (1996) On the experience of keeping a therapeutic journal while training. *Therapeutic Communities*, **17**(4), 293–301.

Bettelheim, B. (1976) *The Uses of Enchantment*. London: Penguin.

Beveridge, I. (1997) Teaching your students to think reflectively: the case for reflective journals. *Teaching in Higher Education*, **2**(1), 33–43.

Blake, W. (1958) *Songs of Innocence* (The Divine Image) (A. Lincoln, ed.). Middlesex: Penguin.

Bleakley, A. (1999) From reflective practice to holistic reflexivity. *Studies in Higher Education*, **24**(3), 215–330.

Bleakley, A. (2000a) Adrift without a lifebelt: reflective self-assessment in a post-modern age. *Teaching in Higher Education*, **5**(4), 405–18.

Bleakley, A. (2000b) Writing with invisible ink: narrative, confessionalism and reflective practice. *Reflective Practice*, **1**(1), 11–24.

Bleakley, A. (2002) Pre-registration house officers and ward-based learning: a 'new apprenticeship' model. *Medical Education*, **36**(1), 9–15.

Bleakley, A. (2005) Stories as data, data as stories: making sense of narrative analysis in clinical education. *Medical Education* (forthcoming).

Bleakley, A., Hobbs, A., Boyden, J. and Walsh, L. (2004) Safety in operating theatres: improving teamwork through team resource management. *The Journal of Workplace Learning*, **16**(1/2), 83–91.

Blodgett, H. (1991) *Capacious Holdall: An Anthology of Englishwomen's Diary Writings*. University Press of Virginia.

Bloom, S. (1999) Give sorrow words: emotional disclosure and physical health. *The Psychotherapy Review*, **1**(7), 312–13.

Bolton, G. (1991) Stories at work. *Writers in Education*, **8**, 10–11.

Bolton, G. (1994) Stories at work, fictional-critical writing as a means of professional development. *British Educational Research Journal*, **20**(1), 55–68.

Bolton, G. (1995) Stories at work, writing for professional development. *Issues in Social Work Education*, **14**(2), 21–33.

Bolton, G. (1999a) *Writing Myself: The Therapeutic Potential of Creative Writing*. London: Jessica Kingsley.

Bolton, G. (1999b) Stories at work: reflective writing for practitioners. *The Lancet*, **354**, 243–5.

Bolton, G. (1999c) Reflections through the looking glass: the story of a course of writing as a reflexive practitioner. *Teaching in Higher Education*, **4**(2), 193–212.

Bolton, G. (2003a) Stories of Education. *Cambridge Journal of Education*, **33** (2), 309–10.

Bolton, G. (2003b) Riverside Community Health Project: Experiences told by workers. In J. Kai and C. Drinkwater, *Primary Care in Urban Disadvantaged Communities*. Oxford: Radcliffe Press.

Bolton, G., Howlett, S., Lago, C. and Wright, J. (2004) *Writing Cures: An Introductory Handbook of Writing in Counselling and Psychotherapy*. London: Brunner-Routledge.

Booker, C. (2004) *The Seven Basic Plots: Why We Tell Stories*. London: Continuum. Quoted by Wu D., *Times Higher Education Supplement*, 29 October 2004, 23–4.

Borkan, J., Reis, S., Steinmetz, D. and Medalie, J. (1999) *Patients and Doctors: Life Changing Stories from Primary Care*. University of Wisconsin Press.

Boud, D. (1998) Use and misuse of reflection and reflective practice. Seminar at Sheffield University, February.

Boud, D., Keogh, R. and Walker, D. (1985) *Reflection: Turning Experience into Learning*. London: Kogan Page.

Brimacombe, M. (1996) The emotional release of writing. *GP*, 13 December.

Brockbank, A. and McGill, I. (1998) *Facilitating Reflective Learning in Higher Education*. Buckingham: Open University Press.

Brody, H. (2003) *Stories of Sickness* (2nd edn). Oxford: Oxford University Press.

Brookfield, S. D. (1987) *Developing Critical Thinkers*. Milton Keynes: Open University Press.

Brookfield, S. D. (1995) *Becoming a Critically Reflective Teacher*. San Franscisco: Jossey Bass.

Bruner, J. (2004) *Making Stories: Law, Literature, Life*. Cambridge, Mass.: Harvard University Press.

Burney, F. (1898) *Evelina, or the History of a Young Lady's Entrance into the World*. London: George Bell & Sons.

Butler, J. (1990) *Gender Trouble. Feminism and the Subversion of Identity*. London: Routledge.

Campo, R. (1997) *The Desire to Heal: A Doctor's Education in Empathy, Identity, and Poetry*. New York: Norton.

Carr, W. (1995) *For Education: Towards Critical Education Enquiry*. Buckingham: Open University Press.

Carr, W. and Kemmis, S. (1986) *Becoming Critical: Education, Knowledge and Action Research*. Lewes: Falmer.

Carroll, L. ([1865] 1954) *Alice's Adventures in Wonderland*, London: Dent & Sons.

Carson, R. (1994) Teaching ethics in the context of the medical humanities. *Journal of Medical Ethics*, **20**, 235–8.

Casement, P. (1990) *Further Learning from the Patient*. London: Routledge.

Cavallaro-Johnson, G. (2004) Reconceptualising the visual in narrative inquiry into teaching. *Teaching and Teacher Education*, **20**, 423–34.

Charmaz, K. and Mitchell, R.G. (1997) The myth of silent authorship: self, substance and style in ethnographic writing. In R. Hertz (ed.) *Reflexivity and Voice*. London: Sage.

Charon, R. (2000a) Medicine, the novel and the passage of time. *Annals of Internal Medicine*, **132**(1), 63–8.

Charon, R. (2000b) Literature and Medicine: origins and destinies. *Academic Medicine*, **75**, 23–7.

Charon, R. (2000c) Informed consent: the imperative and the therapeutic dividend of showing patients what we write about them. Paper presented at the Narrative Matters: Personal Stories and the Making of Health Policy Conference. Airlie Virginia, March.

Charon, R. (2004) Narrative and medicine. *New England Journal of Medicine*, **350**(9), 862–4.

Charon, R. and Montello, M. (2002) *Stories Matter: The Role of Narrative in Medical Ethics*. New York: Routledge.

Chowaniec, J. (2005) Exploring Identity. *Teaching in Higher Education*, 10(2) 265–70.

Chuang Tsu (trans. 1974, trans. Gia-Fu Feng and J. English) *Inner Chapters*. London: Wildwood House.

Cixous, H. (1991) *Coming to Writing and other Essays* (ed. D. Jenson). Cambridge, Mass.: Harvard University Press.

Cixous, H. (1995) Castration or decapitation? In S. Burke (ed.) *Authorship from Plato to the Postmodernists: A Reader*. University of Edinburgh Press, pp. 162–77.

Clandinin, D.J. and Connelly, F.M. (1990) Narrative experience and the study of curriculum. *Cambridge Journal of Education*, **20**(3), 25–37.

Clandinin, D.J. and Connelly, F.M. (1994) Personal Experience Methods. In N.K. Denzin and Y. Lincoln (eds) *Handbook of Qualitative Research*. London: Sage.

Clandinin, D.J., Davies, A., Hogan, P. and Kennard, B. (1992) *Learning to Teach: Teaching to Learn: Stories of Collaboration in Teacher Education*. New York: Teachers College Press.

Clark, P.G. (2002) Values and voices in teaching gerontology and geriatrics: case studies as stories. *The Gerontologist*, **42**, 297–303.

Clark, R. and Ivanič, R. (1997) *The Politics of Writing*. London: Routledge.

Clarke, A. (1998) Born of incidents but thematic in nature. *Canadian Journal of Education*, **23**(1), 47–62.

Clifford, J. (1986) Introduction: partial truths, and On ethnographic allegory. In J. Clifford and G.E. Marcus (eds) *Writing Culture: The Poetics and Politics of Ethnography*. Berkeley: University of California Press, pp. 1–26 and 98–121.

Clough, P. (1996) 'Again fathers and sons': the mutual construction of self, story and special educational needs. *Disability and Society*, **11**(1), 71–81.

Clough, P. (2002) *Narratives and Fictions in Educational Research*. Buckingham: Open University Press.

Clutterbuck, D. (1998) *Learning Alliances*. London: Institute of Personnel and Development.

Clutterbuck, D. and Megginson, D. (1999) *Mentoring Executives and Directors*. Oxford: Butterworth-Heinemann.

Cocteau, J. ([1930] 1968) *Opium: The Diary of a Cure*. London: Peter Owen.

Coleridge, S.T. (1817) *Biographia Literaria*, ch. 14.

Coleridge, S.T. ([1798] 1969) *Poetical Works* (The Rime of the Ancient Mariner) Oxford: Oxford University Press.

Coleridge, S.T. ([1834] 1978) *The Rime of the Ancient Mariner*. New York: Harper & Brothers.

Connolly, D.M. and Clandinin, D.J. (2000) Teacher education: a question of teacher knowledge. In J. Freeman-Moir and A. Scott (eds) *Tomorrow's Teachers: International and Critical Perspectives on Teacher Education*. Christchurch, New Zealand: Canterbury University Press and Christchurch College of Education, pp. 89–105.

Copeland, W.D., Birmingham, C., La Cruz, E. and Lewin, B. (1993) The reflective practitioner in teaching: toward a research agenda. *Teaching and Teacher Education*, 9(4), 347–59.

Cox, A. (1996) Writing the self. In J. Singleton and M. Luckhurst (eds) *The Creative Writing Handbook*. London: Macmillan.

Crockett, M.D. (2000) Inquiry as professional development: creating dilemmas through teachers' work. *Teaching and Teacher Education*, **18**, 609–24.

Cupitt, D. (1991) Interviewed by Neville Glasgow. BBC Radio 4. 8 September.

Cutcliffe, J.R., Epling, M., Cassedy, P., McGregor, J., Plant, N. and Butterworth, T. (1998) Ethical dilemmas in clinical supervision. *British Journal of Nursing*, 7(15), 920–3.

Daloz, L. (1999) *Guiding the Journey of Adult Learners* (2nd edn). San Francisco: Jossey Bass.

Dante Alighieri (trans. 1985, T. Philips) *Dante's Inferno*. New York: Thames & Hudson.

DasGupta, S. (2003) Reading bodies, writing bodies: self-reflection and cultural criticism in a narrative medicine curriculum. *Literature and Medicine*, **22**(2), 241–56.

DasGupta, S. and Charon, R. (2004) Personal illness narratives: using reflective writing to teach empathy. *Academic Medicine*, **79**(4), 351–6.

Davidson, B. (1999) Writing as a tool of reflective practice. *Group analysis*, **32**(1), 109–24.

Davis, C. and Schaefer, J. (eds) (2003) *Intensive Care: more poetry and prose by nurses*. University of Iowa Press.

Deal, D. (1998) Portfolios, learning logs, and eulogies: using expressive writing in a science method class. In E.G. Sturtevant, J.A. Dugan, P. Linder and W.M. Linek. *Literacy and Community*. Texas: The College Reading Association.

Denyer, S., Boydell, L., Wilde, J. and Herne, U. (2003) *Reflecting Leadership: Leadership for Building a Healthy Society*. Dublin and Belfast: Institute of Public Health in Ireland.

Denzin, N.K. (1992) The many faces of emotionality: reading *persona*. In C. Ellis and M.G. Flaherty (eds) *Investigating Subjectivity: Research on Lived Experience*. London: Sage, pp. 17–30.

Department of Education and Science (1978) *Primary Education in England*. London: HMSO.

Dinkelman, T. (2000) An inquiry into the development of critical reflection in secondary student teachers. *Teaching and Teacher Education*, **16**, 195–222.

Diski, J. (2005) Your dinner is the dog. *The Guardian Review*, 15 January, 31.

Dixon, D.M., Sweeney, K.G. and Periera, G. (1999) The physician healer: ancient magic or modern science? *British Journal of General Practice*, **49**, 309–12.

Doubtfire, D. (1996) *Teach Yourself Creative Writing*. London: Hodder Headline.

Doyle, W. (2004) Heard any good stories lately? A critique of the critics of narrative in educational research. *Teaching and Teacher Education*, **13**(1), 93–9.

Doyle, W. and Carter, K. (2003) Narrative and learning to teach: implications for teacher-education curriculum. *Journal of Curriculum Studies*, **35**(2), 129–37.

Drabble, M. (ed.) (2000) *The Oxford Companion to English Literature*. Oxford: Oxford University Press.

Drucquer, H. (2004) in Bolton, G., Allan, H.S. and Drucquer, H. Black and blue writing for reflective practice. In G. Bolton, S. Howlett, C. Lago, and J. Wright *Writing Cures: An Introductory Handbook of Writing in Counselling and Psychotherapy*. London: Brunner-Routledge

Duffy, C.A. (1999) *The World's Wife* (Mrs Midas). London: Picador, Macmillan.

Durgahee, T. (1997) Reflective practice: nursing ethics through story telling. *Nursing Ethics*, **4**(2), 135–46.

Eagleton, T. (1983) *Literary Theory: An Introduction*. Oxford: Basil Blackwell.

Eastaugh, A. (1998a) The pursuit of self knowledge through a study of myself as a member of a group of co-tutoring facilitators. Unpublished MA dissertation.

Eastaugh, A. (1998b) Abstract for paper presented to the International World Organisation of Family Doctors Conference, Dublin.

Einstein, A. (2002) Interview with Sylvester Viereck 1929, Berlin. Quoted by K. Taylor, When fact and fantasy collide. *Times Higher Educational Supplement*, 20/27 December, viii.

Eisner, M. (2000) A villanelle: writing in strict form. In G. Bolton (ed.) Opening the word hoard. *Journal of Medical Humanities*, **26**(1), 55–7.

Elbasch-Lewis, F. (2002) Writing as enquiry: storying the teaching of self in writing workshops. *Curriculum Enquiry*, **32**(4), 403–28.

Eliot, T.S. ([1936] 1974) *Collected Poems*. London: Faber & Faber.

Eliot, T.S. (1994) *Four Quartets*. London: Faber & Faber.

Elkind, A. (1998) Using metaphor to read the organisation of the NHS. *Social Science Medicine*, **47**(11), 1715–27.

Ellis, C. and Bochner, A.P. (2000) Autoethnography, Personal Narrative, Reflexivity: Researcher as Subject. In N. Denzin and Y. Lincoln (eds) *Handbook of Qualitative Research* 2nd edn. London: Sage.

Ellos, W.J. (1998) Some narrative methologies for clinical ethics. *Cambridge Quarterly of Healthcare Ethics*, 7, 315–22.

Engel, J.D., Pethel, L. and Zarconi, J. (2002) Hearing the patient's story. *Sacred Space*, **3**(1), 24–32.

Epstein, R.M. (1999) Mindful practice. *Journal of the American Medical Association*, **282**(9), 833–9.

Eraut, M. (1994) *Developing Professional Knowledge and Competence*. London: Falmer Press.

Etherington, K. (2004) *Becoming a Reflexive Researcher: Using Ourselves in Research*. London: Jessica Kingsley.

Evison, R. (2001) Helping individuals manage emotional responses. In R.L Payne and C.L.Cooper (eds) *Emotions at Work: Theory, Research, and Applications in management*. Chichester: Wiley & Sons, pp. 241–68.

Exley, H. (ed.) (1991) *A Writer's Notebook*. Watford: Exley.

Fanghanel, J. (2004) Capturing dissonance in university teacher education environments. *Studies in Higher Education*, **29**(5), 575–90.

Feltham, C. (2004) *Problems are us: or is it just me?* Felixstowe, Suffolk: Braiswick.

Ferry, N.M. and Ross-Gordon, N. (1998) An enquiry into Schon's epistemology of practice: exploring links between experience and reflective practice. *Adult Education Quarterly*, **48**(2), 98–112.

Fins, J.J., Gentilesco, B.J., Carber, A., Lister, P., Acres, C.A., Payne, R. and C. Storey-Johnson (2003) Reflective practice and palliative care education: a clerkship responds to the informal and hidden curricula. *Academic Medicine*, **78**(3), 307–12.

Flax, J. (1990) *Thinking Fragments*. Berkeley: University of California Press.

Fowler, J. and Chevannes, M. (1998) Evaluating the efficacy of reflective practice within the context of clinical supervision. *Journal of Advanced Nursing*, 27, 379–82.

Fox, D. (1983) Personal theories of teaching. *Studies in Higher Education*, **8**(2), 151–63.

Frank, A. (1947) *The Diary of Anne Frank*. London: Macmillan Children's Books.

Frank, A. (1995) *The Wounded Storyteller: Body Illness and Ethics*. The University of Chicago Press.

Frank, A. (2004) Asking the right question about pain: narrative and phronesis. *Literature and Medicine*, **23**(2), 209–25.

Frankenberg, R. (1986) Sickness as cultural performance: drama, trajectory, and pilgrimage root metaphors and the making social of disease. *International Journal of Health Services*, **16**(4), 603–27.

Frankl, V.E., (1985) *Man's Search for Meaning* (5th edn). New York: Washington Square Press.

Freire, P. (1972) *Pedagogy of the Oppressed*. London: Penguin.

Freire, P. (1998) *Pedagogy of Freedom: Ethics, Democracy, and Civic Courage*. Maryland: Rowman & Littlefield.

Freud, A. (1950) Foreword. In M. Milner, *On Not Being Able to Paint*. London: Heinemann Educational.

Freud, S. ([1910] 1962) *Two Short Accounts of Psychoanalysis*. London: Penguin.

Freud, S. (1995) Creative writers and day-dreaming. In S. Burke (ed.) *Authorship from Plato to the Postmodernists: A Reader*. University of Edinburgh Press, pp. 54–62.

Garro, L.C. and Mattingley, C. (2000) In C. Mattingley and L.C. Garro (eds) *Narrative and cultural construction of illness and healing*. Berkeley: University of California Press.

Gee, S. (2002) *Thin Air*. London: Headline Review.

Geertz, C. ([1973] 1993) *The Interpretation of Culture*. London: HarperCollins.

Gerber, L. (1994) Psychotherapy with Southeast Asian refugees: implications for treatment of western patients. *American Journal of Psychotherapy*, **48**(2), 280–93.

Gerber, L. (1996) We must hear each other's cry: lessons from Pol Pot survivors. In C. Strozier and F. Flynn *Genocide, War, and Human Survival*. New York: Rowman & Littlefield, pp. 297–305.

Gersie, A. (1992) *Storymaking in Bereavement*. London: Jessica Kingsley.

Gherardi, S. and Turner, B. (2002) Real men don't collect soft data. In A.M. Huberman and M.B. Miles *The Qualitative Researcher's Companion*. London: Sage, pp. 81–101.

Gibbons, N. (2003) Portrait by a patient. In G. Bolton (ed.) Opening the word hoard. *Journal of Medical Humanities*, **29**(2), 97–103.

Gibran, K. ([1926] 1994) *The Prophet*. London: Bracken Books.

Glaister, L. (1999) *Sheer Blue Bliss*. London: Bloomsbury.

Glaze, J. (2002) Ph.D. study and the use of a reflective diary: a dialogue with self. *Reflective Practice*, **3**(2), 153–66.

Glen, S., Clark, A. and Nicol, M. (1995) Reflecting on reflection: a personal encounter. *Nurse Education Today*, **15**, 61–8.

Goethe (1998) (D. Seamon and A. Zajonc, eds) Goethe's way of science; a phenomenology of nature. New York: SUNY Press. Review: http//www.datadiwan.de/ SciMedNet/library/reviewsN69+N69Goethesci.htm: accessed on 27 October 2004.

Goffman, E. (1990) *The Presentation of Self in Everyday Life*. Harmondsworth: Penguin.

Goldberg, N. (1986) *Writing Down the Bones*. Boston: Shambhala.

Goldberg, N. (1991) *Wild Mind: Living the Writer's Life*. London: Rider.

Gomez, M.S., Burda Walker, A. and Page, M.L. (2000) Personal experience as a guide to teaching. *Teaching and Teacher Education*, **16**, 731–47.

Goodson, I. (1998) Storying the self. In W. Pinar (ed.) *Curriculum: Towards New Identities*. New York and London: Taylor & Francis, pp. 3–20.

Goodson, I. (2004) Representing teachers. *Teaching and Teacher Education*, **13**(1), 111–17.

Gough, N. (1998) Reflections and diffractions: functions of fiction in curriculum inquiry. In W. Pinar (ed.) *Curriculum: Towards New Identities*. New York and London: Taylor & Francis, pp. 91–129.

Greenhalgh, T. and Hurwitz, B. (eds) (1998) *Narrative Based Medicine: Dialogue and Discourse in Clinical Practice*. London: BMJ Books.

Greenwood, J. (1995) Treatment with dignity. *Nursing Times*, **91**(17), 65–6.

Grumet, M.R. (1981) Restitution and reconstruction of educational experience: an autobiographical method for curriculum theory. In M. Lawn and L. Barton (eds) *Rethinking Curriculum Studies: a Radical Approach*. London: Croom Helm, pp. 115–30.

Guppy, S. (2000) Feminist witness to the century. *Times Educational Supplement*, February, 27.

Hamberger, R. (1995) Acts of parting. *New Statesman*, 24 November, 49.

Hancock, P. (1998) Reflective Practice: using a learning journal. *Nursing Standard* 13 (17) pp. 37–40.

Hargreaves, J. (1997) Using patients: exploring the ethical dimension of reflective practice in nurse education. *Journal of Advanced Nursing*, **25**, 223–8.

Harris, J. (2003) *Signifying Pain: Constructing and Healing the Self through Writing*. New York: SUNY Press.

Harrison, R. (2004) Telling stories about learners and learning. In J. Satterthwaite et al. (eds) *The Disciplining of Education: New Languages of Power and Resistance*. Stoke-on-Trent: Trentham Books, pp. 169–80.

Hartley, L.P. (1953) *The Go Between*. London: Hamish Hamilton.

Hatem, D. and Ferrara, E. (2001) Becoming a doctor: fostering humane caregivers through creative writing. *Patient Education and Counselling*, **45**, 13–22.

Hatton, N. and Smith, D. (1995) Reflection in teacher eduction: towards definition and implementation. *Teacher and Teacher Education*, **11**(1), 33–49.

Heaney, S. (1980a) *Selected Prose 1968–1978*. London: Faber & Faber, p. 47.

Heaney, S. (1980b) *Selected Poems* ('Digging'). London: Faber & Faber, pp. 10–11.

Heifetz, R.A. and Linsky, M. (2002) *Leadership on the line*. Boston: Harvard Business School Press.

Heilbrun, C. (1988) *Writing a Woman's Life*. New York: W.W. Norton.

Heitsch, D.B. (2000) Approaching death by writing: Montaigne's *Essays* and the literature of consolation. *Literature and Medicine*, **19**(1), 96–106.

Heller, T. (1996) Doing being human: reflective practice in mental health work. In T. Heller et al. (eds.) *Mental Health Matters*. London: Macmillan.

Helman, C. (ed.) (2003) *Doctors and Patients: An Anthology*. Abingdon Radcliffe Press.

Hesse, H. ([1927] 1965) *Steppenwolf*. London: Penguin.

Hildebrand, J. (1995) Learning through supervision: a systemic approach. In M. Yelloly and M. Henkel (eds) *Teaching and Learning in Social Work: Towards Reflective Practice*. London: Jessica Kingsley.

Hilfiker, D. (1985) *Healing the Wounds: a Physician Looks at his Work*. New York: Pantheon.

Holly, M.L. (1988) Reflective writing and the spirit of enquiry. *Cambridge Journal of Education*, **19**(1), 71–80.

Holly, M.L. (1989) *Writing to Grow: Keeping a Personal-Professional Journal*. Portsmouth, NH: Heinemann.

Homer (trans. 1996, R. Fagles) *The Odyssey*. London: Viking Penguin.

Hoover, L.A. (1994) Reflective writing as a window on preservice teachers' thought processes. *Teacher and Teaching Education*, **10**(1), 83–93.

Horowitz, C.R., Suchman, A.L., Branch, W.T. and Frankel, R.M. (2003) What do doctors find meaningful about their work? *Annals of Internal Medicine*, **138**(9), 772–6.

Howard, J. (1997) The emotional diary: a framework for reflective practice. *Education for General Practice*, **8**, 288–91.

Huber, M., Huber, J., Clandinin, J. and Clandinin, D.J. (2004) Moments of tension: resistance as expressions of narrative coherence in stories. *Reflective Practice*, **5**(2), 182–98.

Hudson Jones, A. (1998) Narrative in medical ethics. In T. Greenhalgh and B. Hurwitz (eds) *Narrative Based Medicine: Dialogue and Discourse in Clinical Practice*. London: BMJ Books, pp. 217–24.

Hughes, T. (1967) *Poetry in the Making*. ('The Thought Fox') London: Faber & Faber, pp. 19–20.

Hughes, T. (1982) Foreword. In S. Brownjohn, *What Rhymes with Secret?* London: Hodder & Stoughton.

Hughes, T. (1995) Interview, *Paris Review*. http://stinfwww.informatik.uni-leipzig.de/~beckmann/plath/thint.html Accessed 8 September 2004.

Hughes, L. and Pengelly, P. (1995) Who cares if the room is cold? Practicalities, projections, and the trainer's authority. In M. Yelloly and M. Henkel (eds) *Teaching and Learning in Social Work: Towards Reflective Practice*. London: Jessica Kingsley.

Hulatt, I. (1995) A sad reflection. *Nursing Standard*, **9**(20), 22–3.

Hunt, C. and Sampson, F. (1998) *The Self on the Page: Theory and Practice of Creative Writing in Personal Development*. London: Jessica Kingsley.

Huxley, A.J. ([1932] 1994) *Brave New World*. London: Flamingo.

Hwu, Wen-Song (1998) Curriculum, transcendence and Zen/Taoism: critical ontology of the self. In W. Pinar (ed.) *Curriculum: Towards New Identities*. New York and London: Taylor & Francis, pp. 21–4.

Illes, K. (2003) The patchwork text and business education: rethinking the importance of personal reflection and co-operative cultures. *Innovations in Education and Teaching International*, **40**(2), 209–15.

Ixer, G. (1999) There's no such thing as reflection. *British Journal of Social Work*, **29**(4), 513–27.

Johns, C. (1995) Framing learning through reflection within Carper's fundamental ways of knowing in nursing. *Journal of Advanced Nursing*, **22**, 222–34.

Johns, C. (2004) *Being Mindful, Easing Suffering: Reflections on Palliative Care*. London: Jessica Kingsley.

Joyce, J. (1944) *Stephen Hero* (T. Spencer, ed.) New York: New Directions Press.

Joy-Matthews, J., Megginson, D. and Surtees, M. (2004) *Human Resource Development* (2nd edn). London: Kogan Page.

Keats, J. (1818). Letter to John Taylor, 27 February.

Kember, D. et al. (1996) Encouraging critical reflection through small group discussion of journal writing. *Innovations in Education Training International*, **33**(4), 313–20.

Kemp, M. (2001) Fictioning Identities: A course on narrative and fictional approaches to educational practice. *Reflective Practice*, **2**(3), 345–55.

Keys, C.W. (1999) Revitalising instruction in scientific genres: connecting knowledge production with writing to learn in science. *Science Education*, **83**, 115–30.

Kim, H.S. (1999) Critical reflective inquiry for knowledge development in nursing practice. *Journal of Advanced Nursing*, **29**(5), 1205–12.

Kipling, R. (1902) *Just So Stories*. London: Macmillan.

Kirkham, M. (1997) Reflection in midwifery: professional narcissism or seeing with women? *British Journal of Midwifery*, **5**(5), 259–62.

Kirkham, M. (1999) The wisdom of nausea. *Midwifery Today*, **52**, 15.

Kolb, D.A. (1984) *Experiential Learning*. London: Prentice Hall.

Kruse, S.D. (1997) Reflective activity in practice. *Journal of Research and Development in Education*, **31**(1), 46–60.

Kyeremateng, S. (2003) Jug. In G. Bolton (ed.) Opening the word hoard. *Journal of Medical Humanities*, **29**(2), 97–103.

Lakoff, G. (1991) Metaphor and war: the metaphor system used to justify war in the gulf. *Viet Nam Generation Journal*. V3, N3 November http://lists.village. virginia.edu/sixyties/HTML_Texts/Scholarly/Lakoff_Gulf_Metap.

Lakoff, G. and Johnson, M. (1980) *Metaphors We Live By*. University of Chicago Press.

Landgrebe, B. and Winter, R. (1994) Reflective writing on practice: professional support for the dying? *Educational Action Research*, **2**(1), 83–94.

Lao Tsu (trans. 1973, Gia Fu Feng and J. English) *Tao Te Ching*. London: Wildwood House.

Lepore, S.J. (1997) Expressive writing moderates the relation between intrusive thoughts and depressive symptoms. *Journal of Personality and Social Psychology*, **73**(5), 1030–7.

Lepore, S.J. and Smyth, J.M. (2002) *The Writing Cure: How Expressive Writing Promotes Health and Emotional Well-being*. Washington, DC: American Psychological Association.

Levi, P. (1988) *The Wrench*. London: Abacus.

Levi-Strauss, C. (1966) *The Savage Mind*. London: Wiedenfeld.

Lévi-Strauss, C. (1978) *Myth and Meaning*. London: Routledge & Kegan Paul.

Lewis, C.S. (1961) *A Grief Observed*. London: Faber & Faber.

Lewis, R. (1992) Autobiography and biography as legitimate educational tasks or pedagogic terrorism. Paper presented to Teachers' Stories of Life and Work Conference, Chester.

Lillis, T.M. (2001) *Student Writing. Access, Regulation, Desire*. London: Routledge.

Llosa, M.V. (1991) *A Writer's Reality*. Syracuse, NY: Syracuse University Press.

Longfellow, H.W. (1960) *The Song of Hiawatha*. London: Dent.

Loughran, J. (2004) Review essay. *Teaching and Teacher Education*, **20**, 655–60.

Love, C. (1996) Using a diary to learn the patient's perspective. *Professional Nurse*, **11**(5), 286–8.

Lyotard, J.P. (1992) *The Postmodern Explained to Children*. London: Turnaround.

Maclure, M. (2003) *Discourse in Educational and Social Research*. Buckingham: Open University Press.

Macnaughton, J. (1998) Anecdote in clinical practice, in T. Greenhalgh and B. Hurwitz (eds) *Narrative Based Medicine: Dialogue and Discourse in Clinical Practice*. London: BMJ Books.

Maisch, M. (2003) Structuring a Masters degree dissertation from Patchwork Text. *Innovations in Education and Teaching International*, **40**(2), 194–201.

Mantzoukas, S. and Jasper, M.A. (2004) Reflective practice and daily ward reality: a covert power game. *Journal of Clinical Nursing*, **13**(8), 925–33.

Marrow, C.E., MacAuley, D.M. and Crumbie, A. (1997) Promoting reflective practice through structured clinical supervision. *Journal of Nursing Management*, **5**, 77–82.

Marshall, J. and Reason, P. (1997) Collaborative and self-reflective forms of inquiry in management research. In J. Burgoyne and M. Reynolds, *Values and Purposes in Business Management*. London: Sage.

Marx, K. (1962) *Writings of the Young Marx on Philosophy and Society* (ed. and trans. L.D. Easton and K.H. Gudat) New York: Anchor Books.

Mattingley, C. (2000) Emergent narratives. In C. Mattingley and L.C. Garro (eds) *Narrative and Cultural Construction of Illness and Healing*. Berkeley: University of California Press, pp. 181–211.

Mazza, N. (2003) *Poetry Therapy: Theory and Practice*. London: Brunner-Routledge.

McDonell, J., Lloyd, P. and Valkenberg, R.C. (2004) Developing design expertise through the construction of video stories. *Design Studies*, **25**, 509–25.

McGill, I. and Brockbank, A. (2004) *The Action Learning Handbook*. London: RoutledgeFalmer

McKenzie, J. (2003) The student as an active agent in a disciplinary structure: introducing the patchwork text in teaching sociology. *Innovations in Education and Teaching International*, **40**(2), 152–60.

McKenzie, J., Sheely, S. and Trigwell, K. (1998) An holistic approach to student evaluation of courses. *Assessment and Evaluation in Higher Education*, **23**(2), 153–63.

McMahon, S.I. (1997) Using documented oral and written dialogue to understand and challenge preservice teachers' reflection. *Teacher and Teacher Education*, **13**(2), 199–213.

Mearns, D. (1994) Person Centred Counselling with Configurations of Self. *Counselling*, May, 125–30.

Meath Lang, B. (1996) Cultural and language diversity in the curriculum: towards reflective practice. In I. Parasnis (ed.) *Cultural and Language Diversity and the Deaf Experience*. Cambridge: Cambridge University Press, pp. 160–70.

Megginson, D. and Whitaker, V. (2003) *Continuing Professional Development*. London: Chartered Institute of Personnel and Development.

Mezirow, J. (1981) A critical theory of adult learning and education. *Adult Education*, **32**(1), 3–24.

Mezirow, J. (1991) *Transformative Dimensions of Adult Learning*. San Francisco: Jossey Bass.

Middlebrook, D. (2003) *Her Husband. Ted Hughes and Sylvia Plath: A Marriage*. London: Penguin.

Miles, M.B. and Huberman, A.M. (1994) *Qualitative Data Analysis: An Expanded Sourcebook*. London: Sage.

Milne, A.A. ([1924] 1959) *The World of Christopher Robin (When We Were Very Young)*. London: Methuen.

Milne, A.A. ([1928] 1958) *The World of Pooh (The House at Pooh Corner)*. London: Methuen.

Modell, A.H (1997) Reflections on metaphor and affects. *Annals of Psychoanalysis*, **25**, 219–33.

Moi, T. (1985) *Sexual Textual Politics*. London: Routledge.

Montgomery, K., Chambers, T. and Reifler, D.R. (2003) Humanities education at Northwestern University Feinberg school of medicine. *Academic Medicine*, **78**(10), 958–62.

Montgomery Hunter, K. (1991) *Doctors' Stories: The narrative Structure of Medical Knowledge*. Princeton: Princeton University Press.

Moon, J. (1999a) *Learning Journals: A Handbook for Academics, Students and Professional Development*. London: Kogan Page.

Moon, J. (1999b) Reflect on the inner 'I'. *Times Higher Education Supplement*, 15 October, 34–5.

Moon, J.A. (2003) *Reflection in Learning and Professional Development*. London: Kogan Page.

Moon, J.A. (2004) *A Handbook of Reflective and Experiential Learning: Theory and Practice*. London: RoutledgeFalmer.

Morrison, K. (1996) Developing reflective practice in higher degree students through a learning journal. *Studies in Higher Education*, **21**(3), 317–31.

Moustakas, C. (1990) *Heuristic Research Design, Methodology and Applications*. London: Sage.

Murray, D. (1982) *Learning by Teaching*. New Jersey: Boynton Cook.

Newton, R. (1996) Getting to grips with barriers to reflection. *SCUTREA Conference Papers*, pp. 142–5.

Nias, J. and Aspinwall, K. (1992) Paper presented to the Teachers' Stories of Life and Work Conference, Chester.

Nin, A. *The diary of Anais Nin 1939–44*. New York: Harcourt Brace. As quoted in Epstein 1999, p. 834.

Oriah, M.D. (2000) *The Invitation*. London: Thorsons.

Orwell, G. ([1949] 1987) *1984*. London: Penguin.

Osborn, J. (1993) AIDS – science, medicine, and metaphor (editorial). *Western Journal of Medicine*, **158**(3), 305–7.

Parker, J. (2003) The patchwork text in reading Greek tragedy. *Innovations in Education and Teaching International*, **40**(2), 180–93.

Paterson, B.L. (1995) Developing and maintaining reflection in clinical journals, *Nurse Education Today*, **15**, 211–20.

Pattison, S. Dickenson, D. Parker, M. and Heller, T. (1999a) Do case studies mislead about the nature of reality? *Journal of Medical Ethics*, **25b**, 42–6.

Pattison, S., Manning, S. and Malby, B. (1999b) I want to tell you a story. *Health Services Journal*, 25 February, 6.

Paula, C. (2003) Bubbles in a pond: reflections in clinical practice. *Clinical Psychology*, **27**, July, 27–9.

Pennebaker, J.W. (2000) Telling stories: the health benefits of narrative. *Literature and Medicine*, **19**(1), 3–18.

Pennebaker, J.W., Kiecolt Glaser, J. and Glaser, R. (1988) Disclosure of traumas and immune function: health implications for psychotherapy. *Journal of Consulting and Clinical Psychology*, **56**, 239–45.

Perry, C. and Cooper, M. (2001) Metaphors are good mirrors: reflecting on change for teacher education. *Reflective Practice*, **2**(1), 41–51.

Phillion, J. (2002a) Narrative multiculturalism. *Journal of Curriculum Studies*, **34**(3), 265–79.

Phillion, J. (2002b) Becoming a narrative inquirer in a multicultural landscape. *Journal of Curriculum Studies*, **34**(5), 535–56.

Phillion, J.A. and Connelly, F.M. (2004) Narrative, diversity, and teacher education. *Teaching and Teacher Education*, **20**, 457–71.

Phye, G.D. (ed.) (1997) *Handbook of Academic Learning*. San Diego, California: Academic Press.

Picasso, P. http://www.cyber-nation.com/victory/quotations/authors/quotes_picasso_ pablo.html (accessed 14 February 2005).

Pickering, N. (1999) Metaphors and models in medicine. *Theoretical Medicine and Bioethics*, **20**, 361–75.

Pietroni, M. (1995) The nature and aims of professional education for social workers: a postmodern perspective. In M. Yelloly and M. Henkel (eds) *Learning and Teaching in Social Work: Towards Reflective Practice*. London: Jessica Kingsley.

Pinar, W.F. (1975) Currere: towards reconceptualisation. In W.F. Pinar (ed.) *Curriculum Theorising: the Reconceptualists*. Berkeley: McCutchan, pp. 396–414.

Plato (trans. 1955) *The Republic* (trans. D. Lee). London: Penguin.

Plato (trans. 1958) *The Protogoras and Meno* (trans. W.K.C. Guthrie). London: Penguin.

Plato (trans. 2000) Apology of Socrates in *Selected Dialogues of Plato* (trans. B. Jowett). New York: Random House.

Plummer, K. (2001) *Documents of Life 2: An Invitation to Critical Humanism*. London: Sage.

Poitier, S. (2000) *The Measure of a Man: A Memoir*. London: Simon & Schuster.

Prigogine, I. (1999) Review of *Doubt and Certainty* by T. Rothman and G. Sudarshan. *Times Higher Education Supplement*, 24 September, 26.

Progoff, I. (1987) *At a Journal Workshop*. New York: Dialogue House.

Pullman, P. (1995) *His Dark Materials*. London: Scholastic.

Purdy, R. (1996) Writing refreshes my practice. *Medical Monitor*, 6 March.

Rainer, T. (1978) *The New Diary: How to Use a Journal for Self-Guidance and Expanded Creativity*. London: Angus & Robertson.

Reason, P. (ed.) (1988) *Human Enquiry in Action: Developments in New Paradigm Research*. London: Sage.

Reid, A. and O'Donohue, M. (2004) Revisiting enquiry-based teacher education in neo-liberal times. *Teaching and Teacher Education*, **20**, 559–70.

Reifler, D.R. (1996) 'I actually don't mind the bone saw': narratives from gross anatomy. *Literature and Medicine*, **15**, 183–99.

Reynolds, M. (1997) Learning styles: a critique. *Management Learning*, **28**(2), 115–33.

Rich, A. (1995) *What is Found There: Notebooks on Poetry and Politics*. London: Virago.

Richardson, L. (1992) The consequences of poetic representation: writing the other, rewriting the self. In C. Ellis and M.G. Flaherty (eds) *Investigating Subjectivity: Research on Lived Experience*. London: Sage, pp. 125–40.

Richardson, L. (2000) Writing: A Method of Inquiry. In N. Denzin and Y. Lincoln (eds) *Handbook of Qualitative Research* (2nd edn). London: Sage, pp. 923–47.

Richardson, L. (2001) Getting personal: writing stories. *Qualitative Studies in Education*, **14**(1), 33–8.

Ricoeur, P. (1978) *The Rule of Metaphor: multi-disciplinary studies in the creation of meaning of language* (trans. R. Czerny). London: Routledge & Kegan Paul.

Rigano, D. and Edwards, J. (1998) Incorporating reflection into work practice. *Management Learning*, **29**(4), 431–6.

Rilke, R.M. ([1934] 1993) *Letters to a Young Poet* (trans. H. Norton). New York: W.W. Norton & Co.

Robertson, P. (1999) Talk to King's Fund 'Arts in Hospital' Forum. December.

Rockwell, J. (1974) *Fact in Fiction*. London: Routledge.

Rogers, C. (1969) *Freedom to Learn: a View of What Education Might Become*. Columbus: Charles E. Merrill.

Rogers, J. (1991) *Mr Wroe's Virgins*. London: Faber & Faber.

Rolfe, G. (2002) A lie that helps us see the truth: research, truth and fiction in the helping professions. *Reflective Practice*, **3**(1), 89–102.

Rowan, J. (1990) *Subpersonalities: The People Inside Us*. London: Routledge.

Rowe, J. and Halling, S. (1998) Psychology of forgiveness. In R.S. Valle (ed.) *Phenomenological Inquiry in Psychology: Existential and Transpersonal Dimensions*. New York: Plenum, pp. 227–46.

Rowe, J., Halling, S., Davies Leifer, M., Powers, D. and van Bronkhurst, J. (1989) The psychology of forgiving another: a dialogical research approach. In R.S. Valle and S. Halling (eds) *Existential-Phenomenological Perspectives in Psychology: Exploring the Breadth of Human Experience*. New York: Plenum.

Rowland, S. (1984) *The Enquiring Classroom*. Lewes: Falmer.

Rowland, S. (1991) The power of silence: an enquiry through fictional writing. *British Educational Research Journal*, **17**(2), 95–113.

Rowland, S. (1993) *The Enquiring Tutor*. Lewes: Falmer.

Rowland, S. (1999) The role of theory in a pedagogical model for lecturers in Higher Education. *Studies in Higher Education*, **24**(3), 303–14.

Rowland, S. (2000) *The Enquiring University Lecturer*. Buckingham: Society for Research into Higher Education and Open University Press.

Rowland, S. and Barton, L. (1994) Making things difficult: developing a research approach to teaching in higher education. *Studies in Higher Education*, **19**(3), 367–74.

Rowland (Bolton), G., Rowland, S. and Winter, R. (1990) Writing fiction as enquiry into professional practice. *Journal of Curriculum Studies*, **22**(3), 291–3.

Rust, C. (2002) The impact of assessment on student learning. *Active Learning in Higher Education*, **3**(2), 145–58.

Sacks, O. (1985) *The Man who Mistook his Wife for a Hat*. London: Picador, Macmillan.

Salvio, P. (1998) On using the literacy portfolio to prepare teachers for 'willful world travelling' in W.F. Pinar (ed.) *Curriculum: Towards New Identities*. New York and London: Taylor & Francis, pp. 41–75.

Saran, R. and Neisser, B. (2004) *Enquiring Minds: Socratic Dialogue in Education*. Stoke-on-Trent, Staffs: Trentham Books.

Sartre, J.P. ([1938] 1963) *Nausea*. Harmondsworth: Penguin.

Sartre, J.P. ([1948] 1950) *What is Literature?* London: Methuen.

Schneider, M. and Killick, J. (1998) *Writing for Self-Discovery: a Personal Approach to Creative Writing*. Shaftesbury: Element.

Schon, D.A. (1983) *The Reflective Practitioner: How Professionals Think in Action*. New York: Basic Books.

Schon, D.A. (1987) *Educating the Reflective Practitioner*. San Francisco: Jossey Bass.

Schratz, M. (1993) Researching while teaching: promoting reflective professionality in higher education. *Educational Action Research*, **1**(1), 111–33.

Scott-Hoy, K. (2002) The visitor: juggling life in the grip of the text. In A.P. Bochner and C. Ellis (eds) *Ethnographically Speaking: Autoethnography, Literature and Aesthetics*. New York: Altamira Press.

Scruton, R. (1982) *Kant*. Oxford: Oxford University Press.

Shafer, A. (1995) Metaphor and anaesthesia. *Anesthiology*, **83**(6), 1331–42.

Sharkey, J. (2004) Lives stories don't tell: exploring the untold in autobiographies. *Curriculum Enquiry*, **34**(4), 495–512.

Shelley, M. ([1820] 1994) *Frankenstein*. Ware: Wordsworth.

Shem, S. (2002) Fiction as Resistance (Medical Writings: Physician-Writers reflections on their work). *Annals of Internal Medicine*, **137**(11), 934–7.

Shepherd, M. (2004) Reflections on developing a reflective journal as a management adviser. *Reflective Practice*, **5**(2), 199–208.

Simons, J. (1990) *Diaries and Journals of Literary Women from Fanny Burney to Virginia Woolf*. London: Macmillan.

Simpson, J. (1988) *Touching the Void*. London: Vintage.

Smith, S. in Astley, N. (2002) *Staying Alive: Real Poems for Unreal Times* Northumberland: Bloodaxe.

Smith, L. and Winter, R. (2003) Applied epistemology for community nurses: evaluating the impact of the patchwork text. *Innovations in Education and Teaching International*, **40**(2), 161–72.

Smyth, J.M. et al. (1999) Effects of writing about stressful experiences on symptom reduction in patients with asthma or rheumatoid arthritis. *Journal of the American Medical Association*, **281**(14), 130–49.

Smyth, T. (1996) Reinstating the personal in the professional: reflections on empathy and aesthetic experience. *Journal of Advanced Nursing*, **24**, 932–7.

Sontag, S. (1991) *Illness as Metaphor; Aids and its Metaphors*. London: Penguin.

Sophocles (trans. 1982, R. Fagles) *Antigone*. New York: Penguin.

Sparkes, A.C. (2002) Autoethnography: self-indulgence of something more? In A.P. Bochner and C. Ellis (eds) *Ethnographically Speaking: Autoethnography, Literature and Aesthetics*. New York: Altamira Press.

Sparkes, A.C. (2003) Bodies, identities, selves: autoethnograhic fragments and reflections. In J. Denison and P. Markula '*Moving Writing': Crafting Movement and Sport Research*. New York: Peter Lang.

Spiegel, D. (1999) Editorial: Healing words: emotional expression and disease outcome. *Journal of the American Medical Association*, **281**(14), 1328–9.

Standard for Chartered Teacher: Scottish Executive Education Department (2002) *Standard for Chartered Teacher*. http://www.teachingscotland.com (assessed 2 October 2004).

Stedmon, J., Mitchell, A. Johnstone, L. and Staite, S. (2003) Making reflective practice real: problems and solutions in the South West. *Clinical Psychology*, **27**, July, 30–3.

Stefano, G. (2004) George Stefano quoted by Ian Simple, The new pleasure seekers. *The Guardian Life*, 16 December, 4–5.

Sterne, L. ([1760] 1980) *Tristram Shandy* (Vol. 2, ch. 11). London: W.W. Norton.

Stevenson, R.L. ([1886] 1984) *Dr Jekyll and Mr Hyde*. London: Penguin.

Stoker, B. ([1897] 1994) *Dracula*. London: Penguin.

Strawson, G. (2004a) Tales of the Unexpected. *The Guardian Saturday Review*. 10 January, 19.

Strawson, G. (2004b) A fallacy of our age: not every life is a narrative. *Times Literary Supplement*. 15 October, 13–15.

Street, B. (1995) *Social Literacies*. London: Longman.

Sumsion, J. and Fleet, A. (1996) Reflection: can we assess it? Should we assess it? *Assessment and Evaluation in Higher Education*, **21**(2), 121–30.

Sydney, Sir Philip (1965) *The Poems of Sir Philip Sydney* W.A. Ringler (ed.). London: Oxford University Press.

Tennyson, A. ([1886] 1932) 'The Lady of Shalott'. In J. Wain (ed.) *The Oxford Library of English Poetry*. Oxford University Press, pp. 79–83.

Thomas, R.S. (1986) *Selected Poems* ('Poetry for Supper'). Newcastle-upon-Tyne: Bloodaxe.

Tripp, D. (1995a) *Critical Incidents in Teaching*. London: Routledge.

Tripp, D. (1995b) SCOPE facilitator training. *NPDP SCOPE Project Draft*. Western Australia: Murdoch University.

Trotter, S. (1999) Journal writing to promote reflective practice in pre-service teachers. Paper presented to the International Human Science Research Conference, Sheffield, July.

Truscott, D.M. and Walker, B.J. (1998) The influence of portfolio selection on reflective thinking. In E.G. Sturtevant, J.A. Dugan, P. Linder and W.M. Linek, *Literacy and Community*. Texas: The College Reading Association.

Tsai Chi Chung (trans. 1994, B. Bruya) *Zen Speaks*. London: HarperCollins.

Tyler, S.A. (1986) Post-modern ethnography: from occult to occult document, in J. Clifford and G.E. Marcus (eds) *Writing Culture*. Berkeley: University of California Press.

Usher, R. (1993) From process to practice: research reflexivity and writing in adult education. *Studies in Continuing Education*, **15**(2), 98–116.

Usher, R., Bryant, I. and Jones, R. (1997) *Adult Education and the Postmodern Challenge: Learning Beyond the Limits*. London: Routledge.

van Manen, M. (1995) On the epistemology of reflective practice. *Teachers and Teaching: Theory and Practice*, **1**(1), 33–49.

Verghese, A. (2001) The physician as storyteller. *Annals of Internal Medicine*, **135**(11), 1012–17.

von Klitzing, W. (1999) Evaluation of reflective learning in a psychodynamic group of nurses caring for terminally ill patients. *Journal of Advanced Nursing*, **30**(5), 1213–21.

Wade, S. (1994) *Writing and Publishing Poetry*. Oxford: How To Books.

Ward, J.R. and McCotter, S.S. (2004) Reflection as a visible outcome for preservice teachers. *Teaching and Teacher Education*, **20**, 243–57.

Warner, M. (1998) *No Go the Bogeyman: Scaring, Lulling and Making Mock*. London: Chatto & Windus.

Weedon, C. (1987) *Feminist Practice and Post-Structuralist Theory*. Oxford: Basil Blackwell.

Wellard, S.J. and Bethune, E. (1996) Reflective journal writing in nurse education: whose interests does it serve? *Journal of Advanced Nursing*, **24**, 1077–82.

Wilde, O. ([1891] 1949) *The Picture of Dorian Gray*. London: Penguin.

Williams, W.C. (1951) *Selected Poems*. London: Penguin, p. 231.

Winter, R. (1988) Fictional-critical writing, in J. Nias and S. Groundwater-Smith (eds), *The Enquiring Teacher*. London: Falmer, pp. 231–48.

Winter, R. (1989) *Learning from Experience*. London: Falmer Press.

Winter, R. (1991) Fictional-critical writing as a method for educational research. *British Educational Research Journal*, **17**(3), 251–62.

Winter, R. (2003) Contextualising the patchwork text: problems of coursework assignment in higher education. *Innovations in Education and Teaching International*, **40**(2), 112–22.

Winter, R., Buck, A. and Sobiechowska, P. (1999) *Professional Experience and the Investigative Imagination: The Art of Reflective Writing*. London: Routledge.

Woolf, V. (1977, 1978, 1980) *The Diary of Virginia Woolf* (3 vols). London: Hogarth Press.

Woolf, V. ([1928] 1992) *Orlando*. Oxford: Oxford University Press.

Wordsworth, W. ([1802] 1992) *The Lyrical Ballads*: Preface. Harlow: Longman, p. 82.

Wordsworth, W. ([1880] 2004) *The Prelude*. In *Selected Poems* (D. Walford Davies, ed) London: Dent.

Yeats, W.B. (1962) *Selected Poetry*. London: Macmillan.

Yelloly, M. and Henkel, M. (eds) (1995) Introduction. In: *Teaching and Learning in Social Work: Reflective Practice*. London: Jessica Kingsley.

Zeichner, K.M. (1994) Research on teacher thinking and different views of reflective practice in teaching and teacher education. In I. Carlgren, G. Handel and S. Vaage (eds) *Research on Teacher's Thinking and Practice*. London: Falmer Press.

INDEX